Regional Policy in Europe

Sergey S Artobolevskiy

Regional Policy and Development Series 11

Jessica Kingsley Publishers
London and Bristol, Pennsylvania

Regional Studies Association
London

First published in the United Kingdom in 1997 by
Jessica Kingsley Publishers Ltd
116 Pentonville Road
London N1 9JB, England
and
1900 Frost Road, Suite 101
Bristol, PA 19007, U S A

with
the Regional Studies Association
Registered Charity 252269

Copyright © 1997 Sergey Artobolevskiy

Library of Congress Cataloging in Publication Data
Artoboloevskiy, S.S.
Regional policy in Europe / S.S. Artobolevskiy.
p.   cm. -- (Regional policy and development ; 11)
Includes bibliographical references and index.
ISBN 1-85302-308-6 (alk. paper)
1. Regional planning--Europe. I. Title. II. Series: Regional
policy and development series : 11.
HT395,E8A83   1997
337.4--dc20   95-41246
                                        CIP

British Library Cataloguing in Publication Data
A CIP catalogue record for this book is available from the British Library

ISBN 1-85302-308-6

Printed and Bound in Great Britain by
Athenaeum Press, Gateshead, Tyne and Wear

Regional Policy in Europe

Regional Policy and Development Series

Series Editor: Ron Martin, Department of Geography, University of Cambridge

Throughout the industrialised world, widespread economic restructuring, rapid techno-logical change, the reconfiguration of State intervention, and increasing globalisation are giving greater prominence to the nature and performance of individual regional and local economies within nations. The old patterns and processes of regional development that characterised the post-war period are being fundamentally redrawn, creating new problems of uneven development and new theoretical and policy challenges. Whatever interpretation of this contemporary transformation is adopted, regions and localities are back on the academic and political agenda. *Regional Policy and Development* is an international series which aims to provide authoritative analyses of this new regional political economy. It seeks to combine fresh theoretical insights with detailed empirical enquiry and constructive policy debate to produce a comprehensive set of conceptual, practical and topical studies in this field. The series is not intended as a collection of synthetic reviews, but rather as original contributions to understanding the processes, problems and policies of regional and local economic development in today's changing world.

Contents

List of Figures   vi

List of Tables   vii

Introduction   1

1. Regional Policy within a System
   of State Socio-Economic Activity   15

2. The Main Directions of Regional Policy   51

3. The Mechanism of Regional Policy Realization   105

4. Regional Policy in USSR/CIS/Russia and the
   Opportunities for the Practical Implementation
   of Foreign Experience   130

   Conclusion   152

   References   167

   Author Index   179
   Geographical Index   181
   Subject Index   182

List of Figures

1.1	Regional policy in Britain (pre-war period)	39
1.2	Regional policy in Britain 1945–1960	40
1.3	Regional policy in Britain 1966	41
1.4	Regional policy in Britain 1979	42
1.5	Regional policy in Britain 1989	43
1.6	Regional policy in Britain 1992	44
2.1	Quality of life in EU less developed regions	65
2.2	Dynamics of population in capitals and capital agglomerations of some European countries	75
2.3	Level of unemployment in Ile-de-France, 1987	80
2.4	Level of unemployment in Greater London, 1986	81
2.5	Poverty in Greater London	82
2.6	Dynamics of unemployment in EU	91
2.7	Types of EU regions economy	92
4.1	Transfers from federal budget to regional budgets (grants, loans, privileges) per head of population, 1992	146
5.1	Efficiency of regional policy	154

List of Tables

1.1 State aid for economic development in EU countries. Average per year – 1981–1986, (mln ecu)   25

1.2 Grants from the ERDF and capital investments stimulated by them, 1985, (mln ecu)   27

2.1 Old-developed regions of EU (beginning of the 1990s)   55

2.2 Underdeveloped regions of EU (end of 1980s – beginning of 1990s)   64

2.3 Regional social-economic differences in Italy   67

2.4 Role of capital agglomerations, 1980s   74

2.5 Inter- and intra-regional differences in level of unemployment, mid-1980s   83

2.6 Social-economic indicators of EU problem regions, end of the 1980s   90

2.7 Share of population living in EU problem regions, 1989 (%)   93

2.8 The role of structural funds for underdeveloped regions (%)   94

2.9 Criteria for problem regions apportionment, installed by the EU Commission   98

3.1 Share of population living in problem regions (%)   112

3.2 Rates of grants in problem regions,1991 (% of investments)   120

3.3 Direct financial help within the framework of regional policy (1990 prices)   123

Introduction

In advanced capitalist countries many aspects of economic, and especially social, life have been determined for decades by the state. Within Soviet socio-economic literature, authors describe a system state-monopolistic capitalism, and in western texts, the 'welfare state' is discussed. Without judging between the two 'terms', the differences in these approaches can be seen: an economic focus in the East, and socio-political one in the West. The solution of regional socio-economic problems has always been an important component of state intervention in the West. In political declarations and scientific publications it has been called 'regional policy', although the understanding of this term differs greatly between various authors and frequently includes an unjustifiably large part of state activity.

Regional strategy and regional policy

Every state (with the possible exception of the Vatican) has a certain given territory and cannot function without a regional strategy, that is a clear plan of how its space (economy, population, environment) should be organized. This strategy reflects (or can be derived from) the macro-aims established by the state for itself: these can include the continued effective functioning of the economy, the unity of the country, the maintenance of a certain standard of living for the population etc. In turn, these aims are determined by the 'ruling' (prevailing) ideology, the latter depending on the political 'orientation' of the party or parties in power, as well as on the peculiarities of each period of development.

Changing approaches within Conservative-liberal and Social-democratic parties to the problems of nationalization/privatization in the post-war period (in western Europe) is an excellent example of this. However, it is also apparent from an analysis of the transformation of regional policy (see Chapter One). Frequently, the real course of events infringes on the 'plans' of a state, necessitating some form of intervention. The determining territorial structure of an economy/population can interfere to increase or preserve the competitiveness of the country's production, to create significant spatial disparities in the quality of life, to threaten national unity or to stratify society to a level which is unacceptable (from the point of view of a particular ideology). In such cases, the need for intervention through government regional policy and adjustments in the activities of the state emerges. Such intervention is designed to change the territorial structure of the economy and population in a given direction and, for the achievement of its aims, to stimulate or restrict the development of selected regions/areas. Thus, if a regional strategy is a *permanent* phenomenon (part of the *ideology* of any state), then regional policy is required only when critical deviations from the macro-economic goals of the state occur. The significance of such deviations are, once again, defined by the state.

During the post-war period in west European countries, there were virtually no periods when regional policy did not operate (although there were significant fluctuations in its scale and shifts in the targets of the policy area – see below). There were some exceptions – at the start of the 1990s, for example, the levelling of regional disparities and the need to increase the competitiveness of the national economy resulted in the almost complete disappearance of centralized regional policy in Denmark and the Netherlands (see Yuill *et al.* 1993). The official regional strategy of the Netherlands includes the stimulation of the Randstad development, but, under current conditions, this goal is achieved within the framework of macro-economic policy and a strict system of physical planning.

Frequently, the term *regional policy* includes distinct regional programmes, the devolution by central government of new rights to lower levels, and the reorganization of the administrative-territorial division etc. In the understanding that terminological disputes in the field of humanitarian sciences have little value, the author asks the readers of this book to accept his definition of regional policy. Regional policy includes any activity of the state where the achievement of predetermined spatial aims (economic, political) is the main priority, and exact and specified spatial purposes underlie the intervention of the state.

Any intervention of the state into socio-economic life clearly has territorial implications, and leads to certain spatial shifts. So programmes of development for individual sectors or industries (high-tech, for example) favour areas in which they are concentrated, promoting, thus, the advantage of these areas over others (in the level of economic development and, naturally, the quality of life of the population). However, in assisting selected sectors/industries, the state is not aiming to develop the areas where that sector/industry is concentrated, but rather wants to increase the competitiveness of a country's economy, to improve the trade balance, and to develop its own R&D etc. At best, such programmes attempt to take into account any regional consequences which are induced by them, although political considerations usually result in the publication of only positive regional consequences. Emphasis tends to be placed on any advantages gained by the crisis regions within the framework of the given sectoral/industry programme, or on opportunities stemming from a general improvement in the national economy.

However, industrial or sectoral programmes can comprise part of regional policy. In some cases where assistance is provided for crisis industries (coal-mining, black metallurgy, ship-building etc.), the state, frequently aware of the absence of development prospects in these industries, and aiming to slow their recession, concentrates on the transformation of the surrounding regions. In this case, the motivation for state intervention is the desire to resolve regional problems.

It is certainly possible to agree on a wider understanding of regional policy, with a further sub-division into different types of policy (including the pure regional policy ascribed to by the author), as seen in the work of Kuklinski (1990). However, here a logical contradiction becomes evident: such a wide definition of regional policy includes various areas of a state's activity which have directly opposing and contradicting consequences (in space). So, a series of state measures may be favourable for the development of crisis regions, but, at the same time, within the frameworks of above mentioned programmes of development for new industries, increase the disparities between the crisis territories and the most prosperous areas of the country. It is doubtful whether measures directed, although not consciously, at the increase of spatial socio-economic disparities should be included within regional policy.

Based on the above ideas, it is possible to formulate two inalienable features of regional policy, in the absence of which the policy area is transformed into something different, and can no longer be said to exist. First, the *positive discrimination* of regions i.e. the granting of advantages to *selected* territorial units (for details see Chapter Three). Regional policy exists only when regions/areas receive unequal levels of support or rights from the state. When all authorities (regional or local) receive state aid in equal part (or identical rights), this is can no longer be classed regional policy, and is a totally different phenomenon. Moreover, the devolution/decentralization of power frequently contradicts the purposes of regional policy and hinders its realization.

Clearly, equal rights can be used to better effect by more advanced regions than by crisis ones as they simply have more means and resources. As a result, the gap in the level of regional socio-economic development will increase (see Chapter One).

The second feature is the centralisation of regional policy. Regional policy is always a policy 'from above'. This does not mean, however, that it is a prerogative only of the central authorities. It is also carried out in 'smaller-sized' territorial units – states, provinces, regions – although these units should have an adequate institutional infrastructure and their own regional strategy. It is interesting that, at a certain level (while moving down through the hierarchy), regional policy (with its approaches and methods) disappears, and is replaced by physical planning, with its own more rigid methods of regulation and problem solution (the issue of planning permission, zoning of a territory, acceptance of strict plans etc.). The transition from larger to smaller-sized units enables the replacement of regional policy by planning (although the topic of spatial planning is not one for discussion in the framework of this book).

The need for decisions to be adopted 'from above' (how otherwise can the problems of regions and their level of crisis be 'weighed') does not mean that regional policy should be realized only from above. Within the framework of adopted decisions, regions/areas can frequently exploit opportunities to greater effect. Additional resources for the development of infrastructure are often better utilized through existing institutions, including local authorities. The discontent of lower territorial units is understandable when strategic decisions are made above, and it is their job simply to carry them out. Who, though, can offer an alternative institutional system for the realization of regional policy aims? The hope that numerous regions/areas can agree on the redistribution of resources and rights seems utopian!

Within the framework of any system, there is always competition between regions/areas for investment, new rights, a privileged position etc. In extreme form, this leads to regional antagonism, the disintegration of the common market and even the country (seen mainly in eastern Europe). Even in 'peaceful' cases, this competition results in regional/local authorities, in the attempt to take the lead over their neighbours, offering new, and often overly expensive, privileges to private business. Regional policy is criticized for over-expenditure of public funds, but unlimited competition between areas has the same financial result and it is unclear which is better. A *united* regional policy is capable of limiting, to a certain extent, the competition between regions/areas and, thus, of helping those problem regions which are clearly losing 'in open struggle' with more prosperous neighbours.

It is clear from the above that in Russia, and earlier in the USSR, regional policy in the western understanding of the term was practically non-existent – although the scientific base did exist. In Poland – during its Socialist period – a considerable amount of scientific research was undertaken, which has now become the basis for the realization of national regional policy. In Hungary, scientific research prompted practical steps such as the decentralisation of economic activity and population from Budapest and the stimulation of depressed areas (for details see Chapter Four).

In discussing the creation of Russian regional policy, it is reasonable to examine, analyze and, where appropriate, utilize the more than half a century of experience accumulated by the countries of the West (see below). In the West, regional policy has always been based on the careful scientific study of all related questions. The first reaction of a state facing any important regional problem is to create a special body, which includes scientists and politicians, to commission research from leading scientific centres.

In indicating the components of regional policy, it is logical to specify the author's understanding of a number of other widely used terms in this book. *Regions* are parts of a country (or the EC/EU), either administrative-territorial, or 'historical', or identified and recognized as units in scientific literature. Thus, for example, in the case of Italy, a region would include the South, and Sicily. *Problem regions* are territories, currently (or previously) included in the sphere of regional policy and subject to state intervention. The understanding of *crisis regions* is a little wider, and includes territories which, although characterized by unsatisfactory social economic parameters, are not officially selected as targets of regional policy. The term *area* applies to a part of a region which is designated officially or in scientific literature or by the author.

The necessity for regional policy

Naturally, many of the author's ideas and approaches are defined by his ideology. Without considering a market economy one of God's best creations, the author recognizes that it works in reality (unlike numerous Socialist models envisaged as the 'ideal' community). However, the market economy in pure form is capable of creating political and social problems of the same scale as those seen in Russia or the former USSR (remember Fascism in Germany). Therefore, state intervention is necessary, although it is frequently inefficient, increases bureaucracy etc. The author has always been on the side of Keynes and his followers.

Regional problems are ranked among the difficulties which are often above the 'ability' of the market to solve –. Moreover, the market, in its very operation, creates many of these regional issues (see Chapter One). Hence, where the market operates, so should regional policy (naturally in a dynamic form which can adapt to changing realities). In a book about London, Hall remarks that the presence of regional planning is ultimately better than its absence (Hall 1989, p.189). The author agrees with this sentiment where regional policy is concerned.

The focus of study

The main subject of investigation in this book is regional policy in advanced countries. Significant differences are apparent – in the extent of regional disparities/problems, in the reaction of a state to their existence, and in its methods of intervention. In this book, the emphasis placed on the study of regional policy in west-European countries can be justified for the following reasons:

1. Connected to a long history of capitalist development, regional problems are sharpest (among advanced countries) in the countries of western Europe. The regional problems in the USA are considerably less marked than in west-European countries (Miernyk 1982).

2. The experience of west-European countries is, as a whole, more suitable for Russia than the experience of other advanced countries. A similarity in natural, historical and even socio-economic conditions between west European countries and Russia means that regions exist with problems of similar origin. Many former members of the USSR and their populations clearly want to be considered part of a united Europe, reflected in their with their favourable disposition towards the EU.

3. Pan-European trends exist in regional development, with a diminishing temporal lag between West and East. In Russia, for example, the processes

of suburbanization and gentrification are occurring simultaneously. There is an interesting opportunity to compare these processes between West and East – not only under various socio-political conditions, but also the differences in how states react to them.

4. The author has for many years studied the problems of development and structural reorganization of 'old industrial' regions, the majority of which are concentrated in western Europe. In addition, he has had numerous opportunities to visit scientific centres in western Europe working in the regional policy field, to gather information and discuss his ideas concerning regional policy. Contacts such as these, including in the EU, provided the author with access to many publications and reports not available in Russian libraries. All this has allowed him, to some degree, to avoid a 'second-hand' approach.

5. In comparison with the USA, a more human model of 'capitalism' has been created in western Europe and is, therefore, more suitable for Russia.

Geographers have always studied regional policy in the countries of the West. Almost all of the largest centres of geography in west-European countries conduct scientific research in the field of regional policy, and carry out studies (scientific and applied) of their own governments and the EU. Many consultancy firms, working within the field of regional policy, use geographers in their work, although their expertise has not been exploited to the full. Only geographers can *link* regional policy with the general trends in the location of economic activities and the population, and 'individualize' adopted measures (i.e. adapt them for particular regions and areas). The geographer is also able to carry out a more exact regional sub-division of territory, which more closely reflects reality.

An interesting paradox has been noted in Harvey (1985): spatial barriers are becoming less important (because of technological progress, the increase of population mobility etc.), but capital is becoming more sensitive to choice of location. In order to influence this through regional policy, it is necessary to understand the reasons for this sensitivity, i.e. the real geography of space.

The totally different nature of regional policy in the USSR was the main reason why geographers were unable to make progress in this field. Geographers can now be near the centre of a domestic *market* regional policy, and this will be beneficial not only for them, but also for business. The geographer, better than representatives of other sciences, understands the real situation within the huge territory of Russia, has the skills of comparative spatial analysis, and can present results in a clear and accessible form (even for politicians). Russian scientists voiced independent opinions even during the worst years of Soviet rule, but unfortunately even within the new era, such opinions are of little interest to a political elite influenced by subjectivity and favouritism.

Naturally, the first step to the creation of a new regional policy should be the designation of problem regions within the country, relying on the analysis of an optimally wide range of socio-economic statistics and a 'qualitative' understanding of the territory. It would be simply foolish to do this job without geographers – 'this is more than a crime: it is an error'. Certainly, work on the creation of a *scientific-practical base* for regional policy should include representatives of various fields – but the desire to include geographers is determined not only by education and the author's place of work, but also by basic logic.

Later in the Introduction a brief analysis of regional policy literature will be given. However, it can be noted now that publications on this theme are numerous in the West and thus the author has tried to identify his own niche in the preparation of this book. Certainly, the reader will find a description of the history of regional policy, its methods and focus etc. Without this, conclusions are impossible, and many of these facts are not widely known to politicians and managers, or to academics in adjacent fields (sociology, economics etc.). An integrated analysis of regional policy in western and eastern Europe (including USSR/Russia) will be attempted for the first time. The author's main purpose, however, is to provide an understanding of the transformation trends in regional policy, to analyze the 'laws' and driving forces underlying these changes, and to highlight the importance of geographical factors within them.

The book focuses on the study of the geographical and evolutionary features (aspects) of regional policy in the advanced countries of Europe. This approach to the study of regional policy allows the integration of original research and, the author hopes, a reduction of any duplication with the extensive scientific literature on the problems of regional policy. The book aims to offer a unique *view* of regional policy in the countries of western Europe.

The purpose and tasks of the book

The scientific bases for regional policy in advanced countries were formulated in the 1950s and 1960s, during a stage of stable economic development. From the mid-1970s, within the framework of general recession and *zero* economic growth, the transition to a post-industrial society, and the crisis of the idea of the *large state*, the existing theory and practice of regional policy was largely rejected (Albrechts, Moulaert and Swyngedouw 1989). Differences increased in the evaluation by experts of the efficiency of regional policy. Questions emerged relating to the existence of common trends in the evolution of regional policy, and its dependence on the stage of development of an economy and society.

Usually, regional policy is considered as only one of a state's areas of activity, not differing significantly from the others. The importance of taking spatial socio-economic distinctions into account in the successful realization of policy aims is underestimated. In turn, each problem region/area has particular requirements relating to the assistance provided to it. A much deeper 'geographization' of regional policy is required, to allow public funds to be saved through the concentration of assistance on those regions which are, first, in greatest need and, second, most in a position to use the aid effectively (provided the aid is in the most appropriate form).

The purpose of this book – on the basis of the analysis and a generalization of experience accumulated in advanced countries – is to try to develop the theoretical and methodological bases of *geographical* regional policy, to reveal the laws of its evolution and the factors determining it, and to define the opportunities and limits for the practical use of western experience in CIS/Russia. The main tasks of this book are defined as follows:

- To establish the extent to which socio-economic features of particular regions/areas can be taken into account in the realization of a regional policy (i.e. the 'geographization' of regional policy).

- To define the dependence of regional policy on real spatial factors or distinct spatial characteristics.

- To reveal the types of regions/areas and the laws of location which are most susceptible to the effects of regional policy.

- To establish the extent to which regional policy can accelerate/slow down the processes of transformation of a territorial structure of an economy and population.

- To reveal the level of dependence within the evolution of regional policy on macro socio-economic factors, such as changes in the territorial structure of an economy and population.

- To give practical recommendations for the use of western experience in the field of regional policy in Russia (and hopefully in the CIS), during the transition to the market.

Analysis of western regional policy will be conducted at three levels: advanced countries of western Europe as a whole (and the EU); the most representative countries individually; and *selected* typical regions. The third area includes all types of problem regions: depressed old-industrial regions, crisis underdeveloped agro-industrial regions and regions with extreme natural conditions… (for details see Chapter Three). Wales and Wallonia, Italy, Sweden and the capital regions of France and Great Britain have been selected for more detailed analysis. However, many problem regions/areas are mentioned in this book, and both unique and typical i.e. inherent to all types of problem regions, regional features are isolated. The way in which these features determine the reaction of regions to the regulation of their development through state policy is also analysed. This approach allows the consideration of the entire process of regional policy: from adopted decisions to their spatial impact.

Review of the literature and statistical sources

In Soviet scientific literature, regional policy is not a theme which has been widely studied. It is possible to note a burst of interest in it at the start of the 1960s and 1970s, when a number of books were published devoted to the analysis of foreign experience (Pavlov 1970, Karpov 1972, Alaev 1973, Karpov and Bogdanov 1974, Volski and Kolosova 1975). In a number of publications (including those of the 1980s) one can find an analysis of regional policy in Europe (Artobolveskiy 1987, a and b, 1989, b), as well as problems of regional policy in the USSR, but basically these works were devoted to the general analysis of territorial shifts, and of adopted regional programmes (Nekrasov 1980, Alymov 1981, Kistanov 1985, Horev 1989).

The author has widely used theoretical and methodological work of experts in social-economic geography. The works of Maergoiz (1964, 1981) should be mentioned in particular, in which the concept of a territorial structure of economy and society was approached for the first time, and methods of its study were proposed. This approach, as well as that offered by Gorkin, Gohman and Smirniagin (1976, 1978), was accepted and used by the author. Ideas contained in the works of Alaev (1973, 1982), Zimin (1976), Baklanov (1986), Privalovskaya (1989), Bandman (1990) were also used.

Analysis of works on the economic and social geography of the USSR and Russia (Ioffe 1987, Lappo and Treivish 1988, Artobolevskiy and Privalovskaya 1989), has provided a more complete understanding of the sharpest regional problems of the country, the extent to which regionalization can be incorporated into management purposes, and the possibilities and restrictions in the use of foreign experience. Much help has been provided by the works of regional economists (Probst 1971, Proposals of reorganisation 1988, Dmitrieva 1990, Territorial organization of economy 1990), in which, especially recently, questions of the possible role of the state in the decision of spatial problems have gained particular importance.

In such scientific centres as the geographical faculties of Moscow and St Petersburg State Universities, and the Institute of Geography of the Russian Academy of Sciences old traditions in the study of advanced countries exist. Publications on social and economic geography of western countries, by Lavrov (1967), Polskaya (1974), Agranat (1984, 1988), Gritzai (1988), Kolosov (1988), Smirniagin (1989), and many others (among which the author wants to highlight Odesser and Shlihter) were very useful in the preparation of this book. First, they were an important source of analytical information about changes in the territorial structure of regions and separate countries, and the driving forces of the processes. Second, the evaluation by the specified authors of the role and forms of regional policy did not always coincide with the author's ideas. This has allowed the author once again to evaluate critically his own position (and to have it confirmed).

Works of Soviet economists on western countries were widely used, especially those devoted to state-monopolistic capitalism and integration. It should be noted that, even before 1985, one could find objective analysis of the processes in many of these works (Maksimova 1971; Raskov 1979; Mileikovski 1981).

Clearly, a large part of the literature used is by western authors. The first works in the field of regional policy appeared at the end of the 1930s and beginning of the 1940s (see, for example, Sickle 1943). Since then, interest in these problems has remained virtually constant. In the West, dozens of publications appear annually on the problems of regional policy including (completely or largely) several scientific journals (Environment and planning. C: Governmental policy, European planning studies, International journal of urban and regional research, Journal of regional policy, Regional studies). Much work is published particularly on regional policy in western Europe – in the region as a whole and in individual countries (Vanhove and Klaassen 1980, Pinder 1983, Berquin 1984, Armstrong and Taylor 1985). Due to the process of integration within the framework of the EU, more attention has been given to the regional policy of this 'group' (Robert 1982, Keating and Jones 1985, The regions of 1987, The regions in 1991).

While in the 1950s and 1960s (and, even, at the start of the 1970s) regional policy was viewed as a positive phenomenon in all publications, the later position of various authors has diverged sharply. Some still consider this policy area absolutely necessary and recognize the need for its reorientation to changing conditions (Gore 1984, Albrechts et al. 1989, Hansen, Higgins and Savoie 1990, Balchin 1990, Freeman 1992). Others, however, consider regional policy a waste of resources and propose to reduce it considerably, or to devote it largely to the solution of pure economic problems (Aldcroft 1984, Regional imbalances 1985, Camagini and Capellin 1985, Muegge and Stohr 1987, Fujita 1988).

In all the works mentioned, regional policy is considered, first of all, as one area of state activity. Even its efficiency is basically evaluated using statistical parameters – the number of new employment places, the decrease in levels of unemployment, the scale of constructed enterprises and establishments etc. (details below). Much less attention is given to the effects of regional policy on the local economy, and its role in moderating and preventing spatial crises. Relatively few authors consider the role of regional policy in the transformation of spatial structures (or its role is simplified). At the same time, regional policy has been considered in many works together with a number of other factors which determine spatial development, and has been evaluated in its role as a factor both of location and of the mobility of capital (Benko 1993, Rodwin and Sazanami 1991, Townroe and Martin 1992, New location 1993).

Traditional geographical descriptions are valuable, especially those devoted to territories with significant spatial problems (John 1984, King 1987, Flockton and Kofman 1989). Many works are devoted to the analysis of the realization of a regional policy in separate regions and centres (Lythe and Majmudar 1982, Seers and Ostrom 1983, The development 1986, Evaluation 1986, Joseph 1989, Thumerel 1989, Sarubbi 1990, Hall 1992). They are a valuable source of information about the efficiency of regional policy and its individual measures. In addition, these works provide the opportunity to assess the parity of the typical and the unique in the understanding of regional policy.

Management bodies of western countries are the largest customers of scientific research on regional problems. For many years this function has been carried out by the Commission of the EU, located in Brussels. Reports published by this body, the authors of which are, in many cases, not specified, are scientific publications of a high quality (Peripheral 1986, Europe 1991, European 1987, The regions 1991, European 1987). In addition, these reports are a valuable source of up-to-date material (including statistics – see below), compiled specifically within a research framework and, hence, unique. The reports cover territories ranging from Western Europe as a whole to small areas of separate countries (For the Southern 1983, Bachtler 1988, Centre 1988).

One can find experts on regional policy in practically every west European university (many of them also work in private consulting companies, and management bodies). Among the largest scientific departments working in the field of regional policy are the European Policies Research Centre of Strathclyde University, the Department of Geography of Cambridge University (Great Britain), the Institute of Economic Geography of Amsterdam University, the National Economic Institute in Rotterdam (Netherlands), and the Planning Research Centre in Rome (Italy).

This book is based on the analysis of extensive information, mainly statistical in nature. The most valuable sources of information are statistical year-books, including specialized regional ones (published by a number of countries, including Great Britain and France). Particular mention should be made of the year-book of regional statistics of EU countries (Regions), as the data published in it by territorial units of member countries are comparable. At the same time, the use of specified sources is limited by their insufficient territorial sub-division: a significant proportion of statistics cover only large economical-statistical regions or even whole countries. Regional policy frequently operates with considerably smaller territorial units (see Chapter Three), and statistics at this level are either very limited or unpublished.

It has already been said that major sources of statistical information are reports, compiled by, or with the help of, management bodies. Many such reports are published within the framework of the EU, some wholly devoted to regional policy (European 1987, Yuill and Allen 1983, ERDF 1991, Yuill et al. 1993). In addition to statistical information, these reports contain numerous unique maps, data on the institutional organization of regional policy, and texts of the laws and officially adopted decisions. A specialized database on regions also exists in the EU, but unfortunately access to it is limited.

Details on laws and officially adopted plans and programmes (at national, as well as EU levels) are generally available from official publications. At the same time, so much change is adopted each year that the monitoring of laws and official decisions in the field of regional policy represents a separate, rather labour-consuming problem. Therefore, the author was pleased to be able to access a data-bank on regional policy in countries of western Europe, created by the aforementioned European Policies Research Centre (about ten people are engaged in its updating).

Material from population and manufacturing censuses were used on occasion. An important source of information was the directories on companies and state 'bodies', enabling the study of their spatial organization (see, for example, European 1986).

Cartographical materials were also analysed: many maps are directly related to regional policy, showing existing spatial disparities, spatial units receiving state assistance etc. (Hudson, Rhind and Mounsey 1984, Regions 1987).

Valuable data on separate regions and areas, the distribution of state assistance, and planned initiatives in the field of a regional policy were drawn from geographical, economic and, even, political journals and newspapers (Financial Times, Planning Outlook, Scottish Geographical Magazine, Urban Studies etc.). Reports on the work of parliaments, which are also an important source of regional information, were also published in some of them (see, for example, British business – not issued at present). The publications and working reports of DG-XVI (Directorate for regional policy in the EU – see Chapter Two) should be particularly emphasized, and this body commissions and finances research studies, as well as publicizing and distributing them. Many materials are, unfortunately, accessible only directly from DG-XVI. If the Commonwealth of Independent States (CIS) survives, it would be worthwhile considering the creation of a similar body to provide the Commonwealth with regional information.

Given the extent and range of publications on regional policy, the aim of the author has not been to provide a detailed analysis of all, or even a significant part, of the literature in the Introduction. The task has been more modest – to show that the author is acquainted with other research and to try to classify them, having specified the most from his point of view. This analysis indicates that some problems concerning regional policy still have not been investigated and require further research.

The practical importance of the book

In Chapter Four the question of the practical importance and possibilities for using experience in the field of regional policy in Russia (and partly in countries of CIS and East Europe) will be considered separately. It is necessary to note here that the course of reforms in Russia highlight the fact that the need for regional policy is increasing. Regional policy should comprise one of the tools for the improvement of the socio-political situation in the country. This situation was clearly shown in the elections of December 1993 and 1995, when the country 'moved' even further from Communism to a national form of Fascism (a term invented by the author and not intended as a political accuracy).

The second problem for regional policy is the 'struggle' with the disintegration of the country. At present, the main problem is the transition to the formation of a practical regional policy from the basis of development plans for individual regions/cities (developed over decades) which cannot be implemented, and from a period where the state has been 'absent' from regional problems and excessive hopes have been placed on market forces.

Market forces should certainly dominate in an economy, but the state is also obliged to solve regional crises, and indirectly to influence the location of the economy and population. It is necessary to understand that the regional consequences of our reforms will be basically negative and, in the absence of any adjusting measures to combat these spatial effects, the reforms are likely to lose the support of the population and not be completed. The cost of the non-existence of regional policy and, wider, a non-intervention of the state in social problems will be either Fascism, or disorder in the country (or potentially a combination of both of these phenomena).

The experience of western countries in the field of regional policy is great and there is an opportunity to learn from one anothers' errors. Politicians and experts (naturally to differing degrees) should be aware of this. Two things should be avoided at all costs – the direct 'one for one' copying of experience, and the absolute rejection of foreign knowledge, based on the notion that Russian characteristics (geographical, national, economic – see Chapter Four) are completely unique.

The structure and logic of the book

After a general analysis of regional policy, its importance in the state's influence on the economy and society and, among other factors, changing territorial structures (Chapter One), Chapter Two analyses the main directions of regional policy and types of problem regions. Special attention is given in Chapter Two to regional policy at EU level and in peripheral regions, which, by nature of their geographical location, are in a negative position. In Chapter Three, the problems of the practical realization of regional policy aims and its institutional structures are studied. The analysis of domestic regional problems, and the opportunities for using foreign experience (with a comparison of the situation in Russia/CIS with countries of east Europe) is the subject of Chapter Four. Practical recommendations for the use of western experience are provided. In the Conclusion, questions of the efficiency of regional policy, the real extent to which it can be used in the analysis and solution of spatial problems, and the levelling of territorial disparities are considered.

The writing of the last page of the Introduction is always both a pleasant and sad task. While it is good to remember certain periods of one's personal scientific life, it can be slightly sad to realize that they are over. The first person in the list of those whose help to me I should mention is Dr. N.M. Polskaya, who was my scientific tutor for four years in Moscow University. My Ph.D. dissertation was only possible due to the help of professors Gorkin and Mashbitz, and the author is still grateful to them. This book – and the author has not hidden the fact that it is a 'processed' professor's dissertation – has only become a reality through the help of professors Privalovskaya and Kantzebovskaia.

The Institute of Geography of the RAS can be regarded as a collective co-author of this book. I am especially grateful to my socio-economic geography colleagues.

The Netherlands Institute of Advanced Studies (NIAS), having provided the author with the opportunity to work for 10 months on this book, can also be considered a co-author.

The writing of this book would certainly have been impossible without the active and passive help of the author's extended family. I especially want to mention my wife, whose contribution was not limited to the provision of the necessary conditions for scientific work, but also involved typing, making maps etc.

If, despite all the help received, this book still contains any errors, discrepancies or false constructions – which I hope its readers will indicate – these are naturally the author's fault alone.

CHAPTER ONE

Regional Policy within the System of State Socio-Economic Activity

Although this book is devoted to the analysis of regional policy, the author does not overestimate its role in the location of economic activity and the population, and in the solution of territorial problems. Even within the framework of the socio-economic activity of the state (let alone the private sector), there are more powerful factors influencing the processes of regional development.

The main task of this chapter is to show the role of regional policy within an arsenal of state measures, its *uniqueness*, its theoretical bases and the common trends in its development.

The role of the state in the location of the economy and population

The evolution of the capitalist system in advanced countries during post-war periods is staggering. Shocks, connected with the world economic crisis of 1929–1932, and, later, war (partly a consequence of this crisis) threatened the existence of the system and forced a revision of the socio-economic basis of the capitalist system. The state took on responsibility for the social sphere (for the realization of the concept of a welfare state – for details see below) and introduced strict rules for the functioning of the private sector. Now any private company operates, in advanced countries, within the relatively strict framework instituted by the state. A significant part of its decisions must be co-ordinated with the state, including the location of any new 'capacities' (factories, offices etc), and, some-times, the expansion (modernization) of existing ones. This control is actually stricter than in countries with a planned economy (see Chapter Four).

In the mass media, and even in scientific publications, authors frequently speak of a return to the unregulated market of the 19th century as a more effective model of capitalism. In reality, there is a shift in the methods of state control of the economy (and society) from the direct (the existence of a significant state sector, grants etc.) to the indirect (the encouragement of private companies by the removal of administrative restrictions, the provision of necessary information, the creation of a more favourable investment climate etc.). Even at present, in advanced countries, privatization is initiated and carried out by the state, and represents not a withdrawal of the state from the economy, but rather a shift in the method of its management ('The privatization' 1986). In any western model, the market economy is not unregulated. The state does not *abandon* the economy, but changes the arsenal.

Although the concept of the welfare state emerged in the 1920s and 1930s, its realization started at the end of the 1940s and beginning of the 1950s. Programmes of construction of cheap housing (so-called 'social housing') for relatively poor groups of the population in Great Britain, the Netherlands and other countries of the West was undertaken in the 1930s, and the scope of social insurance was expanded etc. However, these programmes were not comparable with those initiated during post-war decades.

At present, in advanced countries, the state guarantees to all citizens a minimum level of income, the availability of affordable housing, education, medical services, and infrastructure (including social). However, the level of state care differs strongly between countries: social housing, for example, is provided almost immediately in the Netherlands, whereas waiting periods are normal within the British system. The quality of the housing, and its position in the *social space* vary. Similarly, the size of pensions and unemployment benefits etc., differ. Theoretically, within an individual country, the state provides assistance to all inhabitants at one level – where they live. In reality, regional distinctions can be observed in this assistance, frequently linked to purely spatial factors (for example, the geographical position of the area).

It would be incorrect to consider the creation of the concept of the welfare state as purely an enforced measure, an answer to crises. At present, the majority of political forces consider the state to be a body which is obliged to take care of human values and, hence, to ensure a minimum quality of life for the whole population. This does not mean, however, the economies of advanced countries should suffer because of state social activity and indeed, only economic success provides the state with the resources for social programmes. Even the Thatcher proposals – the reduction of public spending, the diminishing role of the state, the reliance on market forces etc. – never put in doubt the necessity of state assistance for the unemployed and national minorities. The emphasis was simply placed elsewhere – on delivering this help to those who really need it, to avoid unnecessary overspending on the support of spongers.

The post-war period was characterized by the strengthening of state intervention in the economy. Stricter control of the development of the private sector was introduced, and the state sector increased. The expansion of the latter was encouraged by the nationalization of a number of economic sectors and industries (electrical power production, coal mining, black metallurgy etc.), which were generally unprofitable and required modernization (but, at the same time, were necessary for the functioning of the economy as a whole). However, not only unprofitable old sectors were nationalized, but also modern and more profitable ones (for example, in France and Great Britain). Even after the denationalization campaign in the first half of the 1980s, the state's share in a number of sectors of the economy and industry of western Europe still exceeded 50–75 per cent (Williams 1987, p.83). Thus, although there are sectors and industries with virtually no state control, their number is increasing only gradually. State companies generally functioned under the same rules as private companies. This permitted state assistance to them to be minimized, preventing a monopoly situation in a number of cases, and supporting competition in the market etc.

Within the framework of the welfare state, and in the course of realizing new economic policy, the need to regionalize existing structures has become apparent. This has been reflected in the structure of new management bodies (even those relating purely to the economy), which were decentralized to incorporate regional branches. For example, in Japan, the Ministries of Foreign Trade and Industry and Construction have regional branches. There are also regional branches of the Ministry of Trade and Industry, and a number of other ministries, in Great Britain, as well as in France...

For the maintenance of a certain minimum standard of living for the population in peripheral agricultural areas and in central regions (including wider issues such as a sufficient infrastructural provision), the state has to spend a certain amount per head of population. For peripheral agricultural regions, the creation and repair of roads, the maintenance of regular transport connections, and the support of schools, hospitals and libraries, will often require more resources. Distinct regional characteristics require not only the redistribution of state resources, but also the adaptation of policy methods to fit local conditions. Where, for example, in the southern regions of Scandinavian countries the state can interest private business in the realization of certain industrial and infrastructure projects, in northern regions it frequently has to undertake such projects itself (Diem 1979). A similar picture has been observed in Italy, although there it is the South of the country which is in a similar position to the Scandinavian North (King 1985).

Significant spatial differences can be observed (in advanced countries) in the dependence of both the population on social assistance from the state, and of regional and local authorities on financial flows from central government. In regions where there is a concentration both of new sectors/industries and of relatively well-off groups of the population, regional and local authorities receive more in the form of local tax revenues than their counterparts in areas where there is a dominance of old manufacturing industries, and generally more marginal groups of the population. Accordingly, the state has to grant a greater volume of help to the latter regions.

Even the purely social problems which confront the state cannot be solved simply through the transfer of resources from rich to poor regions. Unemployment benefit only partially compensates for the personal negative social-psychological consequences of not having a permanent job. However, the resolution of purely social problems often cannot be achieved without a link to the economic sphere

– for many years in Great Britain and France, for example, state companies in old sectors were subsidized with the principal purpose of preserving working places in depressed regions (Williams 1987).

The role of the state in the regulation (and stimulation) of internal migration is very important (and this can be partially attributed to regional policy). At the start of the 1950s in many countries of western Europe, and in Japan, the state stimulated the migration of labour to where employment opportunities existed. This was then considered the best way of dealing with unemployment (later the concept of *work to the people* came into vogue).

In the 1960s and 1970s, the state had already stimulated the process of suburbanization, the decentralisation of the largest centres, putting significant resources into housing and infrastructure construction in areas close to agglomerations. The migration of the population from agglomerations, especially the most qualified staff, was directly encouraged (eg. through grants compensating the cost of moving).

In the 1980s, the state began to encourage the process of gentrification and huge sums have been spent on the revitalization of the inner city areas of agglomerations, with the parallel support of suburbanization. In general, the dependence of migration movements on state policy is clear. State help (or the absence of it), granted either directly (through the availability of *state* houses/flats, as in new towns) or indirectly (through the development of infrastructure and the economy in designated areas), leads to the movement of a significant part of the population.

Similarly, the shifts in location of the economy are, to a considerable degree, determined by the state's activity. The state directly owns a significant part of the country's economy, and regulates the activity of the private sector. The activity of the state is often dictated by the need to solve social problems, and is not purely motivated by market reasons. For example, the support of old industries, which cannot survive without assistance, encourages the preservation of an existing pattern of location. At the same time, the support of new sector development – micro-electronics, instrument-making, business services etc. – leads to its concentration, in the initial stages of development, in the largest regions and centres.

The infrastructure created by the state has the same significant effect on the location of various sectors and industries in the economy. New facilities *gravitate* towards highways, new towns, and industrial parks. Among the most dynamic current growth poles are areas adjacent to the largest airports (Schipol in the Netherlands, Orly in France, Heathrow in Great Britain) and ports (Rotterdam, Amsterdam, Antwerp), the development of which is promoted by the state.

The state, largely, supports education and training, culture, public health, the protection of the environment, and housing construction. All this determines the opportunities for a particular region/area.

The power and opportunities for action of local authorities are great, and not only in the social sphere. Current rigid planning control powers can block the progress of any new project, or local authorities can stimulate economic development in an area. Thus, the aims of local authorities can coincide with those of central authorities, although frequently they contradict them (simply because local authorities only take into account the interests of their own areas).

Thus, the dependence of the population and the economy on the state, including in aspects of its location, is clear. In many cases, however, the state does not pursue pre-determined spatial purposes, and does not aim to regulate regional development through intervention. In resolving other problems − such as the improvement of the population's living conditions, the levelling of social disparities, the reduction of unemployment, the increase in economic competitiveness − the state largely defines the processes of regional development. This knock-on effect of the solution of these other problems can, in many cases, also promote, as well as hinder, crisis in regions. Only within the framework of a government regional policy, as already noted, are spatial purposes regarded by a state as the primary ones. Thus, it should be understood, that all the above mentioned areas of state activity have much more significant effects on the spatial structure of the population and economy, than pure regional policy (Higgins and Savoie 1988). At the same time, the latter is an integral part of a state's activity. In an analysis of regional policy, the following two extremes must be avoided: regional policy can do everything or nothing. It is better to accept from the start that it is of *limited validity*.

During the last ten to fifteen years, a key re-evaluation of the role of the state in the regulation of socio-economic development has occurred. Over-expenditure of tax payers' money, the low efficiency of a huge bureaucratic *machine* etc. (see below) has been used to explain the inability of a state to deal with many problems. For advanced countries, such statements are not new: intense discussion on the role of the state began in the 1920s and has been periodically revitalized (McCrone 1969, where it is shown in an example of regional policy). In former Socialist countries (at official level) it was only in the 1980s that any doubt was cast on the positive influence of any socio-economic activity of the state.

Marked synchronization in the appearance of the question relating to the role of the state (as well as similar terms emerging in scientific literature and the media) in both East and West European countries points to the possibility that the processes may be uniform, and may be linked to Kondratiev cycles (ie. the differing cycles have uniform consequences in both East and West).

In the 1970s and 1980s, in the majority of developed countries, regional socio-economic disparities have increased (albeit slightly) (Dunford and Kafkalas 1992). The division of advanced countries into a centre and periphery has become more marked. This division is only partially explained by geographical (and economic) factors, and also has a political and social dimension. The periphery becomes an internal colony, controlled from the centre (see Chapter Two). Differences in the quality of life of the population, in its widest sense, are also amplified, and result in the increase of social, and particularly ethnic, tensions

(Clout 1986, Williams 1987). In many cases there are also national-ethnic and linguistic characteristics which separate the core from the periphery. One can find examples of this in CIS/Russia, Great Britain, Belgium and France (details later in this chapter).

If, previously, the centre and the periphery differed principally in terms of quantitative parameters, more qualitative factors have currently emerged as highly important. The analysis of population censuses in Great Britain from 1951 to 1991 shows that, in the structure of the manufacturing industry (as well as of the service sector and the economy as a whole), the regions of the country are becoming increasingly uniform, and there is a clear trend towards alignment in some the newest sectors/industries. In reality, a significant part of the newest industries in the North are branch plants of companies based in the South or in other countries, and specialize in mass production. Such branch plants are especially vulnerable during crises (Townsend 1983). Thus, the centre is characterized not simply by a high share of electronics, but also by a prevalence of the company headquarters, research and marketing divisions, and specialised enterprises, often exploiting extensively R&D and highly qualified personnel. Analyzing data of directories of research centres in Europe, one can see that their highest concentration is in a limited number of centres – London, Paris, Brussels, Milan etc. A branch plant economy created in crisis regions, having solved neither the problem of unemployment, nor achieved stability of employment, creates a new set of difficulties. The professional and social spectrum of possible employment occupations has been reduced, the problem of male unemployment has become more acute, the disintegration of the local economy has increased, and the influence of the local authorities has been reduced.

Other parameters of backwardness and crisis have required changes in traditional regional policy, which has become less effective under changing conditions (Gorzelak 1988, Hilpert 1991,Townroe and Martin 1992). Details of the evolution of regional policy will be given later, but an initial brief description of its crisis is provided here.

The current crisis of regional policy is linked to the transition to a post-industrial society, the internationalization of the economy, the move away from the idea that 'big is best' in industrial plant size, new stages in technological progress, and the slowing of the rate of economic growth etc. In short, regional policy has ceased to correspond to the new socio-economic reality.

The direction of the reorganization of regional policy is, in many respects, defined by the role of the state in society. In advanced countries, the state accepts responsibility for the solution of social issues (leaving the economy, mainly, to the private sector) and, accordingly, their solution becomes the main focus of regional policy. Clearly, under conditions of low economic growth, the reduction of a state's financial possibilities, and general crisis in the traditional system of state intervention, regional policy has to change.

Traditional regional policy represented a typical variant of 'top-down' development. It entailed limited territorial flexibility, bureaucracy, and the significant use of centralized resources. In the 1980s, greater emphasis was placed on the use of local resources, or development *from below* (Robert 1982). The wider exploitation of local resources is seen as a panacea compared with the branch plant economy created by *conventional* regional policy which, as already mentioned, is unstable during crises, and weakly integrated into the local economy and market (and frequently with local labour). Even the role of local energy resources is being re-evaluated. An example of this is the proposed programme to use peat and bio-mass for energy production, promoted within the framework of regional policy in Finland (Seers and Ostrom 1983). The reorientation of local resources and the new focus of regional policy on small business, (currently flourishing in countries of the West) was the basis of the spring 1988 reform of regional policy in Great Britain.

Emphasis on local resources requires the decentralization of political and economic power, the transfer of certain *executive* rights and, accordingly, the necessary resources to regional and local levels – although not all steps towards the decentralization of power (both political and economic) should be attributed to regional policy.

Both in the West and in Russia/USSR, traditional regional policy (see above) has appeared insufficiently effective, and there are insufficient resources for its realization. The emphasis is placed on its transfer to lower territorial levels, the realization of numerous small-sized projects, and attempts to combine social and economic aims. Questions of its efficiency will be dealt with below.

Certainly, the fact that there is a crisis in traditional regional policy is clear. It has not been able to solve many regional problems: the restriction of the growth of Moscow and other large cities in the USSR; the development of the Non-Black-soil zone (an extensive area in the central and northern parts of European Russia and central and southern parts of Western Siberia); the maintenance of a stable economic situation in depressed regions of France and Great Britain; the elimination of the gap between the South and North in Italy etc. A more efficient regional policy, which is better able to solve the above problems, is now proposed, although, in all probability, it will also not meet all the expectations of its creators.

It is apparent that both the capitalist and socialist systems overestimated the opportunities available to the state to resolve regional problems. At each stage of development, the socio-economic system requires a territorial organization which is adequate for it. Shifts in territorial organization reflect, first of all, macro changes within the system. The outflow of economic activity and population from the largest agglomerations in the West (including London and Birmingham) was less the result of a policy of decentralisation, and more a consequence of the introduction into the mass consciousness of a suburban/rural ideal, the need to locate industry in new greenfield sites, and the progress in transport and methods of communication. All this underlines the 'natural gravitation' of the economy and people to non-agglomeration space. Certainly, the state policy of decentralisation has hastened the outflow of population and employment from agglomerations. Similarly, the observed partial return to cities is a consequence of the supporting effect of other factors of location. Once again, the state merely 'accelerates' the trends which it has not created.

Recognizing the secondary nature of the processes of spatial redistribution of the economy and population, one has to realize the existence of limits in the opportunities available to the state to solve regional problems (Malecki and Nijkamp 1988). These limits are not only the result of limited state resources, the absence of an adequate institutional infrastructure and misdirected efforts, but are also linked to the strength of 'natural' processes (Artobolevskiy, 1990). These include the spatial expression of technological progress, changes in population tastes, the internationalization of the economy etc. Indeed, all these changes were considered by Kondratiev (1928) as major driving forces in his cycles.

It is quite permissible for the state to intervene in the course of specified *natural* processes, on the grounds of needing to resolve social and other problems. First, however, it is necessary to understand clearly that the state must *pay* for any intervention from within the economy. Second, it is necessary to recognize, that while *natural* spatial processes can be slowed down or speeded up, they cannot be reversed. In the 1980s, a concept of determined economic and social predestination for a number of crisis regions in developed countries appeared (Aldcroft 1984). In Russia, the revision of official policy which favoured the development of the North and East took place, and attention was concentrated on the development of the European part.

The process of the creation of branch plants of industrial firms engaged in mass production (and located far from the centres of management) is a *natural* process. The companies are largely free in the choice of their location. This is a wide field of activity for regional policy, as state aid can significantly influence the locational decisions of companies (although in only a limited number of cases will regional policy be the principal motivation behind industrial migration movements).

The significant role of high-tech industries and small-sized business in regional development is currently universally recognized, although research shows that neither neo-liberal, nor neo-Keynesian (i.e. including significant regional policy) approaches are capable of ensuring their development in areas where there are no adequate *natural* conditions for them (Bergman, Maier and Todtling 1991). The state can only regulate their location within certain limits (Hilpert 1991, Artobolevskiy 1992). Once again, the state (including its regional policy) acts here as an additional factor, capable (in a rather limited way) of directing the *locational decisions* of high-tech industries.

Even relatively large scale regional policy can not overcome *natural* trends. In Greece (where regional policy is significantly supplemented by major aid from the EU), large scale grants are available to promote location outside Athens and Salonika, but even this state help cannot overcome the tendency to concentration in these two centres (Tsoukalas 1988). Centripetal tendencies are still dominate in the country, and the period of growth of the largest centres is not yet complete.

The limitation of opportunities of regional policy is amplified by the considerable inertia in territorial structures (in comparison to industrial ones). Spatial inertia is inherent not only in the economy, but also in the population. In the latter case, it is frequently amplified by national/ethnic factors. It is this inertia in the location of the population which has resulted in the greater effectiveness of a policy of *the work to the people*, rather than one of *the people to the work*. Not only the 'movement' of waters (based on the senseless pre-perestroika idea of diverting the Siberian rivers to provide for the Soviet Asian republics), but also of people should be carried out with great care. Occasionally in the West, politicians and scientists return to the people to the work approach, but fail to analyze their own unsuccessful pre- and post-war experience.

A retrospective analysis of western regional policy shows that its current crisis is the deepest in the history of its existence, although the main reasons for this lie outside regional policy. Shifts in the factors of location, *natural* trends, the changing territorial structure of the population and economy, have all resulted in a discrepancy between the old regional policy and new realities (geographical, industrial, and political).

Is regional policy necessary to a market economy? In the West, even supporters of non-controlled capitalism realize the necessity for a regional policy (Higgins and Savoie 1988). In Great Britain, where the deregulation of the economy is more advanced than in other countries of the West, a significant national regional policy, supported by the activity of EU, has survived. Even taking into account the fact that within the EU a process of the partial replacement of national regional policy with a common one is taking place, in general it is not clear whether the combined financial scale of EU and national policies have decreased in the 1980s and 1990s.

Regional disparities in the level of socio-economic development cause a sharp reaction among the population, especially if they are amplified by national-ethnic and/or religious factors. In the mid-1970s, in western Europe, 37 separate ethnic groups were counted, and virtually all of them required self-management (in one form or another) (Williams 1987, p.25). Ethnic/regional problems have become extremely marked in recent years within the boundaries of ex-USSR countries (see detail below).

The market economy does not currently function anywhere in *pure form*, as the state effectively adjusts the majority of economic processes. Even neo-liberals agree on the need for a state response to spatial changes, given that these represent the knock-on consequences of market processes (Higgins and Savoie 1988). It is possible to say that, in Western countries, regional policy has been revamped, but will certainly be preserved as an important component of the social and economic activity of the state. For this reason, a 'growing' similarity in regional policies, as well as spatial problems, within countries of the West and East will doubtless take place (see Chapter Four).

Ongoing macro-economic and social processes are the main underlying reasons for change in the territorial organization of society, their effect being much greater than that of regional policy. Regional policy, therefore, can only affect the speed at which these processes take place and affect the spatial pattern of any redistribution, although this function is seen as very important. Regional policy appears most effective when it follows *natural trends*, although too great a strengthening of these trends can be potentially dangerous.

A return of economic activity to the cities, connected with the transition to post-Fordism, is now predicted (Benko 1993). Without starting a discussion about the accuracy of this forecast, it is reasonable to examine its probable 'consequences' for regional policy. It is clear that in such a case inner-city development will become more successful, and the situation in many peripheral agricultural and 'small-town' areas will deteriorate, leading to the issue of the potential need for increased state aid.

The role of regional policy in the socio-economic life of developed countries

A comparison of state budget figures, or government expenditure on education or public health, drawing out figures for regional policy, would indicate a deficiency in this latter area. This is illustrated by Table 1.1. The low share of regional policy resources, however, is not evidence of its secondary importance.

First, spending on regional policy is much higher in reality. If one takes into account assistance to black metallurgy, ship-building and coal mining, almost all of which goes to old-industrial regions, the spending on regional policy increases greatly in many countries of the EU. The regional policy share in state aid to companies also increases in this case (up to 42.1% in Germany, 41.8% in Great Britain, 37.1% in Belgium – data for 1986–1988, indicated in The Regional Impact 1991). In addition, a significant proportion of resources expended by a state on infrastructure goes to problem regions and increases their appeal for private investment, improving the investment climate. The total volumes are generally higher than they would be if they were defined only by the population size of a region and other similar parameters. It is impossible to establish which part of this infrastructure spending should be classified as regional policy. Similarly, part of education spending is used for the resolving of employment problems in crisis regions.

Second, the importance of regional policy, or any other area of state activity, is not always necessarily defined by the volume of resources.

Table 1.1 indicates that advanced countries cannot be considered as a single bloc – distinctions between them are very significant.

**Table 1.1 State aid for economic development
in EU countries. Average per year: 1981–1986, (mln ecu)**

Country	Total	For regional policy		For development of industry and services
		subtotal	% from total	
Belgium	4000	182	5	1148
Denmark	900	12	1	304
France	16,700	383	2	6695
Germany	19,100	3449	18	3314
Greece	1000	171	17	685
Ireland	1100	176	16	542
Italy	27,700	5855	21	17,886
Luxembourg	200	12	6	77
Netherlands	2200	169	8	902
UK	9400	1372	15	3309
EU	82,300	11,781	14	34,862

Source: Bachtler 1989

Regional policy has huge political and ideological significance. Since the *New Deal* of President F.D. Roosevelt, the state, in advanced countries, has openly stated its responsibility towards the entire population, with particular attention given to minority groups (ethnic, social, *regional*). In turn, the population have become used to the provision of state care, and may often petition the state for assistance. This may even occur in areas outwith the authority or powers of the state – the calls to prevent the closure of Japanese or American multi-national branch plants in Scotland or Lorraine, for example, were addressed to the national governments rather than the headquarters of the companies themselves.

Naturally, the dependence of any population on state aid is greatest in problem regions. Regional policy, always quite widely advertised (including by local politicians), acts as the guarantor of state care to the populations of problem regions.

The misunderstanding of the importance of regional policy in the USSR, and at present in Russia, is partly connected with the traditional view of the majority of the population that assistance to any minority is given only at a minimum level. In developed countries, the situation is completely the reverse, and regional policy is regarded as state care for the minority (ie. inhabitants of problem regions). In the majority of western countries, it is a minority of the population which live in officially designated problem regions (for instance in Sweden – 13.5%), although there are exceptions, such as Greece (58% – Yuill *et al.* 1988, p.86).

The care of minorities has become a component of the political culture of society. Therefore, while it is possible to review and reorganize regional policy, to change the borders of problem regions and/or to reduce resource levels (see below), in reality neither the largest political parties, nor their representatives in parliament and government, will completely abolish regional policy.

The financial scale of regional policy resources is estimated at tens and hundreds of millions (pounds, marks, franks). In 1990, the Member States of the EU spent almost 12 billion ecu on their national regional policies (Allen, Bachtler and Yuill 1994, p.15) as direct financial aid (see Chapter Three). More than one billion ecu was given to them as part of the common regional policy of the EU – see below.

In addition, the resources granted by the state attract considerably higher levels of private investment (EU assistance, for example, attracts both private investment and finance from the budgets of national policy areas, including regional). Table 1.2 testifies to the importance of this multiplier effect. It is also, however, evident from this table that the efficiency of expended resources differs (for details, see Conclusion). Generally, any state aid to problem regions leads to the redistribution, to their advantage, of considerably larger investments from other sources (first of all, private).

Naturally, depending on the acuteness of regional problems and the financial possibilities of the state, the *intensity* of regional policy in countries of Western Europe varies significantly. Italy spends (in direct financial help) more than 1 per cent of GDP on regional policy (more than 8 bln ecu), while Denmark and France spend less than 0.02 per cent. A high 'specific weighting' of expenditure in Spain, Portugal, Greece and Ireland – ranging from 0.4 to 0.6 per cent of GDP (Allen, Bachtler and Yuill 1994, p.16) – is quite natural.

Almost all developed countries have relatively advanced institutional infrastructures for the realization of regional policy. Specific infrastructure also exists within the framework of EU (for details see Chapter Two). For private companies (including multi-nationals), regional policy has become an important factor in determining the location or migration of their capacities, as confirmed by survey results (Clarke 1985).

It can be asserted that regional policy is an important factor in the maintenance of socio-political stability within society. Even directly within the framework of this policy area – at national and EU levels – significant resources are redistributed. Regional policy is taken into account in the location strategy of private business (An empirical 1990), and the activity of local authorities. All these factors mean that it can be considered an important component of state activity and disproves the opinion that it is disappearing as a policy area. It should be remembered that significant groups of the population (of problem areas) and, accordingly, their political representatives in parliament, are interested in the preservation of regional policy. It is necessary to consider the role of regional policy in the stabilization of the economy; Richardson took account of this fact at the start of the 1970s (Richardson 1969).

Certainly, the ideology of the author is clearly seen in this high evaluation of the role of regional policy. Unfortunately, not all geographers, economists and

Table 1.2 Grants from ERDF and capital investments stimulated by them, 1985. (mln ecu)

Countries	Grants from ERDF	'Connected' investments	Ratio of investments and grants
Belgium	24	149	3.8
Denmark	13	67	5.2
France	219	1170	5.3
Germany*	84	1497	17.8
Greece	392	1037	2.6
Ireland	157	577	3.7
Italy	856	1994	2.3
UK	608	2339	3.8
EU*	2370	8945	4.1
Netherlands	17	115	6.8

* without West Berlin
Source: Regions 1987

sociologists share this opinion of the policy area (at present it is more fashionable to criticize it) or are sure of its prospects. All this forces a return to the question of the 'roots' of regional policy and its current and future positions.

The theoretical backing of the need for regional policy

As already noted, large scale regional policy emerged in developed countries (in the 1930s) as part of the 'answer' to the world economic crisis which was threatening the existence of the system. Until then, the dominant theory was that the free market had a sufficient degree of self-regulation, including in the spatial aspects. The latter was ensured by shifts in the spatial preferences of capital (from rich regions to poor with high levels of unemployment and cheap labour – Prestwick and Taylor 1990).

Even now, under considerably more favourable socio-economic conditions, regional problems in their extreme form – Northern Ireland, Corsica, Quebec – lead to bloodshed and threaten the territorial integrity of countries. In CIS/Russia one can find such examples in many areas. The movement of nationalities for independence is the most extreme form (for details see Chapter Four).

The idea that the market can level regional disparities was revitalized and underwent a renaissance in the 1980s. It is necessary to analyze this in detail, with reference to modern conditions. The adherents of this idea base it on the notion of the unlimited mobility of capital (although for a significant proportion of small and medium-sized businesses this mobility is limited), and consider the market within the framework of one country (although the real market is wider, and capital can simply 'leave' the country). The importance of the factors of location, as well as geographical factors in general (not all companies can move to any region), is not taken into account.

Generally speaking, reality appears more complex than the models mentioned above, one of the misfortunes of the real world (Townroe and Martin 1992, p.105). In this book, it is clearly shown in the example of Wales, as well as in the requirement for regional policy in 'weak' regions (*ibid* pp.99–101). The activity of the market *creates* regional problems: the global optimum develops from winning and losing regions/areas (Dunford 1994). In any case, the *non-spatial* policy of the state itself leads to an increase in territorial disparities (Castillo 1989).

Regional policy is part of a wider system of strengthening and modernizing a market economy (the formation of 'capitalism with the human face'). From this standpoint, the reforms of regional policy, and the shift of its *focus*, are the actions of the state directed towards its adaptation to changing conditions. In the 1950s in the Netherlands, the policy of encouraging population migration to the Randstad was changed to a strategy of its decentralisation (Dieleman and Musterd 1992). This was connected to the aggravation of socio-economic problems in the Randstad, and the exacerbated crisis conditions in Groningen and Limburg. Similarly, the policy of active decentralisation of population and economic activities from Paris during the 1960s was linked to the difficulties of development in the capital agglomeration, as well as a sharpening of the problems of the *French desert*, and the heightening of significant inter-regional antagonism (Paris versus the rest of France). The particular attention of the state to the problems of Scotland, Wales and Northern Ireland during the 1970s is linked to the growth of nationalism and the political problems in these regions, as shown in the election results.

The consequences of a well developed regional strategy was a decline in the acuteness of the above-mentioned problems: in Great Britain, for example, nationalism in Scotland and Wales in the 1970s and at the start of the 1980s clearly receded, and adopted a more moderate character. This success has not been achieved every time – as seen in the case of Northern Ireland (or the problem of Wallonia in Belgium), although even in these cases it can be claimed that regional policy has helped to maintain the status-quo. Thus, regional policy is necessary for the maintenance of national-political stability in a country (see below).

The literature on 'territorial justice' is quite extensive (Richardson 1978, Dostal 1984, Higgins and Savoie 1988, Harvey 1985). If one were to summarize the ideas contained in this body of literature, it is possible to come to the following conclusions. First, space determines the existence of socio-economic inequality. For example, certain regions, under any conditions, will remain peripheral. Second, the existence of spatial socio-economic inequality requires state intervention, since, under the conditions of a market economy, only the state is able to solve regional problems. Otherwise social-political instability, a loss of resources for problem regions, and difficulties in solving strategic economic problems are inevitable. The state is ideologically responsible for social justice and this necessitates its intervention through regional (and other) policy areas to solve the problems which exist.

Naturally, an awareness of regional disparities does not mean the automatic intervention of the state. Only when the state perceives their level as 'inadmissible' does state intervention take place. From the point of view of the state, an admissible level of regional disparities is not fixed, but rather is determined by the state of the country's economy, the ideology of ruling parties etc.

Under the conditions at the end of the 1970s and start of the 1980s, the ideas about the requirement of the state to maintain territorial justice, possibly only through a decrease in economic efficiency, were criticized by both politicians and scientists. The practical consequence was the afore-mentioned reduction in the scale of regional policy spending. However, by the end of the 1980s, one can see a crisis of neo-liberal ideas and a partial return to former ideals based on social values. During the 1980s it has become clearer that the market can not guarantee optimum acceptance of decisions from the social point of view.

As a whole, regional policy can be considered a part of the social (socio-political) activity of a state. Regional policy does not simply provide help to designated regions/areas. Within these regions it is really addressed (although not entirely) to certain groups which are the most affected by the crisis – the unemployed, young people etc. In theory, its purpose is the *development* of the local inhabitants, not of the territories (in practice, certainly, this principle is frequently not realized – see Chapter Two). Often it is considered part of the welfare state (Eskelinen 1991).

The theory about the social (socio-political) nature of regional policy is relevant in almost all advanced countries (see, for example, Finnish 1992, Brunt 1993), although it does not exclude other 'motives' for this policy area (Bylund and Wiberg 1986). Economic rationale for the need for regional policy also exist. First, only the state is capable of solving strategic economic problems, like the development of natural resources in regions with external natural conditions (from the market point of view it is frequently more expedient to import them). Second, regional policy reduces the level of loss of resources (territorial, human, economic) from problem regions, and saves them for subsequent stages of development. During the 1960s, the sharply increased attractiveness of non-metropolitan areas caused companies undergoing relocation to exploit extensively the infrastructure (for example, new cities and industrial parks, roads etc.) created within the framework of regional policy in the 1950s. Third, the achievement of a certain regional balance can promote the *prosperity* of countries as a whole, for example through a reduction of social costs (Healey and Ilbery 1990).

On occasion, regional policy can also be a tool to increase the *current* efficiency of an economy. In the absence, at a given stage, of serious regional disparities in a country, it is possible to concentrate temporarily on the development of the most competitive areas. Currently, in the Netherlands, an attempt to increase the competitiveness of the national economy has led to a return to the policy of developing the Randstad (Houterman 1992). In London, the policy of promoting development of the docks area is also an attempt to encourage City 'expansion', i.e. one of the most prestigious and prosperous areas in western Europe.

The effect of regional policy on the level of inflation is weakly investigated, although there is evidence that the reduction of unemployment in problem regions leads to lower inflation growth than would occur in more prosperous ones (Stillwell 1972). Regional policy increases the efficiency of the economy through the agglomeration effect – it effectively stimulates development in a limited number of growth poles (Richardson 1969, 1979). It is clear, even from the two works mentioned above, that ideas about the economic efficiency of regional policy became popular at the end of the 1960s and start of the 1970s. In the 1980s, a second peak in the popularity of this idea was evident, leading to attempts to 'economize' regional policy, frequently to the detriment of social purposes.

The majority of researchers and politicians agree that the market does not solve, but rather creates, social, political, environmental etc. problems at regional level which then require state intervention. In the evaluation of the necessary scale of such *intervention*, opinions vary greatly. A further interesting point can be noted. The market creates regional economic problems which cannot be solved without state assistance. This opposes the popular idea that the market can tackle all economic problems, leading only to difficulties in related areas (eg. social life, environmental conditions etc.).

In many cases, national and regional interests, both economic and social, contradict each other. One can clearly see the conflict between the two problems: the need to maximize national income on the one hand, and reduce disparities in the standard of living between regions on the other. In the literature, this contradiction is called the *efficiency or equity* debate (Richardson 1978). The curve presented by Richardson clearly shows an inverse dependence between efficiency and equity. In the identification of a location for almost any industrial unit, it is possible to find a place where the parameters for its operation will ensure greatest efficiency or success, and, conversely, where it will make the maximum contribution to the development of the local economy and the resolution of social problems (for example, the reduction of unemployment levels). The state uses regional policy first and foremost for the resolution of equity problems, although the realization of regional policy cannot be detached from the need to solve economic problems (confirmed by the experience of west European countries).

However, the general impossibility of achieving both efficiency and equity at the same time is not recognized by everybody. Economists particularly want to trust in the possibility of being simultaneously *rich and healthy*, although the constant reappearance of regional disparities highlights the existence of the afore-mentioned inverse dependence between efficiency and equity. Even if one were to consider this 'pair' only in relation to the economy (equity being seen as the alignment in the level of economic development of regions, and efficiency the receipt of maximum output from all regions) there can be no reliance on the likelihood of simultaneously achieving both purposes. The consideration of efficiency and equity is only possible under conditions of homogeneous development levels within countries (for example in the Netherlands). In countries with slightly higher regional disparities, the concept of equity gains a social-political dimension.

Clearly, private companies, interested in maximum profit, will be motivated by their own efficiency, and this will lead to their concentration in a limited number of regions/centres. If the decision-making process is simplified slightly, it can be assumed that these companies aim to minimize their production costs. If this is the case, the state can only influence their location decisions when its assistance becomes an important factor in this cost reduction, i.e. counteracting of the poor factors of location in problem regions (eg. high transport costs, the absence of qualified staff etc.). Regional policy is one of the main channels for achieving such aims, and is therefore a factor of location within the economy (and population), but acting indirectly, changing the 'weight' of other factors such as transport, capital, cost etc.

An analysis of the shifts in the territorial structure of the economy and population in developed countries (see, for example, Artobolevskiy 1992) shows that, since the Industrial Revolution, radical changes in location have taken place. Whereas the economy and population were initially attracted to regions of natural resource concentration, they now prefer regions with a high quality of life, advanced infrastructure, and a position close to the market. Whereas the labour force formerly followed employment opportunities, the location of economic activities is now increasingly defined by the territorial preferences of the staff, particularly the highest qualified (Gudgin 1978, Goddard 1987).

At each stage of socio-economic development (see details below), there have been prosperous and crisis regions. Their changing pattern was determined by shifts in the location factors, tastes and preferences of the people. It can easily be shown, therefore, that the *natural* trends in the location of the economy and population (see above), are connected only weakly with state activity, and determined more by the market. These trends were only partly accelerated during the post-war period by state aid for the development of the newest industries, business services, state sector etc.

The enforced intervention of the state in regional disparities is already a new artificial factor of location. However, in solving social and strategic economic problems, regional policy reduces the efficiency of the economy.

For two centuries, the market has created numerous regional problems and their number increases with each decade. Regional policy provides *a controllable inequality* (term of the author), i.e. it does not represent a danger to the system, the unity of the country etc. There are two main reasons for its occurrence and functioning: purely social (the maintenance of equal rights and opportunities for all inhabitants of the country) and socio-political (the maintenance of national unity).

In the majority of cases, the resolution of economic problems takes second place within regional policy. It is interesting that the people on the street have defined the purpose of regional policy more unanimously than the experts. A survey conducted in the EU (Ravet 1993) has shown what the majority consider the main purpose of EU regional policy to be: that is, to provide all regions with equal opportunities and to raise the standard of living in problem regions (the latter answer is more characteristic for poorer countries). Although both specified purposes are unequivocally social, they assume different approaches to regional policy. In the first case, the balance of opportunities/chances within the national space is required (naturally with subsequent competition), while in the second, an increase in the standard of living is the primary and supreme objective (i.e. intervention with predetermined results).

The next section attempts to show that social objectives have been the most important ones throughout the existence of regional policy.

The evolution of regional policy in developed countries

Throughout the 60 years of its existence in the countries of the West, regional policy has experienced periods of decline and increase, and its territorial and financial scope has varied very significantly. Were these changes accidental or subject to the determining laws/trends of regional policy development?

As already noted, regional policy (in the modern understanding) was introduced in countries of western Europe during the 1920s as a reaction to the strengthening of spatial disparities and the emergence of the first depressed regions, induced by sectoral crises. These were, basically, the regions where the old industries of the Industrial Revolution – coal mining, black metallurgy, textiles – were concentrated. Governments decided separate programmes of aid to help areas dominated by these industries. Finally, regional policy in advanced capitalist countries was 'legitimized' with the effect of the world economic crisis of 1929–1932, which had uneven spatial effects. It was especially deep in areas dominated by the afore-mentioned traditional industries (but also took place in underdeveloped agrarian areas).

The crisis was especially bad in the old-industrial regions of western Europe, and in Great Britain, the native country of the Industrial Revolution, in particular. In a number of areas in South Wales, Scotland, and the Northern region, the level of unemployment exceeded 50 per cent (Fogarthy 1949). Also in the USA – in New England – there were old-industrial areas with a similar situation in terms of employment. In Great Britain, the first law on regional policy was adopted in 1934: four old-industrial areas (see Figure 1.1) were designated and assistance measures for them were determined. In the first period of regional policy, the efforts of state were directed towards the stabilization of old industries, and steps were taken to develop an infrastructure, and retrain staff (McCrone 1969). In other countries of western Europe, although separate territorial programmes were developed, regional policy did not receive official status during the pre-war period.

During the crisis of the 1930s, the first regional governmental programme in the USA was adopted: on the basis of the hydro-electric potential of the Tennessee river, a complex development of its valley was planned. Only the opposition from conservative forces stopped, in the same period, the acceptance in the USA of a number of other regional programmes (see Miernyk 1982). However, it was also clear in this country that state intervention was required to solve regional problems.

During the 1930s, an important distinction between the American and west European approach to regional policy came to light: in the USA, priority was given to development programmes for individual cities, areas, and states, while in western Europe, the state produced a national strategy of regional development with defined foci of activity based on it. Thus the scale of regional policy in western Europe was far greater. This is linked to the lesser development of *state-monopolistic capitalism* in the USA, and to the federal organization of the state, with autonomous states. These distinctions in approach were maintained, as shown in the programme for Appalachian region development accepted in 1965. It is interesting that in Japan, regional policy followed the American pattern during the 1950s, but adopted the western European approach in the 1960s (Glickman 1979).

There is one more reason for the specified distinctions between western Europe and the USA. Capitalism in western Europe is 'older' and has survived more stages of transformation, each of which was derived in problem regions (see details below). Deeper spatial distinctions between the countries of western Europe have also determined the state's fuller answer to this situation. In addition, it should be remembered that the idea of helping the weak, and caring for minorities, was always more characteristic in west European countries than in the USA (without analyzing the reasons of this phenomenon). Therefore, problem regions have demanded more state attention in the countries of western Europe.

During the post-war years, a boom in regional policy was observed. The end of economic growth, connected with war (for the USA) and post-war reconstruction (in the countries of western Europe), resulted in a new sharpening of crisis phenomena. The crisis of traditional industries (including, in addition to those already mentioned, a number of engineering sub-sectors) 'promoted' an increase in economic and social problems in Alsace, Lorraine and Northern France, Southern Belgium, the Ruhr and the Saarland in Germany, and in a number of regions in the north and west of Great Britain. The development of agrarian and agro-industrial regions in west European countries, mainly Italy, became a major problem. The resource requirements stimulated a strengthening of state intervention in the development of northern regions of Scandinavia (as well as of Canada and the USA).

In the second half of the 1940s and the start of the 1950s, a wide range of depressed regions in Great Britain were allocated aid, and in Italy the 'Cassa' of the South (for many years the main governmental body for the development of the region) was created in 1950. The scale of regional policy in France and other west European countries also increased. The relative 'wealth' of the USA, in comparison with countries of western Europe, resulted in the later rise of regional policy in this country, from the mid-1950s. The adopted programmes stimulated the development of individual areas and states (by the end of the 1950s, more than 400 specialized official bodies were engaged in this work). It was only in 1957 that the National Association of Planning declared that depressed areas were a national problem, although it failed to provide them with sufficient aid.

Regional policy was not officially 'born' simultaneously in all west European countries, although it is possible to say that, by the start of the 1960s, regional policy existed as a distinct area of state activity in all of these countries. In many countries, the mass media and scientific publications created *symbols or buzz words* of regional policy – key words which immediately described for everybody the main problems and regions of a country. In Italy it was the South and *Cassa* of the South, in France, Paris and French desert, in Germany, the Ruhr, in Norway, Sweden and Finland, the North, and in Belgium, Wallonia and Borinaige. Although many of these words are still widely used, early symbols now already no longer correspond to the changing reality – in many cases because there is increasing differentiation within individual crisis regions (see below).

During the post-war period, a further direction of regional policy emerged ie. the decentralisation of the largest regions and agglomerations. The excessive concentration of economic activity and population in these regions had resulted in a heightening of social problems (criminality, use of drugs etc.), and a deterioration of the environment and housing conditions and had also become economically unprofitable. In addition, without decentralizing the largest regions and agglomerations, it would have been impossible to ensure the development of depressed and underdeveloped regions. The problem of decentralisation in Great Britain, France, the Netherlands and Italy was particularly marked. The policy of decentralizing the largest agglomeration began in Great Britain immediately after the war (with the creation of the first new town, close to London, in 1947). In France, it began only in the mid-1950s, and in Italy and the Netherlands in the 1960s. Before the beginning of World War II, a commission was created to study the location of the employed population in Great Britain, and its conclusions included the need to decentralize Greater London with the help of the state (Royal 1940). The realization of its proposals began straight after the end of the war.

After World War II, the rise of regional policy was underscored by a number of political reasons. The victory of the USSR in the war increased the attractiveness of the idea of planning (it is interesting that currently planning, including regional planning, is more popular in the West than in the former USSR and other 'Socialist' countries, and many western experts engaged in the 'solving' of problems in the former 'Socialist' countries, base their ideas on planning possibilities). This provided an impetus for the development of *state-monopolistic capitalism*, including regional policy. In the post-war period, in many countries of western Europe,

Socialist and social-democratic parties came to power, supporting the idea of regulated capitalism. Their activity gave a new thrust to regional policy and, as already noted, it become a natural part of the *welfare state.*

On the whole, the 1950s and 1960s can be considered the renaissance of regional policy, a period of constant increase in its scale. New regions/areas (depressed old-industrial, underdeveloped, of excessive concentration) became part of its remit. This was possible because of the steady rates of economic growth in advanced capitalist countries, which permitted the allocation of significant resources for regional policy.

The development of crisis regions was based on the attraction of capital from outside, mainly through the establishment of the newest industrial sectors. Even the term *migration of industry* was coined, which included the physical moving of the enterprise, as well as the creation of new facilities in territorial isolation from existing ones by a company already operating in the country (in 'new' regions/areas).

Certainly, throughout its development, regional policy has not been without criticism – both from scientists and politicians (the latter prevailing). In western European countries, the criticism of regional policy became more intense during the crisis years of the 1970s and 1980s. Most attention was focused on the contradiction between the aims of regional policy and the problem of increasing economic efficiency in the country. Now, even in scientific publications, it is possible to find calls for the abolition of regional policy.

Many developed countries, during the 1980s and 1990s, have followed the route of the partial curtailment of regional policy and its reorientation from social to economic objectives (rather than increasing its scale, as has happened in previous periods of crisis). The state has concentrated more on macro-economic purposes, although political and social factors do not permit the abolition of regional policy. In reality, even the scale of *intervention* frequently does not decrease, but rather its form is altered ('privatization' and 'economization' etc. of regional policy – see below). In many respects, the nature of the current transformation of regional policy (i.e. from the mid-1970s) is explained by the characteristics of this new period of socio-economic development.

As already noted, the system of regional policy instruments was mainly developed during the 1950s and 1960s, when there were high rates of growth in the manufacturing industry and employment levels in advanced countries. Its measures were directed towards the attraction of new industrial capacities to crisis regions (or the limitation of their creation in other regions). Under conditions of economic crisis in the 1970s to 1980s, zero economic growth was typical and so the total volume of production remained constant. Clearly, an increase was registered in some industries, while a reduction occurred in others. These differences in production levels between industries provided some scope for the spatial redistribution of economic activity within the framework of regional policy. However, while in periods of rapid growth regional policy principally influences the location of new plants, offices etc., under crisis conditions, such opportunities are more limited and more attention must be paid to existing capacities. In depressed and underdeveloped regions, considerably more attention has been given to the stimulation of local and, hence, small-sized business. However, the majority of regional policy measures are still focused on large companies, operating, at the very least, in the country as a whole (see Chapter Three).

The crisis of the 1970s and 1980s was closely linked to a new stage in the scientific and technological 'revolution'. What happened to regional policy at this stage? The characteristics of this stage should now be examined briefly. It is generally connected with the wide-spread introduction of micro-electronics, computers, and the development of bio-technology. New engineering methods and technology are generally initially labour-saving. This stage has resulted in the reduction of employment in industry, and an *office revolution* may very soon become apparent, which could deprive millions of people of work. According to some forecasts, by the beginning of 21st century, the development of science and technology could lower the requirement for labour by a factor of ten. It is difficult to imagine that developed countries (for example, in western Europe) could *allow* a 90 per cent level of unemployment. Even if this forecast is only partially correct, an expansion of the social activity of the state is inevitable.

The current stage of the scientific and technological revolution promotes an even sharper core-periphery division in west European countries. The development of communication systems facilitates the management from the centre of manufacturing units located on the periphery, and provides servicing opportunities (throughout the country and even further afield) from a limited number of centres. At the same time, the majority of high-tech industries, R&D units, and business services only have development prospects in central regions: proximity to each other, the availability of diverse consumers, and direct contact with state bodies etc. are important for them. Moreover, scientific and technological progress results in the 'core–periphery' model being evident not only within individual countries, but also in western Europe as a whole. All these factors lead to the strengthening of regional disparities, and suggests that they will continue to increase in the future (Massey 1984, Oakey 1984, Rees 1986). During the 1950s and 1960s, the economic development of problem regions was promoted through the inflow of capital from large outside companies, whereas, in the 1980s, the revival of small-sized (and, accordingly, local) business was observed. Objectively speaking, all the above mentioned processes heighten the need for regional governmental policy and an increase in its scale. However, the latest conditions in the operation of the economy and enterprises have presented new requirements to regional policy. The current reorganization of regional policy can be described in the following way:

1. The government reduces the financial and territorial scale of regional policy, but while abolishing some instruments, introduces other new ones. A greater socio-economic fragmentation of space leads to the increased

territorial selectivity of regional policy. Even a classical problem region, such as South Italy, becomes increasingly internally differentiated during its development. As a result, in the 1990s, the level of assistance for the most 'prosperous' areas within South Italy was lowered, while simultaneously particular emphasis was placed on the development of its most backward parts (Yuill *et al.* 1993). At the same time, in previously wealthy regions, crisis areas are now appearing (eg. in Great Britain and Switzerland) which fall within the remit of regional policy. The change in the assisted areas map of Great Britain in the summer of 1993 (see Figure 1.6) is further confirmation of this.

2. Ever increasing attention is given to the development of services, especially business services, tourism etc. West European countries, in reality, are more successful in the development of routine services in problem regions than of professional ones. Suitable economic and social conditions do not exist for the development of professional services, eg. the availability of qualified labour, modern infrastructure, a large internal market etc.

3. Emphasis is placed on the exploitation of the internal resources of problem regions, and the development of local business. In the case of local business, the regional multiplier effect is higher than for branch plants of large multi-regional companies. The use of local resources is therefore stimulated by central management bodies. Without this centralization, it is impossible 'to support' uniform regional policy.

4. The government tries to attract the private sector to crisis regions. Opportunities for the development of such crisis regions through nationalized industries and the state sector as a whole are decreasing.

5. The state attempts to promote the development of a number of areas through the removal of restrictions on private sector activity which accelerates and facilitates project realization.

6. Some functions of central government and regional authorities are transferred to local level. These steps are dictated principally by political reasons.

The privatization and decentralization of regional policy is ongoing, reflecting a certain level of disillusionment with the efficiency of state activity and the crisis in the idea of 'large government'. This is the second main reason for the crisis in, and reorganization of, regional policy. Economic crisis conditions have limited the opportunities available to the state to finance regional policy. However, the crisis has also demonstrated the limited efficiency of all state activities, given that they proved unable to prevent it. Under these conditions, all dirigible models of economic management have been subjected to criticism, and the increased popularity of neo-liberal approaches had its greatest practical realization in the policies of Thatcher (and Reagan in the USA).

A further reason for the 'economization' of regional policy, and its reorientation towards *efficiency* (and away from *equity*) can be assumed. The internationalization of the economy has resulted in a huge dependence in all west European countries on the world market, and the heightening of competition. Within the framework of the world market, individual countries can be considered as regions, competing with other similar 'regions'. Naturally, the authorities of these *regions* are concerned less by internal problems than by competitiveness etc. The pursuing of such goals is only possible by developing the most prosperous areas ('internal' regions) i.e. growth poles, although their development does not guarantee an improvement in the situation of the inhabitants of crisis regions (the success of the development of Milan, for example, is of little significance for the inhabitants of Palermo).

Another interpretation of the 'economization' of regional policy exists – the achievement of the same (or better) results at a lower cost. This subject will be dealt with in more detail in Chapter Three, but this approach should not be rejected completely. However, the practice of regional policy indicates just how difficult it is to compare the efficiency of various measures (see Conclusion).

The transfer of certain rights to regional and local authorities (in the sphere of regional policy) can increase efficiency. The central question is which powers should be transferred to lower levels, and which should be left to the management of central authorities. Excessive decentralization can create areas which compete with one another, and this is not the aim of regional policy (as already mentioned in the Introduction). A more productive approach may be one of unequal decentralization, where certain powers are transferred, but only to selected territories (depending on the tasks of regional policy). Examples of this kind of approach can be found in France, Denmark, and other countries, but this method is insufficiently exploited. Regional and local levels should be involved, but to transfer the operation of regional policy to all of them is impossible and would lead to the disappearance of this policy area and its replacement by inefficient and expensive competition between regional and local authorities (Castillo 1989, Hansen *et al.* 1990).

The attempt to achieve the development of crisis regions purely through local business and local authorities, and the creation of cooperatives etc. is utopian. The state is certainly limited in the extent to which it can regulate the regional strategies of national companies and multi-nationals (even if it wanted to do so). The use of local resources and small businesses etc. is not, however, a panacea (details in Chapter Two). The current reorganization of regional policy is evidence of the decreasing effectiveness of conventional methods in the solution of territorial development problems. The curtailing of state assistance for the solution of social problems is a clear trend, regional policy providing only one example of this development.

In the last two to three years, a gradual withdrawal from a neo-liberal ideology has been observed. In the area of regional policy, a new wave of increased state interest in this field can be observed even earlier (The Regions 1991). The most

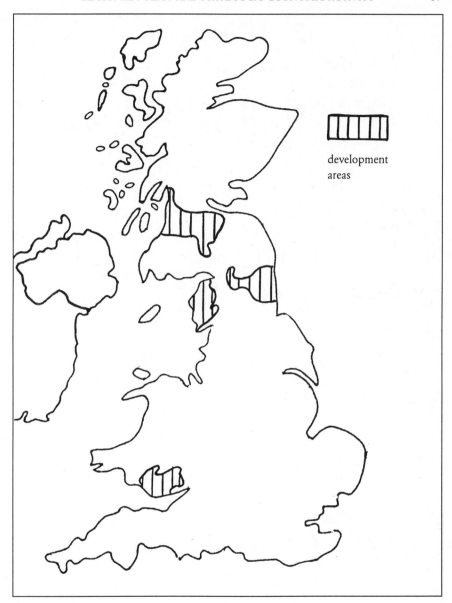

Figure 1.1 Regional policy in Britain (pre-war period)

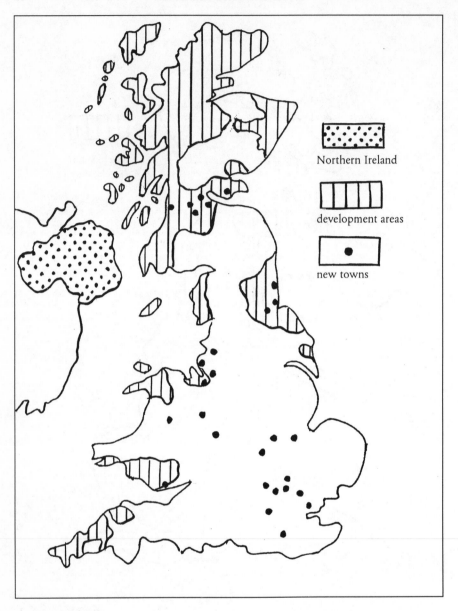

Figure 1.2 Regional policy in Britain 1945–1960

Figure 1.3 Regional policy in Britain 1966

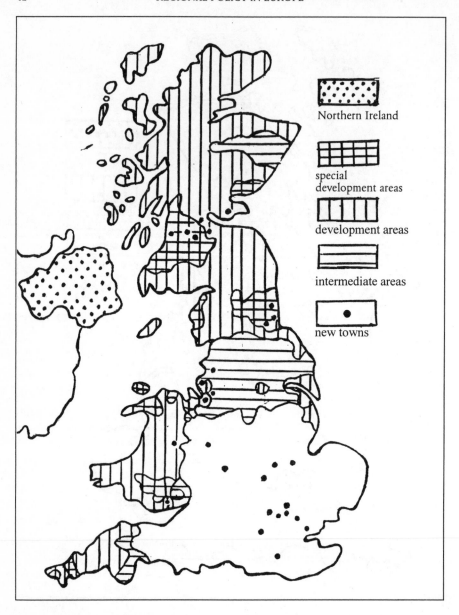

Figure 1.4 Regional policy in Britain 1979

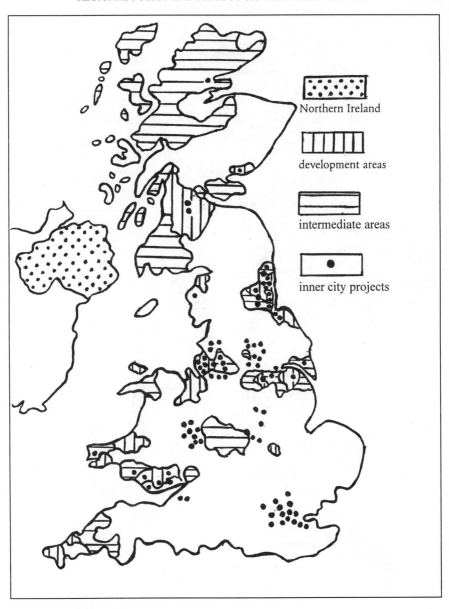

Figure 1.5 Regional policy in Britain 1989

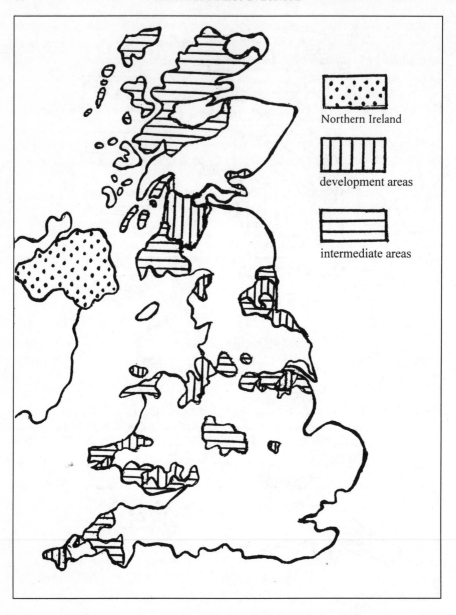

Figure 1.6 Regional policy in Britain 1992

radical reform of regional policy was carried out by the Thatcher government in Great Britain. However, even in this country, there was no debate on the abolition of regional policy, merely about its reform. The continuity within regional policy, including in its spatial coverage, is great (compare figures 1.1–1.6). Moreover, this continuity can be seen in the cycles of problem region designation (details below).

In the light of the above analysis, it is possible to divide the stages of regional policy as follows. The first stage – from the 1920s to the 1930s – was the emergence of an understanding of the existence of regional problems, and the adoption of the first programmes for old-industrial and underdeveloped area development. The second stage – from the 1940s to the 1950s – was the stage of legislative and institutional legitimization of regional policy (including the decen-tralisation of the largest agglomerations and regions, starting with the capitals). The third stage – from the 1960s to the beginning of the 1970s – was a period of flourishing regional policy, supported by both politicians and the population, and the expansion of its spatial and financial scale. The current fourth stage of regional policy – starting at the end of the 1970s – is characterised by the curtailment, as well as the reorganization, of regional policy. The focus of assistance has shifted from large areas to the development of smaller ones. The support of the decentralisation of agglomerations has been replaced by a policy of develop-ment of their inner city areas (with particular attention given to the problems of ethnic minorities within these areas). Regional policy is subject to criticism both from the Left, but particularly from the Right, and is accused of being a waste of taxpayers' money. However, even by the end of the 1980s and start of the 1990s, there was some evidence of a future revival of regional policy. This can be seen in the increasing criticism in scientific literature of the neo-liberal approach, as well as in changing positions and opinions even within Conservative parties in favour of the state's role in the solution of regional problems.

In the analysis of the stages of regional policy, one has to take a certain temporal lag into account: Great Britain has moved first through the stages, followed by France, and then the other advanced countries of the region.

In conclusion, it is logical to return to a question posed at the start of this chapter. Do internal laws governing the evolution of regional policy exist, and, if so, what are they? If one accepts the theory of the large cycles of Kondratiev (1928), almost the entire history of regional policy in developed countries is concentrated in the fourth cycle. The *decreasing wave* of the third (the 1930s, the first regional programmes) and fourth (the 1970s to the 1980s) cycles have resulted in the sharpening of regional socio-economic disparities, and the increasing focus of attention on the state to solve them. However, an obvious contradiction is evident here. In the 1930s, the scale of regional policy increased, while the 1970s, 1980s and 1990s was the period of its curtailment. The last statement is not strictly accurate. A reorganization, rather than curtailment, of regional policy is underway. Kondratiev considered each new cycle to be a radical shift in all the conditions governing the operation of economy and society. Clearly, in the field of regional policy, new conditions of operation should also lead to its reorganization. Thus, during the period of the *decreasing wave*, a sharpening of spatial disparities and a rise in the interest in these problems occurs, resulting in a reorganization of regional policy (as a part of general reorganization of the economy and society).

The *increasing wave* of the fourth cycle – from the end of the 1940s to the beginning of the 1970s – was characterized by a general rise in regional policy. The stable rate of economic development allowed the state to allocate significant resources for its finance. In the 1990s, the start of the *increasing wave* of the fifth cycle can be expected and, thus, the increase in importance of regional policy. Under the new conditions, new spatial priorities, sectoral foci, methods of assistance and institutional systems within regional policy should be anticipated.

What general conclusion can be made from the analysis of regional policy evolution? It has been constantly adapted to the changing conditions of regional policy functioning (the same general conclusion is made in Hansen *et al.* 1990). Only in this way could it survive and prove the need for its existence. Any delay in its reorganization, or attempts to operate using old methods under new conditions, always resulted in deep crisis. In this book, six maps are provided showing the changing borders of designated crisis regions in Great Britain. The cyclical nature of these changes can be clearly seen (moving from small areas to extensive regions, and then back to more limited territorial coverage), as well as certain adjustments to the designated areas receiving regional policy assistance.

In the Introduction, the greater *sensitivity* of capital to its location in space was mentioned (Harvey 1985). The fragmentation of space, where even areas located close to one another are not interchangeable, explains perfectly this space selectivity of capital. Even in a small country such as the Netherlands, the development of small-sized business is better in the Randstad than outside it. Under modern conditions, such fragmentation requires regional policy to move towards the use of smaller territorial units, the diversification of instruments and development methods, and to take greater account of the influence of problem areas on adjacent territories. While all these developments are taking place (see Chapter Three), the policy transition is insufficient, not rapid enough, and not always consistent.

The dependence of regional policy on changes in the socio-economic situation can be illustrated through the example of the 'evolution' of political parties. Generally speaking, social-democratic parties devote considerably more attention to regional policy than conservative-liberal ones. There are numerous examples of this: the notable rise of interest in regional policy during the last period of power of the Labour party in Great Britain (1974–1979); its renaissance in France during the years of Socialist power in the past decade etc. This is linked partly to the struggle for votes. In reality, many crisis regions – in Great Britain, France, Belgium, and Germany – traditionally vote for social-democratic parties, although the distinction between the party approaches is also rooted in their ideologies.

However, an analysis of regional policy history also shows that, at certain times, conservative-liberal parties have also undertaken intensive regional policy activity (eg. the Conservative party of Great Britain in the 1960s), while at other times, social-democrats have curtailed it (eg. France at the start of the 1990s). This indicates that electoral, as well as ideological, factors appear less important than changes in socio-economic conditions. It is possible to conclude generally that, for each stage of socio-economic development, a specific regional policy approach is required. This fact should be taken into account by all parties in the practical activities, although ideology can create different nuances in approach).

Regional policy and political life

The role of regional policy in the stabilization of socio-political life and the preservation of national unity has already been noted. In developed countries, it is not revolutions but ethnic (religious) problems which pose the real threats (Amersfoort and Knippenberg, 1991). Even in the wealthy and relatively mono-ethnic countries of western Europe, there are more than 30 national movements (Williams 1987), and the spectrum of their demands ranges from cultural autonomy to complete political independence. The nature of the struggle within these movements to achieve their goals also varies: in the Basque country, on the island of Corsica, and in Northern Ireland, military methods (terrorism) are used. In Brittany, Catalonia and Wales, a ethno-cultural opposition to central government exists, while in Alsace, Galicia and Scotland, emphasis is placed on the support of nationalist parties (Williams 1987, pp.251–252). In a number of cases – such as Canada and Belgium – a real threat to the territorial unity of these countries exists. The rise of such nationalism has a cyclical character – the previous period of increase occurring in the 1960s (Chisnolm and Smith 1990).

In western Europe, there are 30 territorially concentrated linguistic minorities, 'conterminous' in part with national movements (Minorities 1991). In the majority of cases, they are concentrated in problem regions, thus necessitating a greater degree of attention from the state.

These processes are even more characteristic for the CIS/Russia. Recent events in the countries of eastern Europe (the former Yugoslavia and Czechoslovakia), never mind in the territory of the former USSR, have often been accompanied by violence and have sharply increased the attention paid to problems of nationalism in developed countries. The mass media has even linked the current rise of nationalism in western Europe with the events in eastern Europe.

Other forms of national/ethnic problems are linked to the presence of a significant number of immigrants, especially non-whites, in many advanced countries. During the 1950s and 1960s, Great Britain, France, Belgium, the Netherlands, Germany and Switzerland encouraged the entrance of immigrants from developing countries to compensate for internal deficits in unskilled labour. The majority of these immigrants settled in the largest agglomerations, in central areas and certain suburbs, i.e. where they could find cheap housing. It is easy now to identify areas of concentration of coloured immigrants in almost all large cities, often distinguished visibly by a poorer quality of life. In many of these areas, considerable social tension exists (see below).

A particular ethno-regional problem is religious conflict. For more than 20 years, Great Britain, for example, has not been able to prevent terrorism in Northern Ireland resulting from the disharmony between two Christian churches. The problems of ethno-religious areas attract particular attention in developed countries. Northern Ireland, for example, receives (per head of the population) two to three times more assistance than crisis regions in Great Britain. Almost all regions and areas in which ethnic problems are acute earn the highest priority attention within their countries – in France, Great Britain, Spain – ie. within the framework of regional policy, they receive the maximum level of assistance. This is justified and generally concerns inner city areas of the largest agglomerations.

The reliance on regional policy support of ethnic-related problems can be analysed in detail in the example of Belgium. The areas in receipt of the maximum levels of assistance within regional policy do not always coincide with the regions where the population has the lowest standard of living. In Wallonia, for example, relatively prosperous areas are included within regional policy activity, but the genuine danger of the disintegration of the country and potential 'transfer' of the region to France, necessitates the provision of particular assistance to the development of Wallonia. At the same time, Belgian regional policy has to include many areas in Flanders due to the 'dualism' of the country. Nationality-related problems, therefore, are the major determining factor of regional policy in Belgium.

The intensity of regional policy in advanced countries is often directly proportional to the acuteness of nationality-related problems, and the existence of ethnic (or religious) minorities. As the crisis of the 1970s and 1980s forced developed countries towards the operation of a scaled-down regional policy, at the same time, problems related to nationalities (concentrated in certain regions/areas) demanded its strengthening. As a result, a shift of spatial targets of the state took place and, in many respects, it is ethno-territorial problems which fundamentally determine the present reorganization of regional policy. On the whole, the rise of nationalism, and an intensification of relations between the immigrant and 'native' populations, promotes a strengthening of regional policy. Thus, adopted decisions are defined more by political-national factors than by existing spatial disparities in levels of income, unemployment etc.

In general, if regions do not recognize national aims – as is the case in Belgium, which is close to a confederation in structure – then regional policy will be undertaken at regional level ie. in Belgium, separate regional policies in Flanders and Wallonia. However, in all federal states, there are two levels of regional policy – one at national level, and one at the level of the federation subjects eg. the German *Lander*. The parity of their rights shifts, as shown in an extreme case in Belgium. However, in Germany, Switzerland and Austria, the objects of federation also have significant rights in this area. Related to the progress of federalism in Spain, a redistribution of rights in the field of regional policy is also evident (see Chapter Three). An analysis of the German and Swiss experience, never mind the situation in the former Yugoslavia, highlights the complexity of regional policy in federal states. These complications are caused less by the operation of one or more levels of management (with the related necessity for coordination, increased bureaucracy etc.) but more by political and psychological factors.

In principle, regional policy should be *long-term*, and not aimed at achieving immediate results. The reorganization of territorial structures is a process requiring decades, but it is carried out by politicians (at different levels) whose time horizons are a maximum of five years. For victory in the next elections they require rapid results. They concentrate their efforts, therefore, on the most visible symptoms of crisis – treating the symptoms of the illness rather than its root cause. In addition, politicians only start to provide assistance once the crisis has already taken place, although in many cases the problems could have been predicted beforehand, and their impact softened. The logic of political life, however, does not allow such a preventative approach to be followed within regional policy. Analysis of regional policy in Sweden and Great Britain (Larsson 1989) confirms the theory that this policy area is focused more on the solution of short-term political (and economic) problems, although, in theory, a longer-term approach is required.

Decisions taken by politicians are often dictated less by the genuine economic and social situation of the area, and more by its ethnic and religious structure, the dominance of certain parties, the mass media etc. Under the majoritarian electoral system, deputies from individual districts lobby for their own areas, and much depends on their weight in the party hierarchy and their ability 'to push' the decision through the necessary channels. This naturally leads to a level of subjectivity within regional policy. It is interesting that the adopted laws and decisions in the field of regional policy (in individual countries as well as the EU), although formally quite strict and frequently incorporating quantitative criteria, almost always leave room for such subjectivism (this is clear from an analysis of the texts of the relevant documentation). Purely political factors play an important role in the formulation and realization of decisions. It is similar to USSR/Russian practice, where the term 'by way of exception' is a popular political formula!

The interests of local political elites (in each case with the support of the majority of the population) naturally conflict within regional policy. As regional policy redistributes resources from rich to poor regions, the first group complains that too much is given, while the second claim that too little is received. In Spain, for example, relatively poor central and southern regions require more assistance, but the richer regions – eg. the Basque country and Catalonia – consider that they are overpaid (Barquero and Hebbert 1985).

In western Europe, it is possible to differentiate three levels of regional policy: the EU, individual countries, and their regions. This means that, within the framework of the EU, regional policy is carried out under a principally social-democratic approach, while in many countries, the methods are more neo-liberal. Despite these differences, all three levels work together. This means that western European politicians are often willing to come up with pragmatic compromises. Political realities, therefore, can both hinder the realization of regional policy (as can be seen from the above discussion), but can also frequently assist it.

It has been noted that the decentralization of power (currently quite fashionable) hinders the realization of regional policy. The creation of regional governments and mini-parliaments complicates the operation of a regional policy which encompasses the whole country. However, the approach (already mentioned) within which regions/areas receive unequal rights is a way in which decentralization can be part of regional policy – although this method is not currently widely exploited. In Great Britain, for example, this occurred in the case of the Greater London Council, which promoted the decentralization of the capital. At the start of the 1960s, the Ile-de-France authorities were also awarded special rights, while in Italy, five *special regions* were granted particular wider rights. This is evidence of *positive discrimination*, the 'beginning' of regional policy.

CHAPTER TWO

The Main Directions of Regional Policy

In official government documentation, as well as in scientific literature, there is no standard classification of regions/areas where development is regulated by the state. Usually, they are called crisis or problem regions (see Introduction), and are further classified by sector (agricultural, industrial) or the historical reason for the current crisis ('principal of origin') (Stillwell 1972). The latter approach is more logical and, therefore, depressed old-industrial regions, underdeveloped (in relation to the other regions in the country) and problem areas within the largest agglomerations will be analysed in this book.

The first type of region, depressed old industrial, which formed the basis of many countries' economies, initially became the target of regional policy between the 1930s and the 1950s. Underdeveloped regions, classified most often as agro-industrial or regions with extreme natural conditions, have generally become targets of regional policy a little later ie. during the 1950s and 1960s. Finally, the crisis areas within the largest agglomerations are a phenomenon of the 1970s. These are usually called inner city areas, although in a number of agglomerations they are located in the suburbs (eg. in Paris and Amsterdam – see Chapter Three). These areas, in kind with depressed regions, previously flourished, and their current crisis is a result of the structural reorganization of the economy, and a change in the factors of location.

If agro-industrial regions can be classed as crisis regions, then territories with extreme natural conditions can only be treated as crisis territories with certain provisos. Although they are sparsely populated, they contain important resources and are of strategic significance within their countries. In these regions, the problem is not a 'struggle' with crisis, but rather the impossibility of their development in the absence of state assistance. For the majority of problem regions, the current crisis is a result of an insufficient level of development in the past, or, in the case of previously wealthy regions, the inability to adapt to new conditions.

Each of the specified types of problem region has common features – a high level of dependence on old industries or agriculture, a peripheral position, a low share of qualified professionals etc. The existence of such features means that the state (or the EU) can often carry out a certain standard form of regional policy for each 'class' of problem region (to jump ahead, it is possible to observe a fairly typical set of regional policy measures in the countries under analysis).

At the same time, each problem region/area also has certain unique features which distinguish it from the *'brothers in its class'*. These features, specific to each region, can include its geographical position and the internal territorial structure of its economy and population. In many respects, the unique features of a given region/area are of central importance to its receptiveness to various regional policy measures. Certainly, regional policy measures take these unique features into account in the graduation of assistance, often with maximum levels of aid being given to the most peripheral regions. However, on the whole, regional policy is oriented more towards the overcoming of the typical 'deficiencies' (structural backwardness etc.), rather than individual ones.

It should be remembered that problem regions often incorporate smaller areas of very different characteristics. In regions officially designated as 'depressed old-industrial', it is frequently only small areas within the overall designated region which can genuinely be classified purely under this description. The reaction to a*typical* regional policy will thus vary within the designated region. The efficiency of regional policy measures, therefore, depends on the balance between the consideration of typical and unique problems.

The development of depressed old-industrial regions

As already noted, some depressed old-industrial regions were previously flourishing and formed the basis of their country's economy. At certain given times, these regions reached their maximum level of development, and only later conceded their leading position to other regions. This loss of position, and the difficulties related to it, are defined within the term *depressed*. The distinctive feature of such regions, taken into account in the realization of regional policy, is their huge resource and potential base, both material and human, accumulated during the previous stages of development. Frequently the main problem is not the creation of new capacities, but the modernization of existing ones, and equally, not the training of personnel, but their retraining. Simultaneously, this accumulated capacity and resource base contribute to a development inertia: it is much more difficult, for example, for former coal-miners or shipbuilders to find a niche in the service sphere, than it is for young people leaving school, or similarly, it is often cheaper to construct, say, a new electronics plant, in a completely new location.

In describing a region as 'old-industrial', most researchers emphasize not only the start of the development in that region, but also the level of economic growth which has been achieved and the current economic difficulties. Thus, this category can include regions which are reasonably developed, but which would not currently be classified as among the most prosperous. Strictly speaking, the South East region of Great Britain, the Paris region and the Randstad should be described as old-industrial (see below), although this has not happened. Therefore, the widely used term *old-industrial region* has a distinctly negative connotation. The term *crisis industrial region* is almost synonymous with 'old-industrial'.

Old-industrial regions exist in the mother-countries of modern capitalism, i.e. in Europe and the USA. They also exist in the CIS/Russia, Poland, and the former Czechoslovakia, but appeared, as was the case in the West, during the capitalist period of development in the eighteenth and nineteenth centuries.

Modern capitalism began in the Industrial Revolution, i.e. at the end of the eighteenth and the beginning of the nineteenth centuries, and regions connected with its *development* are among the oldest old-industrial regions. The Industrial Revolution brought about huge changes in the development and location not only of industry, but also of agriculture, services, and the population. Only during the Industrial Revolution did the territorial structure of the economy emerge based on its division into separate sectors – organisational and other differences increased between individual sectors, and distinct areas became more specialized (Artobolevskiy 1992).

It is clear that regions in which sectors such as textiles, coal-mining, and black metallurgy emerged (the symbols of the Industrial Revolution) can be classed as 'old-industrial' (Lancashire, Nord Pas-de-Calais, Alsace, Wallonia etc.). In the same period, however, huge progress was also made by central regions of many west European countries, including in capital cities such as London and Paris, through advances in light industry, services and transport (although these regions are not regarded as old industrial).

If it is clear which regions comprise the core of the 'old-industrial' category – ie. the regions of the Industrial Revolution – it is less clear where the cut-off point for inclusion lies. In reality, even during the twentieth century in western Europe and the USA, new regions and areas were involved in a process of rapid development, and many of them radically changed their image and specialization.

Currently, the notion of the cyclical nature of world economic development is widely recognized, linked most often with N.D.Kondratiev (1928). If his approach is accepted, we would currently be at the end of the fourth and the beginning of the fifth cycle (Kondratiev was conducting his research in the 1920s, and had defined three cycles). In the countries of western Europe and in the USA, each new cycle led to the rapid development of new areas, and a shift in the leading position among regions.

The first cycle (from the start of the Industrial Revolution to 1810–1817) began with the rapid growth of the cotton industry and included the transition of the economy to a new power base – coal. The cotton and coal mining industries became the basis for the economic development of regions mentioned above, as well as a number of others. Each different cycle promoted new sectors, and propelled new regions into the leading position within the economy of a country. Although each cycle is linked to certain industries, even during the first cycle, the development of certain central regions/areas, and principally capital regions, was based on their fulfillment of non-productive functions (see above).

Each of the three already *completed* cycles defined the nature of the development in its own regions (although the spatial overlapping of cycles has taken place). Only these regions, in which the reorientation of the 'main capital goods' (Kondratiev's term) inherited from the previous cycles was necessary, should be regarded as old-industrial. At present, in all west European regions, industrial and economic sectors of the fourth cycle are also included, although these came to prominence early in the cycle in some regions, and later in others. While in the capital regions of Belgium, Great Britain, and France, the sectors of each new cycle were developed from the start of the cycle, and gradually replaced the older sectors, these new sectors were 'exported' to regions of the Industrial Revolution on a scale insufficient for the real reorganization of the economy.

As the basis for identifying old-industrial regions, three criteria can therefore be proposed: the time of the original development; the intensity of economic activity (current and former); and the presence of marked socio-economic problems.

Many old-industrial regions have been built up on an agrarian base, having existed prior to the start of the Industrial Revolution. The agricultural sector – and not just industry and services – also has to pass through huge quantitative and qualitative changes, and the areas of its former intensive development can be classified as 'old-developed'. Examples of such old-developed agrarian areas can be found in the Netherlands, France, Germany etc. Even now, a combination of industrial, service sector and agricultural areas can be seen in the majority of old-industrial regions (and, in some regions, also recreational areas).

The acuteness of the social and economic problems of old-industrial regions depends, in many respects, on the scale and nature of development of their newest economic and industrial sectors. The required structural reorganization of the economy can proceed *naturally* if the region proves attractive to the newest sectors or, as in the majority of cases, their location there is encouraged by state measures to increase the potential advantages of these regions. The regions linked principally to the sectors of the three completed cycles are the main targets of regional policy in many of the west European countries. Among the 160 regions of EU, ranked according to their economic situation (from worst to best), old-industrial regions already start to appear between the 31st and 49th rankings (West Midlands and Merseyside agglomerations, Limburg, Hainaut – The Regions 1987). Old-industrial regions thus become identified, to a certain extent, with depressed regions. The industrialisation of virtually all of the regions mentioned in Table 2.1 began during the Industrial Revolution (although at different times in different countries).

However, although regions such as Ile-de-France and the South East of the UK are still undergoing relatively dynamic development, other regions developed between the 1920s and the 1940s are in a state of continual depression. The recession of old sectors has not been compensated for by the emergence of new ones: this situation can be seen, for example, in the Nord-Pas de Calais region (Thumerel, 1989). This region, together with Alsace and Lorraine, has an unfavourable industrial structure in terms of production and organization, dominated by large-scale enterprises. The rate of new firm formation is low, and the relative weight of high-tech industries is minimal (Knaap and Wever, 1987).

Table 2.1 Old-developed regions of the EU (beginning of the 1990s)

Regions	Population		Unemployment %	Share in employment		GDP per head EU–100
	mln	per sq km		industry	services	
Germany:						
Hamburg	1.6	2172	6.1	26	73	183
Nordrhein Westfalen	17.2	506	5.6	42	56	112
Saarland	1.1	416	6.1	38	61	109
France:						
Ile-de-France	10.7	890	7.6	25	74	166
Nord-Pas de Calais	4.0	320	11.6	36	61	91
Est	5.0	105	9.2	29	60	94
Netherlands:						
West	7.0	618	6.7	21	76	110
South	3.3	453	6.7	34	62	95
Belgium:						
Brussels	1.0	5963	9.0	20	80	166
Wallonia	3.3	193	10.0	28	69	85
UK:						
South						
East	17.5	641	7.6	26	73	121
North	3.1	200	11.1	35	63	87
Wales	2.9	139	9.3	33	64	84
EU	328	146	8.5	33	60	100

Source: Regions 1993

In the nineteenth century, there were periods when the regions of the Industrial Revolution in Great Britain and France displayed more dynamic development trends than the capitals, and even overtook them in relation to a number of socio-economic parameters (for details see, for example, Artobolevskiy 1992).

As already noted, the main factors determining the location of economic activity have changed markedly in the time between the Industrial Revolution and the present day, moving from natural resource to more labour force-oriented factors. Many old-industrial regions in peripheral locations and characterised by a poor quality of life (a factor which hinders the inflow and supply of a highly qualified labour force), also show deficits in areas such as R&D, high-tech industries, business services etc. The outflow of the most qualified labour force, ie. young people, results in the marginalization of the population. As a result, many old-industrial regions have obtained a negative image as areas unsuitable for business development and a high standard of living, promoting a certain socio-psychological barrier against their development.

The image of industrial areas in old-developed regions often encompasses whole territories as if the entirety of Wales, Scotland, Alsace, Wallonia etc. were characterized by a poor environment and an unstable social and political life. However, these industrial areas generally occupy no more than 10–20 per cent of the territory. In Wales, for example, they are located on the southern coastal area and the adjacent valleys (plus a small territory in the north), in Scotland, they comprise the central regions, and in Wallonia, the valleys of Maas and Saambr. The agricultural parts of these regions bear no resemblance to old-industrial areas, while the environmental conditions in some of them are better than those found in prosperous capital regions. In some cases, *separate centres* are identified – Corby new town, for example, is an enclave of heavy industry in an area dominated by small trade towns and is not typical for its surrounding area (Grieco 1983).

It is generally necessary to recognize that the environments of old-industrial regions have higher pollution levels than other regions (Europe 1991). This hinders the development of these regions as the state needs to provide higher levels of assistance, and it is more difficult to find private investors and, particularly, to attract qualified staff.

However, old-industrial areas are far from uniform, and many have good prospects of economic and social development. In a similar situation to the nineteenth and early twentieth centuries, it is not entirely fair to talk about uniform crisis regions in the Ruhr or Maas and Saambr valleys as there are relatively prosperous multi-functional centres and areas within these regions.

It is interesting that the 'opening' of many old-industrial areas in west European countries is linked to the activities of multi-nationals. Multi-national corporations, in contrast to domestic capital, are accustomed to a larger territorial scale and can evaluate more objectively the location of future investment in particular re-gions/areas/centres. American multi-nationals stimulated the creation of the new Silicon Valley in central Scotland, Japanese companies, the growth of the southern coastal area of Wales, while German (and American) multi-nations contributed to the stabilization of the economic situation in Alsace (although the role of ethnic/national factors is important in this case). The discovery of oil and gas off the coast of Great Britain and Norway also promoted accelerated development in some coastal old-developed areas of these countries. As a result, they were not longer classed within the 'crisis' category, which became correspondingly consid-erably smaller.

South Limburg (in the Netherlands) provides an example of the successful reorganization of a depressed old-industrial region. In the mid-1960s, the economy of this region depended heavily on coal-mining (accounting for 45,000 jobs). The crisis of this sector, therefore, prompted widespread depression, and by the 1970s, the level of regional unemployment was well above the national average (Kaderabkova 1991). There is no coal mining at all in the region, but new industries have developed strongly (some within the small business sector), and the service sector has also grown. Even within the context of a relatively wealthy country, the region appears to be faring well. It is also possible, however, to identify significant spatial socio-economic disparities within the boundaries of the region (Limburgse 1991).

What factors then have contributed to the successful development of this region? The process of integration within the EU (changing the region's position from peripheral in a national context, to central in a European one), as well as the overall prosperity of the country played an important part. However, the role of regional policy was also considerable. Between the 1960s and the 1980s, the government spent in the order of 200,000 guilders on every employed person in the region. Most effective were the state measures of the second half of the 1970s and the 1980s, where emphasis was placed on an improvement of the regional investment climate, rather than the earlier focus on the provision of support for private business. The state has succeeded in motivating not only local business but also, critically, the regional population. Even the miners and the trade union leaders did not object to the mine closures. This is linked in part to the overall high level of social assistance in the country, i.e. once again, with the wealth of the state.

However, at the same time, areas of crises are also evident in the most prosperous old-developed regions. Among the previously mentioned 160 regions of the EU, for example, the Scottish Grampian region (linked to the oil business) is in 142nd place (i.e. among the most wealthy), while the West Midlands ranks 37th (*The Regions* 1991, part ii, p.61). Thus, an increasing spatial fragmentation has occurred through the improvement of the situation in some old-industrial areas and depression in previously prosperous areas. These shifts also correspond to the changes in Kondratievs' cycles (the transition from the fourth to the fifth). The fifth cycle is currently beginning and it is already possible to class sectors of the fourth cycle as old. This can be seen in the West Midlands region, whose inclusion under regional policy is linked in many respects with the crisis of the automobile industry (an industry of the fourth cycle). The situation of the region has improved appreciably, although the future prospects for development in the West Midlands are a point of debate for both scientists and politicians.

In general, the worst 'conditions' can currently be seen in industrial centres, which flourished in the nineteenth and early twentieth centuries, stretching in a 'band' from northern Italy through eastern and northern France, southern Belgium and the western part of Germany to the Midlands, northern England, southern Wales and north-western Scotland. This picture, however, is a considerable generalization, as the nature of the real socio-economic situation can only truly be seen within smaller territorial units, and not such large regions.

The history of economic development in Scotland and the North West region of England have many similar features – this is also true for the cities of Glasgow and Liverpool. However, Scotland is currently in a considerably better position due to the oil business, the activity of multi-nationals etc. It is interesting to compare the evolution of the two above-mentioned cities. In recent years, Glasgow has developed successfully, rapidly acquiring the image of a modern European city. The reorganization of the city, as well as the creation of new business and trade complexes, is clearly visible. Liverpool, conversely, currently remains dependent on old industries, discouraging potential investors by the existence of *difficult* labour relations and national conflicts.

In general, the situation in west European old-industrial regions/areas is directly proportional to the region's position in space (more peripheral regions usually being worse off). However, the increase in spatial fragmentation of socio-economic development casts doubt on this overall conclusion. Has Glasgow's remoteness from the country's capital, its largest regions and even the centres of western Europe actually been an advantage? The modern organization of national companies, and especially multi-nationals, includes the creation of powerful regional centres of manufacture, sales, services and R&D. The activity of state bodies is similarly organized. Within the context of Scotland's five million population, Glasgow represents the most suitable regional centre (its influence can also be seen in part of northern England). As a result, Glasgow was one of the few large cities in western Europe which achieved significant progress after 1974 (Cheshire, Hay and Carbonaro 1988). Returning to Liverpool, it can be noted that the city is located considerably closer to London and other large centres (mainly Manchester), but its role as a regional centre is not important, and it has lost any significance as a port due to the reorientation of external trade from North America to western Europe. The integration process has also increased its peripherality.

Government regional policy emerged in Great Britain in the 1930s, and in other west European countries (and the USA) in the 1950s, and from the start gave special attention to the development of old-industrial regions/areas as the territories which displayed the worst socio-economic problems – although this is not true for all developed countries. In Italy, for example, small old-industrial depressed areas exist in the North (Yuill, Allen, Bachtler, Wishlade, 1988), but the problems of their development are not comparable to those evident in the South. Similarly, in Scandinavian countries, the principal regional problem is the development of the northern regions. Within western Europe, therefore, one can see a certain trend in the location of problem regions, and this point will be further addressed in the Conclusion.

Depressed old-industrial regions represent the main territorial issue for countries in the central part of western Europe – i.e. its main economic nucleus. This would include Great Britain, France, Belgium, the Netherlands, and Germany (certainly up to the point of re-unification). In the 1950s, central old-industrial regions became the focus of regional policy – at this time, through encouraging the process of decentralisation of the largest agglomerations and entire regions. Attempts were made to link these two directions of regional policy ie. to develop depressed old-industrial regions through the decentralisation and re-direction of economic activity and population from central regions/agglomerations. The most active policy of decentralisation of agglomerations was undertaken in Great Britain, France, the Netherlands and Italy, although, currently, all decentralisation measures have been abolished (for details see Chapter Three).

The process of regional development can sometimes be compared with the diffusion of innovations: new sectors/industries emerge in a centre (or centres) and are then 'diffused' to the periphery. If one were to accept this model, the main purpose of regional policy should be the acceleration of this process of diffusion. The operation of high-tech industries in peripheral areas, and the introduction of innovations, can radically improve the quality of life of the population and create a new investment climate. However, there is a fundamental distinction between these two processes: the new product (innovation) arrives at the periphery unchanged but with a time lag. However, when a new industry or economic activity is diffused from the centre to the periphery, not only a time lag occurs, but also a change in the 'character' of the industry. In the periphery, activities basically comprise mass production and routine services. Even in the case of the transfer of R&D and business service firms, only the units necessary for the functioning of new industrial divisions and their production sales are created. As a result, a branch plant economy is created in old-industrial regions, which can be controlled from outside the region. This has consequences such as the lowering of qualification levels among the population, the relative fall of incomes, the deterioration of the environment etc. (Artobolevskiy 1985). As already mentioned, this type of economic structure appears the most vulnerable during periods of crisis.

The centre – periphery model evident in small West European countries, for example the Netherlands or Belgium, can also be seen in Western Europe as a whole. In the promotion of development in these, or other, old-industrial regions or areas, regional policy should start from the basis of their *indigenous* potential and opportunities. It is unrealistic even to try to create a *uniform* socio-economic space, and it is only possible to stimulate limited changes within the territorial structure of the economy and society. It is necessary, therefore, to understand the various regional 'reactions' to state assistance. In Flanders, for example, even the provision of relatively small amounts of assistance will lead to more significant results than the provision of higher levels of aid in Wallonia (although naturally not in all cases). This is linked principally to the differing rates of development and potential in the two regions (Vandermotten 1989).

The policy for old-industrial regions is defined by macro-economic factors. A comparison of North East England and the Ruhr (Hassink 1992), for example, has shown that in the former region, coal mining was reduced sharply, while in the latter, the process was more gradual, giving more time for the reorganization of the economy. Germany had greater financial resources available for the support of coal-mining, and more opportunities to sell the mined coal – these factors determined, to a large extent, the differences in approach between the two countries.

There are a number of obvious discrepancies between the practice and theory of regional policy in the specified types of regions. In assisting these regions, the state is basically looking to solve social problems, although the grants, loans and other methods of assistance (see Chapter Three) are received by companies. It is clear that without attracting firms, it is impossible to create new jobs, maintain income levels and qualification standards of the population, and develop infra-structure etc. Although the state is aiming to solve social problems, it uses economic development as a tool in this process. As a result, assistance often promotes the 1development of territories, rather than the development of local inhabitants. In the case of old-industrial regions, however, many companies in receipt of state assistance are exploiting only a limited range of local resources (usually cheap labour), and do not promote the development of the territory or integration with the local economy.

Crisis regions officially included under regional policy are defined using a number of criteria: the share of declining or stagnating industries; the level of infrastructure development; the geographical position; the standard of living etc. (see Chapter Three). Parameters such as the level of unemployment are used most often (either alone or in conjunction with other indicators). The negative conse-quences of mass unemployment on the local population and economy have already been described in many publications, and it is not necessary to outline them again. If the level of unemployment is the main indicator of crisis (confirmed by the history of regional policy from the 1930s; Fogarthy 1949, Miernyk 1982), it could be suggested that the clear principal purpose of regional policy is the preservation in a region/area of existing jobs, and the creation of new ones. Accordingly, it would be necessary to concentrate efforts on the development of labour-intensive industries and, particularly, the sphere of services.

In reality, however, regional policy is directed at the attraction, principally, of capital-intensive industries and business services. The state pays a part of the investment costs, permits their accelerated amortization and provides 'low-cost' loans. As a result, the previously mentioned development of branch plants occurs, which undertake mass production and are weakly integrated into the local economy. This form of development creates a relatively small number of new jobs through the multiplier effect due to this general poor integration in the local economy (Watts 1981). It is possible to agree with the assertion that a branch plant economy, created through regional policy, has many disadvantages. However, in the absence of branch plants, the situation in old-industrial regions would be much worse (Fothergill and Guy 1990, p.170), and it is doubtful whether other development routes for such regions existed.

The particular attention given to industry in the realization of regional policy aims is linked to the fact that the opportunities for services development in peripheral old-industrial regions are limited by the small size of the local markets. At the same time, business services are the core of a considerably more effective policy of inner city area development (see Chapter Three). One should remember that in crisis regions, jobs for the male workforce, lost through the crisis in traditional industries (coal mining, black metallurgy, ship-building, heavy engineering etc.) must be found first. In comparison to services, the newest industries provide more male working places.

In the 1980s, greater emphasis was placed in the realization of regional policy on the exploitation of indigenous resources, or on development *from below* (Robert 1982). The renaissance of small business is clearly evident, and the regional multiplier effect of local firms is much higher than for larger firms (Burns and Dewhurst 1986). However, while the indigenous development resources of central regions may be considerable, in peripheral old-industrial ones they are rather limited. In these regions, in addition to their physical remoteness and the small size of the local market etc., one of the most significant restrictions to progress is the industrial-based history of their economic development. The absence of a tradition of individual economic activity and initiative, and the skills of only a collective labour force, result in a lack of people capable of organizing and successfully leading businesses, and of exploiting scarce local resources (The Regions 1991). The population has no experience, and few of the skills, required for independent economic activity. These factors lead to the emergence of internal socio-psychological barriers to development in old-industrial regions, which minimize the extent to which regional policy measures focused on the stimulation of indigenous potential can be exploited. Similar difficulties of development through indigenous resources can be seen in underdeveloped regions.

The progress in transport and communication methods has brought peripheral regions closer to the centre, but the process of creating a new business climate in peripheral regions is considerably more complex and, unfortunately, not sufficiently supported through regional policy. It is necessary not only to provide financial resources for old-industrial regions, but also to create the conditions in which they can be fully exploited.

On the basis of the above, one should once again critically evaluate the present re-focusing of regional policy on the local level – as is occurring in countries such as Great Britain, France, Greece (and the USA). The basis of regional policy is the deliberate designation by the state of regional problem type and areas to receive support. When regional policy is transferred to regional/local levels, it disappears as a 'phenomenon', and is replaced by the expensive (from the state's viewpoint) competition for investment between individual regions, areas and cities (see, for example, Dunford and Kafkalas 1992).

A number of conclusions can be drawn which are of potential practical interest for old-industrial regions in Russia/CIS:

1. In comparison with underdeveloped agrarian and agro-industrial regions, old-industrial regions provide greater opportunities for re-organisation – including through the agglomeration effect, and existing infrastructure and fixed capital.

2. Old-industrial regions in peripheral positions within market space (ie .within individual countries or western Europe as a whole), and with the least diversified economic and industrial structures, are in the worst situation.

3. In regional policy practice, it is impossible to operate with large old-industrial regions (such as the Ruhr, Wallonia, Scotland), given that areas of both rapid growth and depression exist within virtually all of them – although certain broad macro-space trends can be identified. In western Europe as a whole, a decline in the level of development from the centre to the periphery is obvious.

4. Regional policy contributed to the growth in crisis regions (or the stabilization of their position). Intervention, however, is necessary not once the crisis had already taken place, but rather when the situation in the region is stable. At this point, the conditions for the emergence and development of new industries and sectors should be ensured.

5. It is much easier to support the development of a selected territory, than to solve the social problems of its population.

6. The basis of stable development in peripheral old-industrial regions is the promotion of new high-tech industries and the area of business services (or recreation).

7. Development on the basis of external resources is unstable, while exploiting indigenous resources is difficult, if not impossible, without a change in social traditions, lifestyle, and the reorganization of the professional structure of employment. In some cases, this latter route is not possible due to the absence of sufficient internal resources.

Underdeveloped regions

Unlike depressed old-industrial regions, underdeveloped regions never comprised the economic 'base' of west European countries. In previous stages of evolution, they were either purely agrarian (the level of development of this sector not being high), or suppliers of resources (not included in the real market). This is the principal reason for the current dependence of such regions on the economic activities oriented towards the *exploitation of natural resources or primary processing* (agrarian sector, mineral industry, energy), as well as their characteristically underdeveloped infrastructure, low labour force qualification levels, and socio-political and cultural backwardness.

Virtually all underdeveloped regions are characterized by their peripheral location, both within their national context and in the EU/western Europe as a whole. They include Mediterranean regions (of Italy, Portugal, Spain and Greece), northern regions (of Norway, Sweden and Finland), Ireland (not in political borders, but the whole island), and parts of southern and south-western France (although their socio-economic position is better). In global terms, northern regions of Canada, Alaska, and a large part of Australia would be classified under this type (see Karpov 1972).

The progress of west European integration has resulted in several entire countries being included under the 'underdeveloped' classification (if a Europe of regions is considered, rather than a Europe of countries). While essential regional variations are obvious in Ireland, Portugal and Greece (*Regional Problems*, 1981, *Regions* 1987), within the context of the EU as a whole, they are internally relatively uniform territories, particularly if 1-2 of their largest centres (Dublin, Lisbon and Oporto, Athens and Salonika) are excluded. Thus, while existing spatial variations are taken into account in assistance measures through differing rates of award, assistance is available throughout the whole country (Yuill *et al.* 1993).

There are two types of underdeveloped regions. With certain provisos, they can be called agro-industrial and regions with extreme natural conditions. In western Europe, the former is found principally on its southern and western periphery, while the latter is located on its northern periphery. Regions with extreme natural conditions would also include mountain areas, which comprise a relatively small area of western Europe.

Small underdeveloped agro-industrial areas exist in virtually all developed countries – for example, in Scotland and Central Wales, in the centre of France, in the Netherlands etc. Within the framework of national regional policy, all these regions receive a certain level of assistance, while in the EU, they are considered a special type of problem area (see below). However, they bear little resemblance in their level of development (or the acuteness of their problems) to the above-mentioned agro-industrial regions. Taking only agriculture into account, the level of development in these areas is well above that in agro-industrial regions (see data on wheat yields – *Regions* 1987 – which are around the EU average, and much higher than in the large scale agro-industrial regions). These small areas, as well as mountainous ones, are not considered separately in this book. Against the background of the problem regions of western Europe as a whole, the difficulties in mountainous areas of Switzerland seem unimportant (Rossi 1994).

The main aim of regional policy in agro-industrial regions is to ensure the social-cultural development of their populations and the structural reorganization of their economies. The development of regions with extreme natural conditions is promoted by the state first and foremost for strategic (economic and political) reasons. The rich natural resources in these regions can lead to a lower dependency on exports, and, if higher levels of processing and exploitation of resources occur within the regions themselves, can increase the higher-order industrial functions in these areas (details below). Certainly, certain social, national (ie. of the native population), and ecological problems are also solved through policy support.

It is possible to identify a number of common approaches within regional policy to underdeveloped regions. Special attention is given to the creation of an infrastructure which is adequate for modern requirements. The acuteness of the regional problems forces the state to provide the maximum level of assistance for these regions (Yuill *et al.* 1993), and, in a number of cases, the state even participates directly in their development through state companies. It is interesting that this type of approach was used both in Italy, for the development of the South, and in Finland and Norway, for the development of the North.

Agro-industrial regions

Table 2.2 provides a statistical indication of the problems found in underdeveloped regions. It shows a general backwardness, within a national and EU context, in terms of the level of economic development and the quality of life of the population. These are the most basic barriers to unity within their own countries, and within the EU as a whole. It was not without reason that, within the framework of EU regional policy, this type of region receives the main share of assistance (see Chapter Four).

Table 2.2 Underdeveloped regions of EU
(end of the 1980s – beginning of the 1990s)

Countries and regions	Density of population per sq km	Share of working women %	Unemployment %	Share of agriculture in employment	GDP per head	Telephones per 1000 inhabitants
Greece	77	33	7.7	22	47	313
Spain	77	32	16.1	11	75	136
South	82	29	23.9	16	59	81
Italy	191	36	10.2	9	102	274
South	154	31	17.8	17	69	173
Sicily	202	28	21.9	14	66	219
Portugal	107	49	3.6	17	56	–
Ireland	51	35	15.8	14	68	–
UK	235	52	8.8	2	101	293
North Ireland	113	46	16.3	5	74	–
EU	146	43	8.5	6	100	–

– no data

Source: Regions 1993

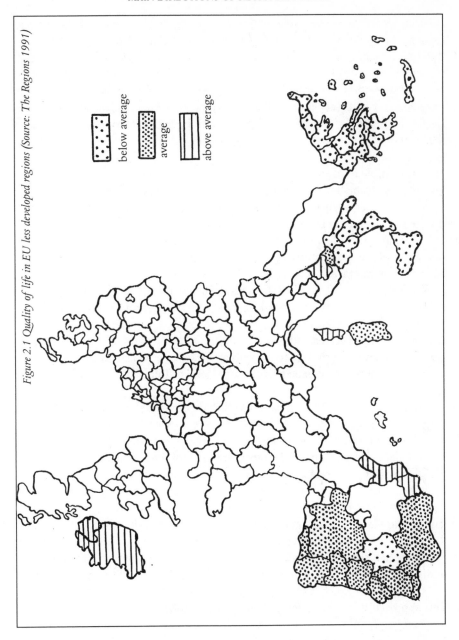

Figure 2.1 Quality of life in EU less developed regions (Source: The Regions 1991)

below average

average

above average

It is clear from the above Table, as well as from Figure 2.1, that problems which exist in the Mediterranean regions, and those in Ireland/Northern Ireland, are different in nature. The latter's degree of dependence on agriculture is lower, and the agricultural sub-sectors are different, comprising principally the production of fruit and vegetables in the Mediterranean, while in Ireland it is more the production of cereals and cattle breeding. The infrastructure provision in Ireland and Northern Ireland is also better, and a different manufacturing and sectoral structure exists in the economy. All these factors dictate certain differences in the approach of regional policy.

It is possible to identify certain stages in regional policy evolution when there was a focus on the development of agro-industrial underdeveloped regions. Such an approach began in the post-war period, and, up to the mid-1950s, it was directed at the modernization of agriculture, and the creation, for this purpose, of the necessary infrastructure. Simultaneously, both directly or indirectly, the out-migration of the population from these regions to more advanced parts of the country or abroad was encouraged.

The subsequent 20 years, to the mid-1970s, was a period of industrialization (of agro-industrial underdeveloped regions), first of all through the attraction of investment from outside, and the creation, in these regions, of branch plants of large companies. The state attempted, through the utilization of a standard set of grants, loans and tax privileges (see Chapter Three), to establish the manufacturing industry as the sole economic basis of these regions (replacing agriculture in this role).

From the mid-1970s, regional policy has encouraged the development of the indigenous resources of agro-industrial regions, as seen in the rise in assistance aimed at small (i.e. local) business, the modernization of the agrarian sector, and the stimulation of tourism development. The crisis of the second half of the 1970s highlighted the vulnerability of the economies of agro-industrial regions, which could be controlled from outside and were overly dependent on industry and/or agriculture. Currently, the state views the more diversified structure of the economy (and its individual sectors), and the increased specific weight of local business, as the guarantor of economic stability in these regions. However, warnings about this new approach should be heeded. For development to be promoted through local (indigenous) resources, it is necessary for a certain base potential to exist, and it is just this potential which is often lacking in the most crisis-ridden peripheral areas. This approach is suitable principally for more wealthy (intermediate) areas (Garofoli 1992).

Throughout the gambit of state activity, among the most important aims for underdeveloped regions have been the creation of infrastructure, the provision of training and retraining for the labour force, and the improvement of the environment and quality of life of the population. A negative image has built up of this type of region: poor roads and housing, significant poverty, a labour force unsuited to work in modern enterprises, and mafia and corruption. In a number of areas and centres, the state has succeeded in changing this image, resulting in the emergence of relatively attractive locations for national companies and multi-nationals. The area of the Shannon airport in Ireland, and certain distinct areas in Italy and Spain, are examples of this.

Virtually every publication on regional policy in western Europe, or indeed in the world, includes a section on Italy. This is completely logical, given that the South of Italy is a text book example of an underdeveloped agro-industrial region, and the country as a whole is ideal for the study of regional socio-economic disparities and regional policy. Such terms as *split nation, cathedrals in deserts, north versus south* were originally created for the Italian case (although they were later widely used in scientific literature to describe regional problems in other countries).

An analysis of Table 2.3 shows not only the clear development lag in the South of Italy as compared to the North, but also the spatial heterogeneity of the South region. Over a period of more than 40 years of the operation of large-scale regional policy, the gap between the North and South has been reduced only very slightly: in 1951, the production per head of the population in the South was 53.2 per cent of the national average, and by 1983 it has risen to 61.7 per cent (King 1987). However, sharply increased spatial distinctions within the South region itself emerged. This is linked to two main factors. First, the northern areas of the South, closest to the capital region with its extensive market (and, in general, to the centres of the EU), have become the most attractive for business. This occurred under conditions in which state assistance took insufficient account of the geographical position of areas within the South region.

Second, prior to the start of the 1970s, regional policy stimulated above all the development of selected poles and areas of growth. The poles selected tended to be the most dynamic areas, rather than crisis ones. The process of spatial fragmentation, therefore, is marked in the South, as well as in the country as a whole. Even within the North, there are areas whose development has been encouraged for many years within the framework of regional policy.

Table 2.3 Regional social-economic differences in Italy

		North and Centre	South	including Sicily	Italy
Population,	1981	36.5	20.1	4.9	56.6
mln	1990	36.5	21.1	5.2	57.6
Child mortality, %	1987	7.8	11.3	12.2	9.5
Migration balance, 1000	1989	81.3	-45.3	-18.4	36.0
Persons per room	1981	0.7	0.9	0.9	0.8
Telephones per 1000 Inhabitants	1987	380	251	269	333

Source: Italian Statistical Abstract 1989, Annuario Statistico Italiano 1990

The notion of polarized development and growth poles etc. has almost always been popular in the field of regional development (Dunford 1988). Indeed, it is difficult to conceive of a different approach within urbanized space, and under the domination of the manufacturing industry and, later, of services. Clearly, however, this approach leads to strengthening of spatial fragmentation.

The non-uniform development of the Italian South underlines the geography of the 1980s crisis. In Abruzzi, Molise and Basilicata, for example, an increase in GDP levels was observed during this period, while a recession emerged even in the main regions of the North and Centre (Nanetti 1988, p.12).

Within the framework of a national regional policy, regular 'deficiencies' or failures to carry out specified measures in the development plans of the South never placed the requirement for state assistance to this region in any doubt. Within regional policy, even during the reforms of the 1980s, only changes to the institutional structure and the nature of the policy instruments took place. Thus, the Cassa of the South disappeared, but the scale of regional policy increased. The development of the South is currently regulated by a special ministry responsible for strategic decision-making, by the Agency of the South (the successor to the Cassa but with more limited powers), and by the Department of the South, responsible for planning and co-ordination (Albrechts et al. 1989).

As previously mentioned, the issue of the extent to which the free market can level regional disparities is currently under discussion (although no practical examples of this exist). The experience of Italy testifies that for more than 100 years, following the unification of the country, only the state (in the post-war period) has promoted the development and solution of the South's problems. Certainly, within the framework of regional policy, the majority of the South's problems have not been resolved, but the absence of this policy area would have made the socio-economic position of the region considerably worse.

Standard assistance measures were used in the South to attract private business, and this was provided at very high rates, often 2-3 times greater than in the majority of depressed old-industrial regions (Yuill et al. 1993). The specific incentives were supplemented by the direct activity of the state, not only through the creation of infrastructure, but also through the social and cultural development of the population. A form of tax was imposed on all state companies (which are relatively important within the Italian economy): from 1957, they were obliged to locate no less than 60 per cent of investment (and later 80%) in the South. Although these limits were never reached, the role of state companies (such as the Industrial Reconstruction Institute, Italsider and others) is very important in the economy of the South. The flip side of such a policy is the poor diversification of the South's industry. The majority of new jobs in industry were created in metallurgy, engineering and chemicals, which are not in the most modern sectors, and are generally weakly integrated with the local economy.

Attempts by the state to encourage the polarized development of the South have already been mentioned. Even in the 1950s and 1960s, however, it proved impossible to follow this principle strictly: the crisis conditions and the struggle for votes forced the inclusion of new areas and centres in the 'selected' growth poles, until 40 per cent of the territory of the South was included. In the 1970s, greater emphasis was placed on the development of the most backward areas. This spatial shift in regional policy – from the most prosperous to the most crisis-dominated areas – correlates with a sectoral shift. The stimulation of small business, the modernization of agriculture, and the development of tourism can be undertaken over larger (and different) territories than the industrialization carried out previously. However, an important question remains: how successful is this new policy?

The new regional policy has a more 'comprehensive' character, paying more attention to the whole of the South, and not simply selected growth poles. The inadequacy of a policy focused purely on growth poles is perfectly illustrated in the example of Basilicata (Sarubbi 1990). The strategy for the South's development was also clearly influenced by political factors, which also prompted an increase in spatial coverage (Goria 1988, Mita 1987).

The realization of regional policy has been hindered by the backwardness of society in the South, and by the people's behaviour. In this area, the state has had only minimal success (Bellu 1988). While regional policy has promoted a rise in the level of socio-economic development in the South, it has also sharply increased its dependence on the North and centre of the country: *all higher level* facilities, exploiting qualified labour, higher levels of R&D etc., were concentrated in these areas.

Within the framework of the EU, the problems of Italian South are generally considered in the context of the Mediterranean region development (For the Southern region 1983). South Italy does share many common features with the regions of Iberian countries and Greece. However, there is one important distinction. Whereas in Italy, an advanced North provides a source of development, this is not the case in the other countries mentioned. Dominant agglomerations do exist in these countries – Madrid, Lisbon and Opporto, Athens and Salonika (and in Ireland – Dublin) – which are clearly distinguished in terms of development from other regions. Thus, the main purpose of Greek regional policy is to achieve a more uniform location of manufacturing industry, but, in reality, it promotes the migration of this industry to areas adjacent to Athens and Salonika agglomerations, thereby promoting the territorial expansion of these centres (Tsoukalas 1988).

Regions with extreme natural conditions

It has already been mentioned in this book that regional policy is directed, first of all, at the resolution of social problems. Therefore its objective is encapsulated in the word *development*, of the population or the economy, but, in the case of the economy, still for the increase in the quality of life of the population. In the case of regions with extreme natural conditions, it is more appropriate to talk of the exploitation of resources as the main purpose of state activity. The most exact definition of all these regions is summed in the word *'new'*, a definition proposed by Karpov (1972) which includes the characteristics of their economies, as well as indicating their role within their national context, and the developed world as a whole. In these regions, the state, within the framework of its overall activity, attempts to resolve social problems, although, in this case, these are of secondary important for regional policy. The level of income per head in new regions is very close to the national average, so the need to struggle with poverty is not relevant as it, for example, in the Mediterranean. As a whole, these regions are relatively wealthy in a pan-European context (Monnesland 1992; Yearbook, 1986, 1989).

However, in all countries where this type of region exists, regional policy does include not only the development of the territories with extreme conditions, but other predominantly social aims (Restructuring 1986, Williams 1987). In Canada, for example, the achievement of social consensus and regional balance is part of the official objective of the state's territorial strategy (Jull 1986).

The delineation of the borders of regions with extreme natural conditions is not the aim of this book: that is a theme for separate research. Regional designations have already been made by state officials for management purposes (Yearbook of Nordic 1990) and by many researchers (Karpov 1972, Diem 1979, Agranat 1984, 1988). It is clear that any differences between objectives and approaches will result in different outcomes. In this book, the author will adhere to officially designated administrative-territorial divisions, and official regional policy areas, as these areas are used in the practical activity of the state. In this book, the Scandinavian North is discussed, including the Arctic islands. Where not otherwise indicated, this includes the counties of Norrbotten and Westerbotten in Sweden, Nordland, Troms and Finnmark in Norway and the Lapland province in Finland.

Practically all the above mentioned regions are very rich in natural resources and, especially, in minerals. In some cases, it would be cheaper for the countries to import raw materials than to mine them in their own northern regions. However, the exploitation of domestic resources by the state is also carried out for strategic reasons, motivated by the desire to lower the dependence on external sources of raw materials, particularly from developing countries where there may be an unstable political-economic situation. This policy has been more actively pursued since the second half of the 1970s. The oil embargo imposed by Arab countries in 1973 highlighted the vulnerability of economies based on the import of raw materials. In addition, encouraging the exploitation of resources in new regions improves the foreign trade balance of the country, promotes the creation of new employment, and encourages the development of higher order manufacturing industries ie. the greater involvement of qualified personnel, R&D etc.

In the case of regions with extreme natural conditions, the policy of Scandinavian countries differs from the North American or Australian approach. Whereas in the latter countries, policy for these regions is a separate part of state activity, in Europe, it is subsumed into the national regional policy. In Sweden, for example, the problem of the development of the North is dealt with in parallel with the decentralisation of the capital and the development of problem territories in the central part of the country (Yuill *et al.* 1990). A hierarchy of problem territories is created (including sub-regions of the North), and northern regions are ranked at the top in accordance with the severity of their problems.

What common features are shared by the northern regions of the three countries? First, their significant territorial scale, in the west European context. It is not only in Russia (and earlier in the USSR) that size can be calculated in 'Belgium-equivalents'. A book by Diem, for example, shows that the Lapland province of Finland is comparable in size to Belgium, the Netherlands and Switzerland combined (Diem 1979, p.362). In addition, these regions have a very low population density – approximately three persons per square kilometre (Yearbook of Nordic 1990).

As a result of this size, the state has to create and support a huge infrastructure, and this comprises one of the major directions of regional policy (although a significant proportion of the resources for this purpose is included under other areas of the budget). In the Norrbotten county (Sweden), around nine thousand km of road are managed by the state, accounting for nine per cent of the total road network in a county which has only just over three per cent of the population (Statistisk 1991). The low population density, the large territorial size, and even the relief of the regions (as in Norway), necessitates the particular focus on infrastructure development within the framework of regional policy (and other areas of state activity), including to help in the struggle against depopulation (Nordic region 1991).

In recent years, there has been a constant out-migration of the population, and particularly young people, from northern regions of all three countries. This is a consequence of insufficient development of the regions' own economic base and the poor system of education and training. The outflow of the population runs against the aims of resource development and economic diversification of these regions. To stabilize the population and attract new inhabitants (labour), the state is creating quality housing and social and cultural services, developing a system of training (including the creation of new universities), and stimulating the development of both *higher order* activities within the manufacturing industry and the service sector (Yuill *et al.* 1993). In recent years, as is the case in other problem regions, particular attention has been paid to the development of small/local business. It is interesting that the greatest willingness to participate in state development programmes is demonstrated by the inhabitants of the most remote areas, displaying the great initiative and willingness to change: here, the success of regional policy depends on psycho-behavioural factors (Bylund and Wiberg 1986).

In recent years, the concepts of creating 'reservations', isolation from the 'centre', and the development of traditional economies etc. have emerged (Nord

REFO 1990). The centre is accused (perhaps fairly) of exploiting northern resources without taking sufficient account of the interests of the regions. However, the proposed strategy (even if it were the right one) cannot be realized without the support of the centre.

In the majority of problem regions, the development of the economy is stimulated with the aim of addressing social problems (see above). In regions with extreme natural conditions, this situation is reversed: social problems are frequently addressed to ensure the continuation of the process of development ie. the realization of economic objectives.

In all three countries, in the formulation and implementation of regional policy, particular attention is paid to the preservation of the environment, which is especially vulnerable under extreme climatic conditions. This environmental focus still exists in this type of region in all advanced countries, despite the higher costs incurred by companies and the state (Agranat 1984, 1988).

Approximately 35,000 Lapps live in the world – including 20,000 in Norway, 10,000 in Sweden and 2,000 in Finland. The process of exploitation of northern regions, including the development of tourism, has led to the destruction of their traditional economy and lifestyle. This is particularly true for the less assimilated Lapps living in central parts of the regions and engaged, largely, in a nomadic life based on reindeer-breeding. Coastal Lapps are more assimilated and 'closer' to modern types of activity (the majority of this nation currently lead a settled lifestyle – Diem 1979). Regional policy in Sweden, Norway and Finland provides protection of Lapp interests, including measures to preserve their traditional economy (through grants, social security payments, the ability to cross state borders free with herds), as well as to help the process of assimilation (through training measures etc.). In addition, the state tries, where possible, to designate separate areas of new development and Lapp activity.

It has already been stated that the role of state companies has been important in the exploitation of the West European North and other regions with extreme conditions, and, thus, that less attention has been given to the more conventional tools of regional policy (see Chapter Three). During the 1980s, however, a certain reorientation of countries towards the indirect participation in the exploitation process could be observed, corresponding to general shifts in economic and regional policy. Greater weight was placed on tax privileges, and grants for environment protection etc. (Agranat 1988).

In Scandinavia, the development process of northern regions has advanced further than in North America or Australia, although the richness of the resource base is lower (Karpov 1972). On the basis of iron ore, non-ferrous metals, wood, hydro-resources etc., a manufacturing industry has grown up, including relatively advanced engineering. The sectoral structure of the economy (and industry) is more diversified (although, certainly, not to the same extent as in southern regions).

The most developed areas within regions of extreme natural conditions are losing their dependency on state assistance and, indeed, are contributing considerable resources to the budget (Agranat 1988). On the basis of many economic and social parameters, the gap between some northern areas and their more advanced southern neighbours is declining.

The regulation of the largest regions and agglomeration development

The key motivation behind the policy of decentralisation (or development restriction) of the largest agglomerations and regions, begun in Great Britain in the 1940s and later in France, the Netherlands, Italy, Sweden and other countries, was the need to resolve two problems. First, the excessive concentration of the economy and population in a limited number of centres hinders their own development and natural sectoral shifts, worsens the quality of life of the population and hampers the efficiency of transport etc. (Cheshire *et al.* 1988). It leads to a deterioration of national production competitiveness, as these centres alone comprise the economic base of the country. Second, under conditions of the 1950s and 1960s, and the nature of regional policy during this period, these agglomerations and their 'hinterlands' were the only possible sources of new jobs and development options for problem territories (see 1 and 2). For this reason, decentralisation measures were accompanied by efforts to steer migrating establishments/enterprises towards problem regions (The intermediate 1969).

The success of the decentralization of agglomerations, promoted through regional policy, led simultaneously to the emergence of a new type of problem area (inner city areas). This once again confirms the validity of the theory that regional disparities are inevitable as an integral feature of any development. It is also still not clear to what extent the real decentralization of the largest regions and agglomerations took place, or how much comprised merely the territorial expansion of adjacent areas (Hall 1989).

The decentralisation of agglomerations (less often of whole regions) was also a part of regional policy in the former Socialist countries – and for some of the same reasons as in the West. However, the results have been considerably more modest. A comparative analysis of differences in efficiency would be useful in the current climate when attempts to utilize western experience in practice are taking place.

The most consistent measures promoting the decentralisation of agglomerations (and their regions) were undertaken for the capital cities. Attention will, therefore, be concentrated on them. In the majority of west European countries, the official capital also comprises the nucleus of the largest agglomeration. The policy of the state regulating the development of the capital differs slightly from that concerning other agglomerations. In many countries, the policy to regulate capital agglomerations was necessary not only in relation to the agglomeration's own problems, but also for the resolution of national problems, including regional inequality (Artobolevskiy, 1989,a).

In the 1970s, it become clear that a policy to decentralize the capital cities – where their success was evident – threatened to reduce the country's competitiveness and decrease its innovative potential. At the same time, however, the creation of jobs in capital agglomerations, and their concentration in elite economic functions, deepened the regional socio-economic disparities in the country and deprived extensive problem areas of new development impulses.

Capital agglomerations suffer from the same problems as agglomerations in other regions: an obsolete transport network and housing stock, the deterioration of the environment, the segregation of the population etc. However, the location of capital agglomerations in the most flourishing regions of the countries, which are attractive to private capital (including multi-nationals), the state, and many sections of the population, helps to solve address these problems. Frequently, the successful tackling of agglomeration problem areas implies the development of the territories themselves (ie. through improved infrastructure, housing, offices etc.) but does little for their inhabitants.

Although the existence of uniform pan-European approaches to the regulation of development in capital agglomerations has been implied, this idea is not well proven. Are there really common features in the approaches of the state to the regulation of capital agglomerations in the countries of western and eastern (including Russia) Europe? With this question in mind, an attempt will be made at a comparative study of state policy in relation to capital agglomerations (principally of the post-war period). Special emphasis will be placed on the study of three west European countries – Great Britain, France and the Netherlands, and, for comparison, two east European countries – Hungary and Russia. It is possible immediately to identify their unifying feature – the key position of the capital agglomeration in many spheres of life, to a much greater extent than their relative population share would suggest (see Table 2.4). The capital agglomerations in these

Table 2.4 Role of capital agglomerations, 1980s

	Share in the country, %					
	population	employment	production	investments	retail trade	number of students
London	12	16	15	–	–	–
Paris	18	21	27	21	22	34
Amsterdam*	16	17	18	17	–	–
Budapest	20	21	30**	28	27	47
Moscow***	6	8	–	5	13	19

–   no data
*   north Holland
**   in industrial production
***   in Russia
Compiled from numerous sources

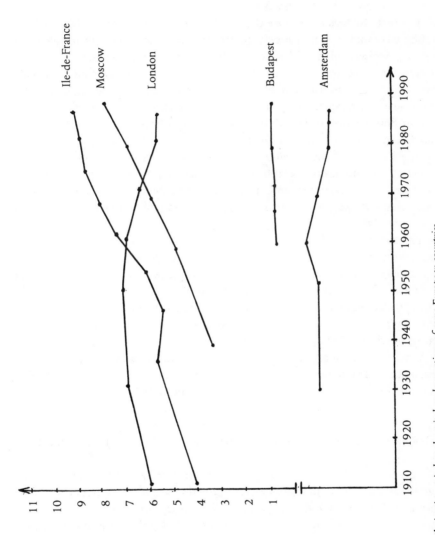

Figure 2.2 Dynamics of population in capitals and capital agglomerations of some European countries

countries (as well as for the majority of other European countries) typically occupy the most wealthy position in the country (Cheshire *et al.* 1988, Lappo and Treivish 1988, Territorial, 1988). In all the above-mentioned countries, the development of the economy of the capital regions was linked with the desire to increase competitiveness and export levels.

The first attempts to regulate the development of the capital and its agglomeration were undertaken in Russia. In 1918, Sakulin developed for Moscow the first real regional plan in the world. The project, which remained unrealized, foresaw the concentration of scientific, cultural and administrative functions in the capital and the transfer of industrial ones to external belts of the agglomeration. In post-war years, exactly these kind of measures would be encouraged by the state in west European countries. In 1931, the decision to limit growth of both the population and new industrial capacities in the capital was accepted. The introduction in 1932 of the *propiska* systems – i.e. the state control of population migration – theoretically strengthened the possibilities for limiting the growth of Moscow. The necessary planning documents were developed, but the attempts to constrain the growth of the Moscow population and economy were not successful (see Figure 2.2).

The state attempted to regulate the growth of Moscow (as well as of other large cities) with the aim of achieving a more uniform location of economic activities and population throughout the territory of the country, as well as developing peripheral regions. The adopted decisions also had political motives: to increase the dependence of individual on the state within framework of the new socio-economic system. From the 1930s until present day, the right to live in Moscow is one of the main 'blessings' which can be bestowed on a person by the state.

Why have all the attempts to stop the growth of Moscow failed (during the post-ward period, similar decisions to those described above were adopted again)? First, they ran against the aspirations of the population to live in areas with a considerably higher quality of life. Second, the state also represented an economic supermonopoly. It was in the interests of this supermonopoly to create new economic capacity in Moscow, and the state was thus forced to make a concession to itself.

New factories, plants and offices, however, required additional labour, which could not be found in Moscow. The growth of Moscow's population was encouraged by the arrival of migrants (called *limiters*) to work in the expanded economic capacity of the city. These migrants were deprived of many civil rights – the right to live in Moscow was related only to the requirement to work for a given number of years on a specified project. In this same period, and in order to tackle similar problems, the countries of western Europe recruited *limiters* from developing countries and less well-off neighbouring countries. The inflow of migrants to the capital cities created similar social problems, such as an increase in the level of crime.

In the USSR, as well as in the countries of western Europe, a post-war spatial segregation of society began to accelerate in the capital cities. More prestigious housing districts and, accordingly, less prestigious ones, began to emerge. Given the lack of sufficient housing and the absence of a housing market, data on housing exchange could provide a ranking of Moscow regions by prestige. Now, this ranking can be confirmed by the price data in the housing market. The most prestigious housing areas of Moscow are concentrated in the centre and to the north-west and south-west of the city.

In Hungary, the situation was similar to that described above. Decisions were adopted as early as the 1950s to restrict growth and decentralize Budapest, and, through this, to develop the periphery of the country. In more western style, measures to promote problem areas outside the capital were adopted at the same time as decentralisation initiatives. In the 1970s, during a period of intensive regional policy, a sharp fall in the rates of growth of Budapest was achieved (both of population and economic activity; see Figure 2.2). However, first, the success was only temporary, and, second, even during the 1970s, the forty-four settlements on the periphery of Budapest all underwent rapid growth. In general terms, and similar to the situation in Moscow, the policy of decentralization of Budapest proved relatively ineffective. The state again had to fight against the *natural gravitation* of the population and economy towards Budapest.

In western Europe, the policy of decentralization of the capital agglomerations was initiated in Great Britain. The need for such a move had become obvious at the end of the 1930s (Royal Commission 1940). The high concentration in the capital of population and economic activity hindered its development, as well as the development of peripheral depressed regions. In 1947, new industrial construction in Greater London was limited through the need to obtain an *industrial development certificate* (cancelled in 1982); later a similar system was implemented for the creation of new office buildings. It was also necessary to gain the usual planning permission from local authorities.

A ring of new towns around London was quickly created (later supplemented by the programme of *expanded towns*). Inhabitants and companies from the capital migrated to these centres, and their migration from the capital into new towns, or other centres, was stimulated by the state. An analysis of manufacturing industries which 'migrated' from Greater London between 1945–1965 (the most intensive period of industrial migration) shows that, although the majority of capacities located in adjacent areas, more than a third migrated into peripheral regions, and the distance migrated for companies leaving the capital was much higher than for companies moving from other areas (The movement 1968).

In 1955, similar restrictions on new industrial construction were introduced in Ile-de-France and, since 1959, they have been extended to offices. Similarly to Great Britain, new towns were created to encourage the decentralization of the capital and the migration of population from Paris was encouraged.

The policy of growth restriction and decentralization of Randstad was started in the Netherlands at the end of the 1950s. It was prompted both by an increase of its problems, and crisis in peripheral regions (partly the result of population movement to the West). Crisis peripheral regions first received official status in 1958. The land-use control system, introduced in 1962, became an important tool in the restriction of Randstad growth. Migration of population and economic activity out of the Randstad was encouraged, particularly to recipient crisis regions. New towns were created near The Hague and Amsterdam. Finally, in 1975, the restriction of economic development in the Randstad were approved (abolished in 1983). The policy of Randstad decentralization had much in common with the similar policies implemented in capital agglomerations in Great Britain and France.

In west European countries, the introduction, in the 1950s and 1960s, of rigid rules of physical planning has helped to resolve regional policy problems. In granting permission for the creation of new economic units in the capital, local authorities, while not declaring it openly, adhered to the same objectives as the national regional policy. They therefore further limited development in the capital agglomerations. Similarly, local authorities in crisis regions were less strict in the area of planning permission.

Physical planning can support the realization of regional policy, but cannot replace it. In the absence of regional policy, local authorities, which all operate at the same level and possess equal powers, will inevitably compete with each other. It areas within their remit are experiencing crisis, they will try to offer the maximum level of assistance to potential investors. Accordingly, the most wealthy authority will be in the best position. The hierarchy of regions/areas by socio-economic position and the corresponding level of state assistance will be lost. This replacement of regional policy by planning is only possible in individual countries, which have, temporarily, reached conditions of relative spatial equality – for example, the Netherlands, although, even in this case, it can be assumed that the current policy of encouraging development in the Randstad will ultimately cause the renewed growth of regional disparities.

The decentralisation of agglomerations has also been accelerated through a significant redistribution of public funds and through channels other than regional policy. In France, for example, it was accelerated by the transfer to 'province' level of significant resources for the development of education and housing construction (National 1988).

The policy of decentralization of capital agglomerations had two principal objectives. First, to improve the living conditions of the population and the functioning of the economy in the capitals. Second, to give a new impulse for the development of other regions and centres, and principally crisis areas.

In west European countries, the second of these objectives was only partially realized. Certainly many new enterprises and offices were created through migration in crisis regions (and especially in growth poles located within them), but, as previously mentioned, they were fundamentally plants for mass production and routine services. Even well-known programmes of enforced decentralization to problem regions of state offices (including R&D units), carried out in Great Britain and France in the 1960s and 1970s, and in the Netherlands and Sweden in the 1970s and the first half of the 1980s, were not fully completed. In the USSR, attempts, in the 1960s, to remove scientific establishments from Moscow were not successful.

The policy to decentralize capital cities has accelerated the structural reorganization of their economies, and their specialization in business services, management and high-tech industries. The rate of suburbanization of the population and economy has also been speeded up – in this case, the policy of the state matched the natural processes, including the *gravitation of the population and economy towards non-agglomeration areas*. In the USSR and Hungary, the state tried to reverse the natural location trends of the population and economy, and because of this, these attempts were not very effective.

Against the background of a continuing policy of decentralization of capital agglomerations, already by the start of the 1970s, the evaluation of this approach had changed in all three countries. The emphasis shifted from the success of the policy to the problems being experienced in the areas 'left' by population and business (*inner city areas*). Thus, the increase in spatial fragmentation became noticeable even within the boundaries of individual cities. These areas (sometimes including blocks of municipal housing on the periphery of agglomerations) became the focus for the location of marginal groups in the population, as well as high levels of unemployment etc. The deterioration of many socio-economic parameters is evident as one travels from the periphery to the centre (see Figures 2.3, 2.4 and 2.5).

Former ports are also included in this type of area in London, Amsterdam, and Rotterdam.

Greater London, Paris, and the Randstad (as well as a number of other west European capitals) are the foci for immigrants (initially from former colonies). Their concentration in inner city areas is natural, given their low qualification and income levels, and they settled in areas offering cheap housing which had been 'left' by the 'original' population. Events in London in the 1980s and, even in the normally peaceful Brussels in the spring of 1991, testify that the problem of *inner city areas* is also a national one (The Brixton 1982). Areas in which the coloured population is concentrated can even differ visually from neighbouring areas, and frequently have a bad reputation.

In the 1970s, an increase on a smaller scale of inner city area problems was also evident in Moscow and Budapest. People on low incomes, pensioners etc. were concentrated in segregated areas in the centre of Moscow in buildings of poor condition. Common flats are also concentrated in these areas.

In the second half of the 1970s, the inner city areas of the largest west European agglomerations emerged as a new class of problem territory. In Great Britain, the first law in this area was adopted in 1978 (the law on urban development was

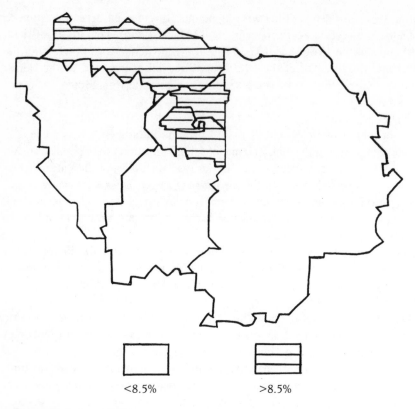

<8.5%   >8.5%

Source: Statistiques 1988

Figure 2.3 Level of unemployment in Ile-de-France, 1987

adopted in 1969, but did not specifically mention inner city areas), and particular emphasis was placed on their development by the 'new' Conservative administration, which came to power in 1979. In France, laws governing the development of inner city areas were adopted earlier (in 1967 and 1975, as well as the programme of La-Defense development which has been in operation since 1955), although the increased scale of action began in the 1980s. Since 1977, the state has provided assistance for the development of the central areas of the largest Randstad cities, although this only became the main direction of regional policy in the mid-1980s (Cheshire *et al.* 1988). Data on other west European countries also testify to the strengthening of state aid to central regions of agglomerations, including the capital cities.

In Great Britain, the emphasis of development methods for inner city areas is placed on market forces, the attraction of the private sector, and privatization. This approach to development has meant that little has been received by the 'native' inhabitants. The policy of inner city area development in France, carried out by the Socialist governments, was focused to a considerably greater degree on social goals (including the problem of ethnic groupings). A similar approach is evident

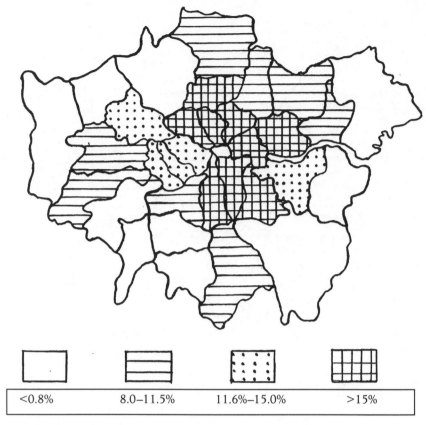

| <0.8% | 8.0–11.5% | 11.6%–15.0% | >15% |

Source: Annual abstract 1987

Figure 2.4 Level of unemployment in Greater London, 1986

from an analysis of the state policy for the Randstad development in one of the most 'Socialist' countries of the continent – the Netherlands.

In Moscow, the accelerated reconstruction of inner city areas began at the start of the 1980s, when even the very first steps towards the introduction of a market highlighted the value of these areas for new banks, exchanges, companies, and cooperatives. The revival of these areas occurred with virtually no state assistance. At a slightly later date, this process extended to include old housing in the centre, now the most popular location for *new Russians*.

The crisis of central areas of capital cities (as well as of other large cities) is frequently considered to be a consequence of the policy of decentralization (Ewers *et al.* 1986). Research in Great Britain, however, has shown that the national regional policy was not the major factor which caused the outflow of enterprises and offices from the capital (Balchin 1990). The space shortage in Greater London, and the correspondingly high prices, played a considerably more important role

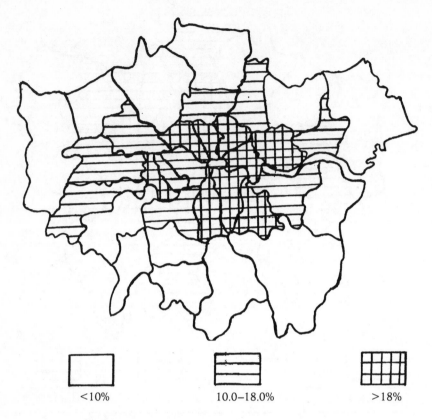

<10%   10.0–18.0%   >18%

Poverty coefficient is sum of shares of population waiting for municial houses
and receiving poverty social benefits

Source: Annual abstract 1987

Figure 2.5 Poverty in Greater London

in this process (Fothergill and Gudgin,1982). At the same time, government
regional policy frequently creates new places for the potential location or residence
of economic activities or population: new or expanded towns, industrial or
scientific parks, depressed or underdeveloped areas etc. This can channel flows out
of the capital.

In many cases, it was not the inhabitants of crisis inner city areas, but rather
those of considerably wealthier peripheral districts who left Greater London. At
the start of the 1980s, all west European countries turned away from policies which
restricted development in capital cities and other large agglomerations (Cheshire
et al. 1988). In parallel, a significant reduction in the scale of traditional regional
policy took place (Albrechts *et al.* 1989). The largest agglomerations now tended
to be considered as places where socio-economic problems were concentrated,

rather than areas of highest economic achievement (Albrechts and Vinikas 1986). The policy of inner city area development is now often regarded as the successor to regional policy. In the 1988–1989 financial year in Great Britain, the state spent £528 million on inner city area development and 463 million on regional policy (the planned expenditure for the 1991–1992 financial year was 570 and 410 million respectively – Balchin 1990, p.96).

The particular focus on inner city areas of capital agglomerations has several underlying reasons. First, their value for the country's economy. Currently, in the Netherlands, only the Randstad provides the country with an opportunity to compete against other countries/regions in Europe and the world and in London, the docks area is a natural continuation of the City. Second, successful development of the capital cities are especially important for ruling political parties, displaying the efficiency of their activity. There is one more reason for 'the switching' of the state's attention from traditional crisis areas to new ones. The socio-economic problems in inner city areas of agglomerations (including the capital cities) are now worse than those experienced in peripheral problem regions (see Table 2.5).

Table 2.5 Inter- and intra-regional differences in level of unemployment, mid-1980s

	Inter-regional differences*	Spatial differences in capitals*
France	1.6	1.3
Netherlands	1.3	3.5**
UK	1.6	2.0

*   ratio of maximum and average levels
**   data on Amsterdam
Source: Statistique 1988, Lambooy 1986, Urban problems 1988, Annual abstract 1987

A similar situation exists in Ireland. The highest level of unemployment in the country is found in the inner city areas of Dublin where, in common with London, the local inhabitants are 'not ready' to work in new enterprises and offices. However, Dublin and its individual areas are not included in the sphere of regional policy (MacLaran 1992, 1993), which is still oriented towards the development of western Ireland – although the real *crisis centre* of the country is moving from West to East with the deepening of problems in the inner city areas of Dublin, and this then requires a different hierarchy of regional policy territories (Drudy 1991).

There are reasons why the development of inner city areas of the largest agglomerations could be considered the new direction of regional policy (although this is not officially recognized). Under many socio-economic parameters, these areas should be treated as 'normal' problem/crisis areas. It should be noted that it is not only the problems of inner city areas which have resulted in a revision of the policy of decentralization. The stronger competition on the world market forced the state to pay greater attention to the development of the national capital (as a way of increasing the competitiveness of the national economy). As a result, the development of Paris, London, and the Randstad can become, for those governments, a priority objective.

Not only the spatial priorities of state activity, but also the methods utilised by the state are changing. Emphasis is being placed on the attraction of private capital, and the stimulation of indigenous regional resources (including small businesses). The selectivity of conventional tools – eg. grants, loans, and various infrastructure projects – is increasing. The state is shifting to the greater use of instruments such as the lessening of administrative controls and tax exemptions in the attraction of the private sector.

It is not easy to know how to evaluate the efficiency of state policy for the development of inner city areas (of the capitals and other agglomerations). While the change in the London docks area is dramatic, this is an example of the successful development of the territory instead of the *native population*. Within the area which comes under the jurisdiction of the development Corporation for the docks, only 13 per cent of the new working places are occupied by the local inhabitants, and, in 1988, the level of unemployment was higher than it had been when the body was created in 1981 (Balchin 1990, p.89).

The success of the development of the inner city areas of Greater London should not be underestimated. The sight of whole blocks of offices and residential buildings, as well as the picture of aeroplanes taking off from the centre of a city of 6.5 million people, is impressive. However, the majority of new employment places and apartments are inaccessible to the local inhabitants: in the former case, because specific qualifications and areas of specialism are required (and the policy of integrated staff retraining has disappeared), and in the latter case because the prices are too high (the cost of an apartment with three bedrooms reached up to ú500,000 at the end of the 1980s – a castle in good condition could be purchased in Wales or Scotland for this price). The new jobs and apartments are occupied by 'newcomers', with higher property-related, professional and socio-economic status. The more marginal population from the docks region is superseded, although their problems are not resolved, but merely moved elsewhere. However, the territorial concentration of the more marginal sections of the population is falling, and the related social and political problems are already less pronounced. This policy can be compared with the processing of dangerous waste: if it cannot be utilized or neutralized, it is better to dilute it to such a degree that it no longer represents a direct danger to the population.

In British cities, it is possible to identify whole areas of non-white population with a visibly lower quality of life than their 'white neighbours'. The further elimination of spatial segregation would significantly modify the acuteness of nationality and ethnic-related problems in British cities. However, data on Greater London indicates an increase in spatial segregation within the capital.

Similar problems are evident in other west European countries – for example, in Brussels (Cheshire *et al.* 1988) and in the cities of the Randstad. In Brussels, native inhabitants prefer not to live in areas with a large proportion of coloured people, despite the fact that visible differences in the quality of life within the Randstad and its individual centres are fewer than in London. The degree of segregation is lower in the Randstad where there have not, as yet, been riots involving immigrants.

The attempt to struggle with the territorial concentration of immigrants from developing countries should be treated with caution, as it is a very difficult area to address. Dependence on the native 'clan' or social group, financial and qualification barriers, as well as the 'spatial behavior' of the native population, all promote their concentration. However, the ideas promoted in Germany – the complete assimilation of migrants – seem more productive, although are longer-term in nature.

Is the process of gentrification the consequence or the reason for inner city area development policy? It is more accurate to speak of parallel processes. A change in taste of a section of the population takes place and young professionals with successful careers prefer to live in the centre of London, Amsterdam or Paris, having enough resources to do so (Lambooy 1986). Thus, their move is amplified by the policy of the state, and encourages the creation of comfortable housing, good infrastructure and overall favourable 'conditions'. Once again, the state channels and enhances the 'natural' flow of migrants.

The transition to a market economy of the CIS/Russia and Hungary, together with the other countries of eastern Europe, will lead to the simultaneous strengthening of the suburbanization and gentrification processes. In Moscow and its vicinity, flats in the centre and houses in close proximity to the capital are the most valuable (some of which are already used not only as second houses, but also as places of permanent residence from which working trips to the capital can be made).

Many Russian and East European economists and politicians have moved exclusively to the use of neo-liberal ideas, and pay no attention to dirigist concepts, based on the ideas of Keins – although these ideas dominated in the West for many decades and are still partially used. At present, even the local authorities (especially in Moscow) are frequently interested more in the generation of maximum profit than the solutions to social problems. The role of state – at all territorial levels – should be precisely defined (within the framework of the ongoing reform).

The experience of west European countries in the regulation of capital agglomerations shows that the state is able slightly to accelerate or slow their *natural* development trends and, to a certain extent, direct existing flows (Hall 1989), although any policy measures which have attempted to reverse these trends do not appear to have had a great deal of success. Even during the official operation of restrictive measures – whether in London, Paris or Moscow – the state itself bypassed them using wordings such as *by way of exception* and *in the interests of the national economy* etc.

In the regulation of capital agglomerations, west European countries used the same approaches, although not simultaneously. In Great Britain, for example, the policy of the decentralization of Greater London began immediately after the war, whereas in Paris it was initiated in the 1950s, and in the Randstad, in the 1960s. In the USSR, the campaign for the decentralization of Moscow was undertaken in the 1960s and 1970s, but again was unsuccessful. In all the countries, the policy was promoted for similar reasons, which have been outlined above.

The encouragement of inner city area development began in Great Britain just at the start of the 1960s and 1970s, in France, in the 1970s, in the Netherlands, in the 1980s. The increasing attention given to the central regions of Moscow can first be identified (mainly in papers) in Moscow development plans of the 1980s. In this policy focus, the time lag between western and eastern Europe is slightly less. The development of inner city areas in western Europe can now be regarded as part of government regional policy (i.e. aid to crisis regions). Processes of social segregation in Moscow and other east European capitals/agglomerations will also force the state to react to them.

At the same time, the state tries to exploit such valuable resources as the territory of the capitals for the stimulation of national economic growth. Any practical steps, therefore, will still be dictated by the compromise between efficiency and equity.

In western and eastern Europe, the policy of the state towards the capital and other large agglomerations had many common features, but with the above-mentioned time lag. The experience of west European countries must be taken into account by both the central government and the local authorities in the eastern part of the continent.

To end this section, a number of conclusions can be drawn from the analysis of state activity:

1. In all western countries, cycles in state policy occur, linked to changes in the prevailing ideology and the tastes of the population (as well as to factors of economic location). It is possible, therefore, to predict a rise in interest in how to tackle social problems which could, potentially, lead to a new phase in the encouragement of a policy of decentralization of agglomerations.

2. The significant similarity in the approach of the state in the countries of both western and eastern Europe is marked. The previously observed time lag is also diminishing.

3. The efficiency of a state's actions depends on the level correlation between the policy and the *natural* processes. It is only possible either to slow or accelerate the latter. A policy of decentralization of the largest regions and agglomerations has merely supported and accelerated a natural process, and, in part, influenced its direction.

4. The policy of the state towards the largest agglomerations often results in the development of the territory or area, rather than of its 'native'

population. This means that many of the problems are not resolved, but merely moved to a different location.

5.   State policy for the largest agglomerations (in developed countries) has largely maintained a social orientation in its objectives. In general, this is in contrast to the nature of such policies in the former Socialist countries of Europe.

6.   The problem areas in agglomerations are, so far, institutionally outside the remit of regional policy. This is linked to political factors and, partly, to the influence of urbanist ideas, where the area of reference is purely the city or town, rather than a consideration of the wider surrounding space (Cheshire and Hay 1989).

Regional policy in the EU

Following the creation of the European Community in 1958, the transfer of a number of functions from national governments to 'uniform' management bodies began. This caused considerable conflicts and debates on issues such as the loss of sovereignty but, in all cases, compromises have been reached (mutually beneficial from a strategic point of view). Thus the powers of common management bodies (located principally in Brussels) have increased. This trend has also been seen in the field of regional policy.

The principle of the need to ensure the 'uniform' development of territory within the framework of the Community and to assist crisis regions, is contained in the Treaty of Rome (the basic document of the Community). The Treaty also gives the Commission rights of monitoring and control in the distribution of state assistance.

The beginning of large-scale regional policy in the EC was the creation – in 1975 – of the European Regional Development Fund (ERDF). This was linked, to a great extent, to the entry in 1973 of Great Britain, Ireland and Denmark to the EC, and the corresponding significant increase of regional socio-economic disparities within the Community. In Great Britain, there existed extensive depressed old-industrial regions, as well as widely known underdeveloped regions such as Northern Ireland. In terms of the level of development, the southern part of the island (ie. the Irish republic) was also similar to its northern counterpart. At the same time, the regional focus of the other two European Structural Funds – the European Social Fund (ESF) and the European Agricultural Guidance and Guarantee Fund (Guidance section) (EAGGF) – was increased.

From this point, two interconnected processes were evident in the EC (now the EU): the spatial expansion of the Community (through the accession of Greece, and later Spain and Portugal and, recently, East Germany) with the corresponding deepening of regional disparities; and the increasing scale of the common regional policy. The above-mentioned acceding countries, for example, undertake the most intensive national regional policy of the EU Member States, and are also the principal targets of common European regional policy. From the initial six Member States, this is also true for Italy and now, to a great extent, for Germany. The extent of regional disparities in the EU can be seen from Table 2.6 and Figures 2.6–2.7. In general terms, significant regional disparities are evident between the centre and the periphery of the EU.

Even before the question of accession into the EU of four new countries was officially resolved, decisions about the list of their crisis regions (to be included in common regional policy) were made and the volume of future help between 1995–1999 was approved (EC Regional N3 1994). These discussions even included (as later came into being) the creation of a new class of problem regions in the Scandinavian countries – Arctic (underdeveloped).

Within the framework of the EU, the concept of problem regions differs markedly from that accepted in the individual countries. While in France, Great Britain and a number of other countries, the EU operates with regions and areas which are largely conterminous with national designated assisted areas, the common European regional policy considers the entirety of Ireland, Portugal, and Greece to be crisis territories (i.e. the whole country is viewed as a single problem region of the EU).

Regional policy in the EU promotes the 'unity' of the European territory (on the basis that real integration is impossible where significant regional disparities exist – Artobolevskiy and Savchenko, 1989). In addition, it aims to compensate, in a number of regions (predominantly crisis/peripheral areas), for the negative consequences of integration.

Two main directions of EU regional policy can be identified. First, the provision of direct financial help for the development of problem territories and second, the co-ordination and control of national regional policies (with powers to overrule and change decisions).

EU 'bodies' designate three types of problem region, where development is encouraged using Community financial resources: underdeveloped regions (so-called Objective 1 regions); crisis old-industrial regions (Objective 2); and agri-cultural regions (Objective 5b). Table 2.7 provides an indication of the relative weight of each of these areas in the individual Member States. A certain lack of logic can be observed in the classification system – underdeveloped regions, for example, can be agricultural and vice versa. However, as will be highlighted below, differing levels of development in the countries and regions are taken into account. The designation in prosperous countries of problem agricultural regions has the underlying aim of ensuring that all Member States of the EU are included within regional policy, to provide support for the majority of the population. Within EU regional policy, a doctrine of *general scope* exists ie. although the spatial targets of the policy can be found in virtually all the countries of the Community, these areas are generally incomparable in terms of socio-economic problems. This is the result of the political influence of all the national governments and the EU authorities (eg. to gain voter support, demonstrate the advantages of integration etc.).

Underdeveloped regions located on the southern and western periphery of the Community (Competitiveness 1994), are designated primarily on the basis of GDP per head: the GDP per head in the region, or in the majority its territorial units, should not exceed 75 per cent of the EU average. In addition, apart from this criteria, certain *special cases* are included ie. regions with well-known development problems. The designation of underdeveloped regions, therefore, is undertaken using both quantitative and qualitative criteria. The highest rates of award (in the EU) are available in underdeveloped regions – up to 75 per cent of the investment cost –, and two-thirds of the Community Structural Fund resources is spent in these regions. The designation of underdeveloped regions for five years (1989–1993, 1994–1999) means that the policy of the EU can be described more as a strategy approach then merely a set of independent measures. The redesignation in 1993 expanded the spatial coverage of underdeveloped regions to include parts of Great Britain (Merseyside, northern Scotland), Germany (the eastern part of country and East Berlin), and Belgium (Hainaut). It is anticipated that the underdeveloped regions will receive up to 70 per cent of the resources granted for problem regions.

A region can be included in the second category of problem region – crisis old-industrial – if the level of unemployment is above the EU average (over the three previous years), and the dependence of the regional economy on industry is higher than average. In addition, an overall reduction of employment in industry, or an acute reduction in certain industries or sectors, is also 'required'. These regions can include those adjacent to *poles of crisis*, areas and centres where the level of unemployment is 50 per cent higher than the EU average, and other areas of employment recession. Once again, a mix of quantitative and qualitative criteria is used, and the scope for EU institutions to play an important role in the designation process is obvious.

As already noted, underdeveloped regions are generally agrarian or, to be more exact, agro-industrial in nature. However, these regions are peripheral and differ from officially designated 'agricultural' regions which are principally concentrated in the central parts of the Community (Competitiveness 1994). They include territories with a high specific weighting of agriculture in the economic structure and a low level of income and socio-economic development. Factors such as depopulation, the level of peripherality in the national context, the size of farms, and the age structure of labour are also taken into account. Within the EU, a special institutional infrastructure exists for the coordination and control of the development of this type of problem region, in addition to the activities of individual countries, which differs slightly from that used for the first two types of problem region. Under many criteria, the average socio-economic situation in agricultural regions is much better than in underdeveloped ones, and thus the level of EU support to these regions is lower. Their problems tend to be acute only at national level, but not within the framework of the EU as a whole (see above).

Regional policy in the EU is implemented principally by the European Commission, located in Brussels. While a special commission also exists in the European Parliament to discuss various questions related to regional policy, the real power lies in the hands of Eurocrats. Its institutional structure is very interesting. In excess of 20 General Directorates exist within Commission, one of which, DG XVI, operates solely in the field of regional policy. It is responsible for underdeveloped and crisis industrial regions, but its activity is coordinated with other DGs engaged in dealing with social and agricultural problems. The DG responsible for agriculture is also responsible for the development of agricultural problem regions, and here DG-XVI plays an auxiliary role.

The existence of DG-XVI is, in itself, a positive phenomenon. This institution is officially responsible for the levelling of spatial disparities in the EU, and has successively increased the scale of the common regional policy over many years, frequently going *against the flow*, as this policy area has been curtailed in many countries.

Financial assistance is distributed through the three above-mentioned Structural Funds and the ERDF in particular. During the 16 years of its operation, ERDF activity has been repeatedly reorganized, the last reform being its 'auditing' in 1993. Even by 1985 its budget comprised around 2.3 bln ecu and by 1993, this level had increased almost three-fold. The spatial coverage of ERDF assistance (and that of the two other Structural Funds) can be seen in Table 2.8, which also indicates the importance of this area of EU activity.

In total, the three Structural Funds 'redistributed' 64 bln ecu between 1989–1993, and it is expected that in the period 1994–1999, this figure will increase to 141 bln ecu (Europe 1994). A significant proportion of the Funds – approximately 118 bln ecu – will go directly to EU problem regions (EC regional N1 1994). The recently created Cohesion Fund, the financing of which has increased rapidly, is intended for transport development and environmental improvement in Ireland, Greece, Portugal and Spain, and will also promote the levelling of regional disparities in the EU.

From 1984, the ERDF has had the power to finance its own programmes and, since 1988, up to 15 per cent of resources has been allocated for this purpose.

**Table 2.6 Social-economic indicators of EU
problem regions, end of the 1980s**

Type of regions	Population density per square km	Unem- ployment %	Share in the economy			GDP per head
			agriculture	industry	service	
Less developed	76	14.3	21	28	51	67
Declining industr.	271	9.5	3	38	58	98
EU average	144	8.3	13	32	59	100

Source: The Regions 1991 p.49.

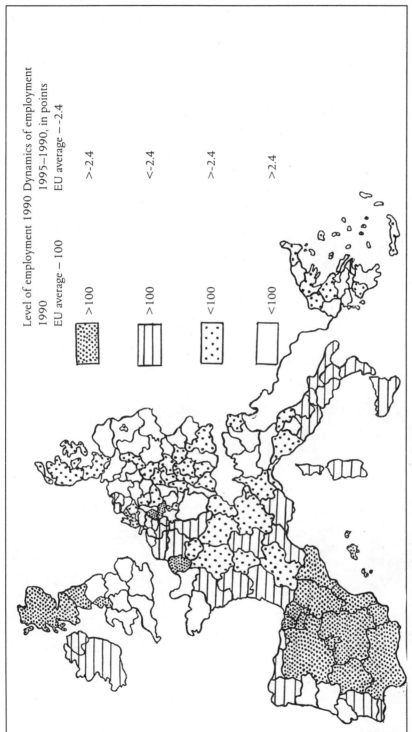

Figure 2.6 Dynamics of unemployment in EU (Source: The Regions 1991)

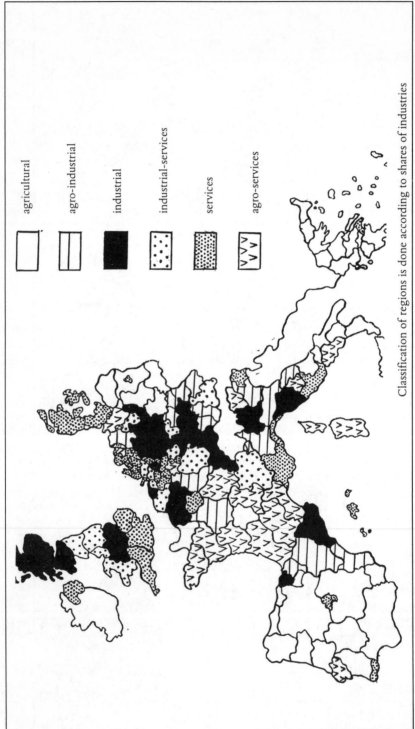

agricultural

agro-industrial

industrial

industrial-services

services

agro-services

Classification of regions is done according to shares of industries

Figure 2.7 Types of EU Regions economy (Source: The Regions 1991)

Other resources are distributed between individual countries. Until 1985, their quotas were strictly fixed, but upper and lower limits have since been designated (i.e. between two specified per centages of the total volume of ERDF resources). Thus, Italy's share in 1985 could range from 31.94 to 42.59 per cent, Great Britain's from 21.42 to 28.56 per cent, Greece's from 12.35 to 15.74 per cent, and France's from 11.05 to 14.74 per cent. The quotas were reassessed in connection with the accession of Spain and Portugal, and again with the unification of Germany. The real quota of each country is therefore defined by the EU institution, and the Commission analyses those situations where the maximum limit is exceeded and implements the final decision (i.e. through the redistribution of millions of ecu).

The EU and national institutions distribute the assistance between countries, types of problem regions and individual areas. As a result, in any set period, each area received a specified level of resources (from the three Funds) for which local *investors* have to compete.

The ERDF's own programmes are particularly oriented towards the development of the Mediterranean. The idea of Integrated Mediterranean Programmes was officially approved in 1985, and two-thirds of their budget is provided by the EU (De Witte 1990). Within their framework, two bln ecu has been provided over

Table 2.7 Share of population living in EU problem regions, 1989 (%)

Country	Problem regions after 1988 reform				Before reform
	Obj.1	Obj.2	Ob.5b	Total	
Belgium	–	22.1	2.7	24.8	33.1
Denmark	–	4.9	2.1	7.0	20.7
Germany	–	11.4	7.4	18.8	37.5
Greece	100	–	–	100	65.7
Spain	57.7	22.2	2.5	82.6	66.4
France	2.7	17.8	9.7	30.2	40.2
Ireland	100	–	–	100	100
Italy	36.4	6.6	5.0	47.8	38.8
Luxembourg	–	38.0	0.8	38.8	79.5
Netherlands	–	9.9	3.0	12.9	14.7
Portugal	100	–	–	100	100
UK	2.8	35.0	2.6	40.4	37.7
EU	21.7	16.4	5.0	43.0	43.8
Population, mln	69.6	52.6	16.0	138.2	–

– absence if this type of problem region
Source: *The Regions* 1991, p.55

Table 2.8 The role of structural funds for underdeveloped regions (%)

Countries and regions	Share of ERDF in investments		Share of ERDF in GDP		Share of structural funds in GDP	
	1989	1993	1989	1993	1989	1993
Greece	6.8	7.8	1.3	1.7	2.3	2.9
Ireland	5.8	6.3	1.0	1.3	2.2	2.7
Portugal	4.9	6.0	1.4	2.1	2.7	3.7
Regions:						
Spain	2.5	3.0	0.6	0.8	1.1	1.2
France	3.1	10.0	0.7	2.2	3.3	4.6
Italy	2.1	2.8	0.5	0.6	0.7	0.9
UK	2.6	2.1	0.6	0.4	1.1	0.9
Total	**3.1**	**4.1**	**0.7**	**0.9**	**1.2**	**1.6**
For all EU	0.5	0.6	0.1	0.1	0.2	0.3

Source: The Regions 1991 p.63

seven years for the development of problem areas in Greece, and 2.1 bln ecu for Italy and France (Cesaretti-Bianca and Torquati 1990). Spain and Portugal only joined the EU in 1986, and although they were not included in these programmes, they are now recipients of significant levels of EU regional assistance. The EU Structural Funds finance more than ten industrial-territorial programmes (see below).

ERDF assistance is oriented more to infrastructure projects (rather than the support of enterprises and offices, an approach found more within national regional policies), and the aid is given to local authorities and companies. In addition to its own programmes, the ERDF prefers to support national programmes (or programmes including several EU countries), particularly those which, if implemented, would be of benefit to the whole Community. Scientific studies in the field of regional development and policy (which can receive up to 100% funding) are financed from the Fund. DG-XVI coordinates all scientific research on regional problems through commissioning projects from several dozen scientific establishments in EU countries. The ERDF is oriented more towards the improvement of the investment climate in problem regions(through the creation of infrastructure, an increase in the quality of life, environmental improvement etc.) rather than aid to particular companies.

In the design and implementation of its own regional policy, the EU tries to take into consideration the priorities of the whole Community, while individual national governments operate only within the borders of their own countries. The parallel operation of two regional policies in each EU Member State is not a fruitless resource overlap, but rather an opportunity to combine national and EU interests to ensure the potential for integration of the majority of the population (and, importantly, EU-wide).

The ESF began its regional *activity* in 1971 (although this Fund has existed since the founding of the Community). Currently, more than 40 per cent of its resources (in 1985, the ESF budget was 2.5 bln ecu) comprises aid to areas with a high level of unemployment, particularly where unemployment levels have stagnated or there is widespread youth unemployment. A significant proportion of its resources go to problem regions, although assistance is often distributed using other criteria (ie. not regional). The EAGGF (Guidance section) finances development in crisis agrarian regions and, at the end the 1980s, its budget was 0.9 bln ecu. Within the framework of the EU's Common Agricultural Policy, the development of agrarian problem regions is certainly a relatively minor component of activity. However, the scale of assistance received by these regions is fully comparable with those granted by national governments.

Every country wishing to receive assistance from the Funds must present a programme, outlining how the Funds will be distributed taking EU priorities into account (this is a precondition). On the basis of national programmes, the Commission produces its own priorities (emphasizing the preference for complex programmes which are multi-annual and multi-sectoral).

The Structural Funds provide assistance in the form of grants. Loans with favourable conditions, for use in the solution of regional problems, can be obtained from the European Investment Bank. In addition, the European coal and steel community finances development of black metallurgy and coal mining regions. In total, 25–30 per cent of the EU budget is directed towards the elimination of regional disparities (The regional 1991, p.12).

Although the operation of all the EU financial institutions engaged in regional policy has a social *objective*, they basically stimulate economic activity (as is the case in national regional policies). As stated in the fourth periodic report on EU regions, if these resources were to be used for consumption, rather than for investment in human and 'physical' capital, one could not expect the growth of industrial potential, output and income levels (The Regions 1991). Ideally, the stimulation of development in problem regions should not lead to the emergence of aid dependency.

In estimating the importance of the common European regional policy, it is necessary to take into account that its growth is set against a background of curtailed activity in this area in the majority of individual EU countries. While the principle of additionality remains central, in reality, the share of the Community in regional policy is increasing (in all EU countries). However, it is possible that just such an increase in a common regional policy allows individual countries to reduce the scale of national policy in this area. The future prospects of a common regional policy are determined by the course of the integration process. Thus, for example, the proposed model for its organisation along German lines (Country – Land, Archibugi 1993) could only be implemented if the EU underwent a transition to a federal structure. This is very unlikely to happen in the near future, given that the transfer of further powers to Brussels is opposed by many countries.

In 1987–88, the EU Commission started to implement four of its own regional programmes – for development in black metallurgy and ship-building areas, for the creation of telecommunication systems in problem regions, and for the development of its energy sector. These programmes were 'designed' for a five year period with an annual budget of 40–150 mln ecu. The realization of 11 more programmes, eight of which are regional, began in 1990 (with annual costs of about 1.3 bln ecu). Among these programmes there were some to stimulate the creation of new infrastructure and R&D activities in crisis areas, as well as to promote environmental improvement etc. All the programmes were focused on the improvement of the investment climate in problem regions.

In some cases, these programmes supplement the activity of national authorities or, if this route is chosen, replace it. In other cases, however, the activity of the specified programmes is completely independent. Private companies and local authorities can approach the Commission for assistance without taking the position of their own government into account (although it would rarely be negative). The EU's own programmes are also financed through the Structural Funds, i.e. ERDF, ESF, EAGGF (Guidance section).

The increase in the financial scale of EU regional policy has led to debate about the real capacity for investment in problem regions. It is not known to what extent assistance, often granted for purely political reasons, is 'superfluous' in a region, if the opportunities for its rational use is limited by the poor real state of the economy and society (*The Regional* 1991).

The budget of the EU is comprised of Member State contributions, and these are not necessarily equal to the financial return. Rich countries give more than they receive, and vice versa for poor countries. This is also true in the field of regional policy, where richer regions subsidize poorer ones (including those in other countries), although there appears to be little ill-feeling about this. It is a necessary penalty for all the advantages of integration.

However, integration would probably be impossible without the co-ordination of the regional policies of individual countries (which, in any case, leads to a common regional policy). Even within the four Nordic countries of northern Europe (Denmark, Sweden, Norway and Finland), whose integration is not comparable in scale to that of the EU, agreements were signed in 1979 and 1989 to co-ordinate regional policies (including the problems of border region development – *Nordic Regions* 1991).

If the redistribution of resources within the framework of a common regional policy is not seriously opposed in the countries, the transfer of certain national powers to EU institutions is not quite as easy. The Commission already has many powers of restriction relating to the level and intensity of regional policy in individual countries, and can 'correct' the designation of problem regions etc. In joining the EU, every country, understanding the advantages of the common market, gives up some of its rights and powers. Article 93 of the Treaty of Rome states that, if the Commission decides that assistance, granted directly by a Member State or on the basis of its resources, is incompatible with the principles of the common market, it can oblige the state to abolish or suspend the assistance. Where the decision of the Commission is disputed by a national government, this can be resolved through the European Court. Equally, the Commission can also apply to the Court where Member States are not fulfilling specified requirements. This rather strict system does have certain exceptions: Commission decisions are not binding for EU countries in cases where extraordinary circumstances and political factors are more important than economic ones, and where large-scale intervention of the state is required. However, the times when EU countries can use this clause are extremely limited, understandably given the otherwise likely disintegration of the Community.

In the area of regional policy, as already mentioned, state assistance in any problem region cannot exceed 75 per cent of the total project costs. There are set limits determining the level of assistance within each category of problem region (based on the level of unemployment and GDP per head, the quality of life, and the severity of the problems). The 'weighting' of a region, therefore, has two stages: an evaluation first of its position within the country and, second, its position with the Community. The determining of the limits for assistance is carried out by DG-IV, and the main purpose of these regulations is to prevent any infringement of the principle of free competition.

The commission has tried to introduce a more *individualized* approach to the designation of problem regions in each country. It is obvious that a crisis area in the Netherlands is a 'dream' for Greece! At the same time, however, this view will not be shared by the inhabitants and companies in the Dutch region. Therefore, a 'weighting' of regions within the country and the EU is necessary. Table 2.9 presents the criteria, drafted by the Commission, which are used in this process. The Commission classifies problem regions by two criteria – GDP per head and the level of unemployment. The base level is less than 85 per cent of the national average GDP per head and in excess of 110 per cent of unemployment. Their criteria are then defined more exactly on the basis of the country's position within the EC. This leads to the criteria shown in Table 2.9. Areas where the GDP per head and unemployment levels are close to the base rates mentioned above can also be included in the category of problem region, following more detailed socio-economic analysis. In these decisions, the Commission shows initiative through the wider consideration of the regional problems and the avoidance of relying entirely on quantitative criteria.

The desire of the Commission to play a more active role in a common regional policy is not always positively received in all Member States. It should, however, be remembered that the 'weakest' countries are interested in a common regional policy and, ultimately, it is part of the political compromise.

Table 2.9 Criteria for problem regions apportionment, installed by the EU Commission

Countries	GDP per head, not more than average level in the country – 100	Level of unemployment, not below average level in the country – 100
Belgium	82	110
Denmark	73	110
France	77	117
Germany	74	145
Greece	83	110
Ireland	85	110
Italy	85	114
Luxembourg	77	145
Netherlands	79	110
Portugal	85	123
Spain	85	110
UK	83	110

Source: Bachtler 1988, p.31

Where the problem regions designated in individual countries do not meet the EU criteria, the Commission can insist on a revision of their borders. This is also true for the rates of award offered in various regions. Such an 'intrusion' of the EU into national regional policy occurred for the first time in 1980 in Denmark, and, by the end of 1988, 13 such cases had transpired, involving Ireland, Great Britain, Belgium, Germany, the Netherlands, Luxembourg and Italy (Bachtler 1988). Commission interference still proved necessary despite the fact that there had been close contact between Community and national institutions during the national decision-making process in this area. It can be seen that the Commission did not interfere in the regional policies of the *weakest* countries – Greece, Portugal and Spain. This is explained by the acute level of spatial problems in these countries, as well as the fact that their regional policies were 'reorganized', with the direct participation of Community institutions, following accession into the EU.

The efforts of the EU to ensure freedom of competition could contradict the interests of regional policy and limit its scale, although the activity of DG-IV actually promotes a strict ranking of EU territory. In many cases, the interference of DG-4 has been in countries with small regional disparities (such as Germany prior to reunification) where national governments have not been permitted to grant large-scale assistance to regions which are healthy in an EU context (Ballantyne and Bachtler 1990).

The activity of the Commission in the field of regional policy (both common and national) is constantly criticized by individual Member States. Criticisms include deficiencies in the statistical base used, a simplistic approach to the designation of problem regions, and the underestimation of the real situation in countries and regions. Additionally, its activity is considered an encroachment on the sovereignty of the Member State as the process of decision-making has moved increasingly to Brussels and the opportunities for the realization of an *independent* regional policy are limited (this process was strengthened after 1992). In addition, it is still unclear whether it is possible for one central authority to resolve the regional problems of every country, given that many of these problems are local. An analysis of regional policy shows that the basic conflict between Member States and EU institutions relates to that of the allocation and balance of powers and rights. If the EU were ultimately to become a single, unified state, an overarching common regional policy will clearly be necessary as a country in which sharp regional disparities exist, and common institutions fail to take adequate measures to overcome them, cannot remain unified in the long-term.

The reorientation of EU regional policy towards closer contact with regional (and even local) authorities is logical within the framework of the creation of a *unified state* (Dunford and Kafkalas 1992). Brussels wants direct contact with its *regional and local partners* and the replacement of part of the national regional policy with a common one strengthens such a transition. If a transition to a *Europe of regions* happens, a common regional policy should operate only with them. In the absence of these EU institutions, inter-regional competition (at EU level) will be exacerbated, and integration will become more difficult (Dunford 1994). It is notable that regions and areas are becoming more and more interested in direct contact with Brussels: their authorities and other institutions have put more active links with Brussels in place, by-passing their national governments (The regions 1991). The notion of a *Europe of regions* is attractive for many 'separatists', as it removes the acuteness of the struggle for independence in a national context – either full independence or administration or cultural autonomy.

The idea of the loss of sovereignty is opposed by various groups of the population and political parties in virtually all the countries of the EU. These feelings are strengthened by the fact that Commission restrictions also apply to the activity of regional and local authorities, attempting to resolve their own spatial problems. The activities of the Community actually limit their powers in the area of their own regional policy.

The supervisory functions of EU institutions – in the field of regional policy – increased sharply from the second half of the 1970s to the start of the 1980s. National governments are obliged to provide the Commission with plans of regional development, and take the position of the Commission into account in areas such as assisted area designation and award rate levels. Conflicts are inevitable, although they are often successfully resolved through compromise. Important features of these conflicts should be pointed out. First, they do not involve large sections of the population. Second, they occur between management institutions, and not between the producers of goods/services. In the resolution of regional problems, governments rarely interfere in private business by placing restrictions on their activity.

The almost complete abolition of obstacles to the movement of goods, capital and people within the EU may increase the significance of national regional policy as one of the last possibilities for the operation of latent protectionist measures in individual countries. Should this occur, the EU control of regional policy in all countries will naturally increase.

Key EU officials (Delores, Millan) have, as would be expected, claimed that the new stage of integration will not have especially adverse consequences for problem regions. However, their optimism appears excessive. A number of research studies (Bachtler and Clement 1990, Yuill *et al.* 1993) have shown that underdeveloped and agro-industrial regions of EU countries will suffer in the transition to a post-Maastrict stage of integration. This will increase the requirement for 'compensation' ie. lead to an increase in common EU regional policy (Submission).

The expansion of the EU through the accession of northern European countries and Austria has created a number of problems for the common regional policy. For example, some regions receiving state assistance in the new Member States are in considerably better socio-economic positions than problem regions in the *original* EU countries (Bachtler, Clement and Raines 1991, Halvorsen 1993). How the various approaches should be unified still remains unclear. It is also expected that the solution of urban problems will become an important part of EU regional policy (EU regional N3 1994).

Despite all the areas of conflict, the peaceful co-existence of national and common regional policies can be seen within the framework of the EU. How will regional problems be addressed in the CIS? More than 30 years of EU experience permits the following conclusions which, let us hope, are of some practical significance:

1. Regional social and economic disparities in the CIS are much more acute than in the EU and the operation of the New Commonwealth would be impossible in the absence of a regional policy.

2. Common institutions for regional policy realization should have two areas of power: the operation of their own *policy measures* within the remit of powers and budgets allocated to them; and powers of limitation over the spatial and financial scale of regional policy in individual sovereign states.

3. Among the first steps in the organization of a regional policy in the New Commonwealth should be the designation of problem regions and their ranking by the severity of the problems and the level of state assistance to be provided.

4. It is important to establish a thorough legal procedure for the resolution of conflicts between the states and the *centre*.

5. A common regional policy in the CIS (or, more likely, in part of it) is not a problem of the near future.

Peripherality and ways of overcoming it

The above analysis of problem regions identifies a range of criteria which describe the nature of the crisis: structural backwardness, poor quality of the labour force, adverse environmental conditions, an insufficient infrastructure provision etc. Correspondingly, within the framework of regional policy, measures exist to attract new industries, develop the service sector, train and re-train labour, improve the environment and level of infrastructure provision, and provide direct state investments. However, a negative feature of many problem regions is their peripherality, and the way in which this can be combated is less clear.

It has already been stated that peripherality should not be perceived as purely the physical remoteness of an area/region within a national or EU context (although this is more widely understood among geographers). It is also possible to talk of areas of social peripherality, including, for example, places of concentration of coloured immigrants in Paris or London, Brussels or Amsterdam. Analysis of statistics and scientific publications on these areas, interviews with populations of these areas as well as experts, and the author's own experience, all testify that these areas are isolated from events and processes in the country, and have a different way of life, culture etc. In extreme cases – as with gypsies and some groups of illegal immigrants – they live in almost completely isolated/closed communities.

The purely physical remoteness of a region/area cannot be a fixed category. Remoteness can be alleviated through progress in methods of transport and communication, and examples of this exist in all the countries of western Europe. At the same time, the construction of the tunnel between Britain and France will exacerbate the peripherality of Ireland within a west European context (MacLaran 1992).

In the French and British national contexts, Brittany and South Wales both occupy peripheral locations, but in an EU context, they are considerably closer to the centre. In the course of west European integration, some regions lose their peripheral nature while in others, such as the northern regions of Great Britain or Scandinavian countries, their peripherality becomes more acute. The expansion of the common economic space inevitably leads to redistribution of regions/areas between the centre and periphery. The creation, and subsequent territorial expansion, of the EU can already be considered a powerful stimulus for the development of certain regions, with the loss of peripheral status for regions and countries central to the EU. While Limburg, for example, is an outlying region of the Netherlands (located in the southern corner of the country), it is simultaneously at the centre of the EU. The process of integration can, in certain respects, thus be considered a *tool* of regional policy, able, for some regions, to solve the problem of peripherality. However, tackling the problems of some regions – through the expansion of a common socio-economic space and integration – also results in a deterioration of the situation in the *new periphery*. Under the strict rules of the EU, the maximum level of state assistance can be provided in regions on the periphery of the Community (Yuill *et al.* 1990, 1993).

Increased peripherality within the framework of the new socio-economic space is not always linked to a deterioration of economic development and the quality of life. Let us again take the example of Scotland. Scotland is clearly on the periphery of the EU, but nevertheless many of its centres and areas are well developed, and even surpass more southerly 'competitors'. This is true not only for the oil-related business centres and areas. It has already been stated, for example, that the largest city of the region – Glasgow – is developing considerably quicker than Liverpool and Manchester (although the reasons for their decline, started in the 1930s, are similar in many respects). However, the very remoteness of Glasgow from the largest centres of the country and the EU has necessitated the creation in the region of a larger service centre. From Russian experience, Novosibirsk provides a similar example. Its remoteness from Moscow permitted the creation of a more liberal political environment, and the needs of a huge regional 'market' promoted the rapid development of the city as an important scientific centre. In many cases, the needs of peripheral regions can be satisfied through their own resources/capacities, and the state can play a role in stimulating this process. This is another route to addressing the problem of peripherality which can be used within the framework of regional policy.

The extent of peripherality can also be altered through the exploitation of new (or the re-evaluation of old) resources. All researchers regard central Wales as on the periphery of Great Britain and the EU (Balchin 1990), while this designation is not currently used anywhere to describe the Aberdeen area (Grampian region). For the last 10–15 years, its rapid development has been linked to the exploitation of oil and gas in the North sea off the coast of Scotland, although physically, and in terms of transport accessibility, Wales is closer to London and the other largest EU centres than the Grampian region. The recreational resources of the Mediterranean coast in Spain and France are also widely recognized, and the increase in demand for these recreational resources has promoted the development of coastal areas in both countries (Europe 1991). Clearly, the state cannot simply exploit new mineral deposits or 'create' natural resources to order. However, within the framework of regional policy, it is possible to focus the stimulation of such resources on peripheral regions (including, for example, recreational potential).

Political change also affects the peripherality of regions. Within the framework of Federal Republic of Germany, areas along the border with the German Democratic Republic were considered as peripheral, and were included among the principal targets for regional policy aid. Now the eastern regions are clearly the periphery of the new Germany, and have become the focus for regional policy action.

Over the last five to ten years, the concept of peripherality has changed. As the already marked degree of spatial fragmentation increases, so the number of territorial levels within which central and peripheral areas can be identified, also rises. At present these include the world, developed countries, western Europe, the EU, individual states, their regions and, even, particular centres. A certain socio-economic inversion can be observed: the inner city areas of many agglomerations of developed countries (for example in London or Brussels) should now be classified as the periphery, while the suburbs and adjacent rural areas count as the centre. However, even within this example, the highly dynamic nature of the processes involved should be noted – the gentrification of inner city areas, for example, would return them to the category of *centre*.

In the majority of cases, peripherality complicates the development of a region's economy and diminishes the quality of life of the population (through enforced migration in search of employment etc.). The state also loses out through the under-exploitation of natural, economic and human resources in peripheral regions, although the question of whether it is necessary to encourage development in all peripheral regions is not as simple as it seems. The rapid development of peripheral regions, and the increase in their population (through the inflow of migrants), as seen through the experience of northern European countries and Scotland, threatens their unique environment and lifestyle, which is different from the dominant one in the country. It should be remembered that national minorities and other population groups, whose economy and lifestyle do not accord with those prevailing in the West, are located in some peripheral regions. Peripheral regions can also be considered as a kind of reserve (territorial, resource etc.) for future development, which would necessitate a policy of preservation.

What practical conclusions can be drawn from these sometimes contradictory ideas? The question about the real level of peripherality of a given region/area, and its inclusion in the sphere of regional policy, should be answered on an individual basis, following the completion of the necessary research. Only some of these regions/areas should be selected as prime targets for development.

The traditional regional policy of the 1950s and 1960s stimulated the creation, in peripheral regions, of new enterprises, offices, infrastructure, labour retraining schemes, and so on. Development was primarily based on the use of 'external' resources. Current regional policy supports the exploitation of indigenous resources in peripheral region, although due to the above-mentioned scarcity of such indigenous resources (particularly of anything that could form the basis of a modern economy), it is unlikely that the new regional policy approach will be effective in peripheral regions. It is impossible to predict the scale of development possible in peripheral regions through high-tech industries, business services etc, although in their absence, it is very difficult to achieve stability in post-industrial society. Many peripheral regions will maintain their agricultural, recreational, or 'environmental' specialization. Given these realities, regional policy must try to find an appropriate way forward, without attempting to stimulate development in all problem regions using a uniform template. The support of the traditional economy will be the right way for some peripheral regions. In practice, these trends can already be observed, and regional policy now more frequently includes support for agrarian sectors.

It has already been stated that technological progress increases the 'penetrability' of space. In Western Europe, telephone, fax and electronic mail connections can now be installed in seconds, face-to-face meetings can be organized in hours, and the transportation of goods takes a maximum of a few days. Peripherality, including physical remoteness, is therefore reduced. Increasing the accessibility of peripheral areas through improved transport and infrastructure links, as well as the stimulation of local resource exploitation, is a natural field of activity for regional policy. It should always be remembered, however, that the 'centre–periphery' balance is the consequence of the diffusion of virtually any development. Progress in the fields of science, economy, culture and other areas will always be distributed from a limited number of centres (which have accumulated a 'critical mass') to peripheral territories. Strictly speaking, an innovation ceases to be an innovation once it has reached peripheral areas.

The phenomenon of peripherality will always exist, although its geography will undergo constant change. The analysis of this shifting spatial pattern of peripherality will allow the correct definition of the targets of regional policy, thereby efficiently using state resources. In the 1980s, when the spatial reduction of official problem regions/areas was taking place in the majority of west Europe countries, the wealthiest of the peripheral areas were excluded from the receipt of state assistance (Yuill and Allen 1983, Yuill et al. 1988, 1993). At the same time, however, 'the eternity' of the peripherality phenomenon may help to guarantee the continuation of regional policy.

CHAPTER THREE

The Mechanism of Regional Policy Realization

Researchers, politicians and companies (let alone the population) have always focused only certain measures of regional policy. Their analysis is based on three questions: who should provide the assistance, who should be assisted, and how should they be assisted? The existence of a variety of approaches in the countries under study, even for the development of the same type of region, permits a comparative analysis of methods with the aim of identifying the most effective ones. It should be remembered, however, that unequivocally *bad* or *good* approaches do not really exist – all of them have plus and minus points. The state, in its choice between them, frequently bases its decisions on political or ideological reasons, rather than on the sole motive of identifying how best to resolve particular socio-economic territorial problems.

The institutional infrastructure of regional policy

In all developed countries, the central authorities hold the main powers in the field of regional policy. The parliament accepts all laws relating to regional policy, i.e. approves (or rejects) assistance measures, their rates of award, the regional designation, and the degree of decentralization, and also creates or abolishes special management bodies etc. Permanent and temporary parliamentary commissions exist, engaged both in regional policy in general and in issues relating to the most critical regional problems. Special attention is given by parliaments to regional problems when the members of parliament not only represent a political party, but also a particular geographical area (for example, the British journal *British Business* publishes a special section detailing government members' answers to the questions of the members of parliament).

Parliamentary budgetary decisions have an important significance for regional policy. A component of regional policy expenditure is passed in separate articles, while another component is contained within the budgets of individual ministries or other state bodies (for example, the ministries of transport or commissions on new towns).

It should be remembered that the main powers at EU level belong to the Commission (i.e. to its government), and, within this body, to a specialized ministry (DG-XVI – see Chapter Two) – although this situation operates against the background of the obvious weakness of the European Parliament.

The central governments of west European countries have more rights (and all the executive power) in the field of regional policy. In developed countries, there are two main institutional models of regional policy. In France and Italy, this policy area is implemented by special national 'bodies' (DATAR in France and the Agency of the South – earlier Cassa – in Italy). Within this model, this body can have its own budget (like a normal ministry), or it can simply monitor the distribution of resources by other institutions (as well as prepare the laws, commission scientific research, consult with state and private offices etc.) In the second model, which operates in countries such as Great Britain, Sweden, and Denmark, regional policy is implemented by several ministries. The relevant ministries are usually engaged in fields such as economic development, environment, labour and social problems. The experience of France shows (with the creation of DATAR in 1963) that the nature of the institutional structure of regional policy in many respects determines its efficiency (Hansen *et al.* 1990). It is impossible to argue unequivocally that either one of these variants – a separate ministry of regional policy or regional policy activity subsumed into other ministries – is better or worse.

The understanding of the term 'environment' is much wider in developed countries than in the USSR/Russia. Correspondingly, the ministries of the environment manage not only ecological problem areas and protected territories, but also inner city areas of agglomerations etc.

The specified ministries (and their regional departments) are involved in the preparation of laws, the granting of various assistance measures, the creation of the necessary infrastructure, the recultivation of lands, and so on. They are not, however, like Russian ministries, which have their own construction companies, factories, and R&D institutes – they are purely management-distribution centres. Decisions adopted by them – on infrastructure development, for example – are financed and adjusted regulated by them alone (as well as by the above mentioned special ministries of regional policy).

The ministries also finance scientific research in the field of regional policy, in addition to special state and non-state bodies (eg. funds, councils, academies etc.). An analysis of the activities of a number of scientific centres working in the field of regional policy in Great Britain, the Netherlands, Belgium and Italy, shows that they could not operate in the absence of commissions and financing from various government ministries. The second main source of financing for these centres are regional and local authorities.

In federal states – such as Germany, Switzerland, and Belgium – the region or state level (eg. the *Lander* in Germany and the cantons in Switzerland) enjoy considerable powers in the field of regional policy, although a range of key decisions are still met at national level (see Chapter One). Political and economic considerations frequently result in *assisted areas* being designated in every federal state/region. This means that the same level of state assistance can be provided for regions which may have quite different socio-economic positions.

As already highlighted in the book, the best example of such a 'mirror-image' approach can be found in Belgium. In the mid-1980s, the level of unemployment was 8.7 per cent in Flanders, but 12.4 per cent in Wallonia (the maximum level in Hainaut at 14.2%), and the GDP per head (as a % of the EU average) was 105 and 87 per cent respectively (and 80 in Hainaut). However, in the officially designated development areas in both Flanders and Wallonia, the maximum rate of grant award was identical – up to 21 per cent of project costs (*Regions* 1987, Yuill *et al.* 1990, 1993). There is a certain parity in the field of regional policy in Belgium. An absence of logic could certainly be argued in this situation, when socio-economic motives are sacrificed to political ones. However, it is possible to analyze this situation from a different point of view. There is a real threat to national unity in Belgium, with an active movement in Wallonia supporting the accession of the region to France and groups in Flanders backing a policy of independence. Under these conditions, it is logical to give more powers to the federal states, including in the field of regional policy. In 'stronger' federations, such as Germany, the *Lander* have certain rights in this policy area (Yuill *et al.* 1993), but comparably far fewer than in Belgium.

The regional authorities (including regional departments of national ministries) are involved in the distribution of assistance, and the control and monitoring of the adopted decisions. In addition, they make independent decisions concerning small-sized projects (the maximum size of investment and the nature of assistance which would fall within their competence is usually officially determined).

In the 1980s in west European countries, there was a typical movement towards a strengthening of regional authorities – examples can be found in France, Italy, and Spain – and this includes regional authorities governing agglomerations. Even the government of the Netherlands wanted to create a management body for the huge Randstad agglomeration (although this issue has been under discussion for years).

Other examples also exist. In Great Britain, under the Thatcher government, management authorities in the regions, as well as the councils of the largest agglomerations, were abolished (making metropolitan counties 'unique' in the country with no united management institutions). Without defending the bureaucracy, it is impossible not to note that the abolished councils were run by the Labour party. The abolition of the Greater London Council, and the institutions linked to it, seriously hindered the integration and adaptation of coloured immigrants in the capital (Hoggard and Green 1991). Everyday realities pushed local authorities towards cooperation, and in the South East and North West regions, county authorities have independently created joint planning bodies (Regional economic 1992).

Local authorities are only slightly involved in regional policy. The state sometimes selectively transfers additional powers to them for regional policy related purposes. In Denmark, for example, only local authorities in problem regions can create *incubator units for new business* (Wise and Chalkley 1990). The allocation of additional resources to local authorities in problem regions (given that their own tax base is small) conforms to and supports the objectives of regional policy and supplements it. Additional resources can be used, for example, for the construction and maintenance of infrastructure. The activities of local authorities certainly significantly contribute to the territorial development of the country, either hindering or 'easing' regional policy.

Local authorities are primarily involved in the improvement of the investment climate in the area (through the development of infrastructure, environmental improvement, housing construction etc.) and the attraction of investment. The interest of local authorities in new investment depends on the socio-economic situation of the area. Where there is a large unemployed pool, insufficient local tax income etc., they are usually interested in encouraging the inflow of investment and developing local business. On the one hand, this coincides with the objectives of regional policy, but, on the other, it can lead to competition between local authorities. Local authorities attempt to offer companies the maximum level of assistance, and present themselves as the *'best of the worst'*. Within the framework of regional policy, however, the state is generally more interested in the development of the worst crisis territories.

In the most wealthy areas, the situation is different. An analysis of the city and county councils in Oxford shows that they are not interested in the inflow of any type of investment, and carry out a selective assistance policy. They have the luxury of not having to accept lower level functions and can, on the contrary, encourage only the newest industries and sectors. In undertaking selective development in the most prosperous areas, the local authorities may indirectly assist the resolution of regional policy problems – some of the 'rejected' projects may 'migrate' to problem regions. However, it would be impossible to evaluate quantitatively the scale of such a flow.

As already mentioned in the book, local authorities have in their power an important tool – that is, the issue of planning permission, without which the construction of new economic activities, or a shift in functions of existing ones, is generally not possible. Theoretically, a refusal on the part of the local authorities can go to appeal through the courts and/or in central management institutions. In practice, however, the potential investor usually tries to reach a compromise with the local authorities. As a result, the project can become more 'tailored' to the needs of the local inhabitants.

The system of planning permission, issued by local authorities, can adjust the industrial structure of new investments, their location in the area and so on. The principal motivation in this process is the interests of the local inhabitants (providing them with employment, a higher quality of life etc.), which can run against the aims of regional policy.

Special management institutions are often created for the management of problem regions/areas. Such institutions exist in new towns, ecologically vulnerable areas, revived inner areas of agglomerations etc. Many of them – for example, the corporations of new town developments in Great Britain – are created only for the period of accelerated growth, and are later abolished. Included within their functions are the development of plans, negotiations with civil engineering firms, the attraction of investors, and interaction with local authorities. These institutions also carry out a number of other functions, such as the creation and maintenance of infrastructure (during a period of rapid growth, the resources required for this purpose are well in excess of the financial reserves of the local authorities). Such temporary authorities tend to be much more dynamic than more permanent ones. They depend not on the population, but on the central authorities. Some of these institutions are created solely within the framework of regional policy while others, although principally connected to non-spatial aims, do pay some attention to the goals of regional policy in their operation.

Even where such special management bodies exist, local authorities reserve a number of functions. They are involved in public health and education, police and fire protection, and environmental control. Usually, as already noted, local authorities carry out planning control in the area although, in a some cases, these powers can temporarily be transferred to management institutions of problem territories. Such a move weakens the planning control, although improves the investment climate. Companies can realize projects considerably faster, as the normal system of planning permission can take many months.

In the management of problem regions conflicts can occur between authorities of various territorial levels (and it should be taken into account that they are frequently led by different political parties). In many cases, these conflicts are related not to the need for a redistribution of functions and powers, but rather to a shortage of resources allocated from higher level authorities. There is not enough money for the realization of social programmes, particularly those carried out by local authorities. Another type of conflict can occur between 'legislative' and executive bodies at one level, or between members of Parliament and the civil service. This last type of conflict is very rare, although the revoking of civil servant decisions by members of Parliament is a much more frequent occurrence (and the final decision rests with the members of Parliament). In any advice on, for example, the refusal of planning permission for the construction of a new factory, the civil servant bases his/her decision on professional grounds – the road network is sufficient, it would necessitate the construction of new waste disposal capacities etc. Members of Parliament, however, who have the final say in the issuing of planning permission, may base decisions on political reasons (for example, a significant part of the population in the affected area are non-white immigrants and employment is required for unskilled labour). Both sides, therefore, are 'right'.

The most painful relations tend to be those between local authorities and special management bodies of problem areas within their territory. These management bodies have generally received, for a fixed period, some of the local authority powers.

The concept of the *devolution* of regional policy, or its transfer to a lower level (including local), is currently quite popular. This idea has already come under criticism in this book, as it leads to the disappearance of regional policy and strengthens the competition between regions/areas etc. These proposals do contain a certain rational component: the specific nature of regional/local problems are better known at lower levels, and frequently money can be spent more effectively. An opportunity exists here to include a geographical approach into regional policy. There are two ways to combine these mutually exclusive approaches to regional policy 196 the centralized and the local. First, maintaining strategic decision-making at the centre (including the designation of problem regions), and then transferring all executive functions to lower levels. In this case, the same method used under the welfare state in the Netherlands would be applied to regional policy: ie. management at local level, within the framework of decisions met at the centre, and financing at national level (Dieleman and Musterd 1992, p.127). Second, the creation of regional policy related opportunities for lower territorial units (within the country), although these units would clearly need to be reasonably large for this type of activity. Regional policy could at least by carried out at the level of large regions. Regional institutions would conduct their own regional policies, in additional to the national regional policy. This model already operates in federal states and can probably be widely recommended. The role of local authorities must obviously be included within the proposed model for regional policy administration.

The designation of problem regions

In Chapter Two, the main types of problem regions/areas were discussed. It is clear that officially designated problem regions cannot completely coincide with all the real areas of crisis. This is linked to the nature of the various designation systems (see below), the limited resources of the state, ethno-political reasons, and the existing administrative-territorial division of the country. As already noted, although the socio-economic situation in Wallonia is much worse than that in Flanders, the latter still contains extensive development regions (Yuill *et al.* 1993). The assessment and comparison of the socio-economic situation of regions/areas is not carried out in a national Belgian context, but rather within each of the two separate regions, and it is these regional authorities who really make the final decision. To a certain extent, regional policy in Belgium depends more on the European Commission than on the national government (although both institutions are in Brussels). While in unitary states, the designation of problem regions is decided by central government, in federal nations, this decision is more commonly made by the authorities of the federal states/regions.

Great attention is paid, within the framework of regional policy, to historical regions/provinces, as seen in the example of Spain and Italy. Even in Great Britain, a country which was unified more than 250 years ago, special attention is given to Scotland and Wales. Emphasis is also placed on the resolution of the problems of national minorities, including immigrants concentrated in the centres of agglomerations. Taking into account all these factors in the designation of problem territories, the state attempts to avoid any social crises (although this has not always been possible eg. the regular riots of immigrants from developing countries in the cities of western Europe – see Chapter Two).

The first problem regions were designated in 1934 in Great Britain, and, after the war, they were 'legalized' in other countries of western Europe, the USA and Canada. There were, and still are, two main approaches to the designation of problem regions: to designate only purely crisis areas; and, to include territories which are adjacent, and therefore closely linked, to them.

During the 1950s and 1960s, relatively extensive problem regions tended to be designated, not simply covering areas of pure crisis – although even within a single type of problem region, 3–4 gradients of area were defined (with a differing regional policy intensity). For example, in Great Britain, at the end of the 1960s, *special development areas*, *development areas* and *intermediate areas* (by decreasing order of state assistance) all existed in Scotland, Wales and the North, encompassing their entire territories. In South Italy, the level of assistance declined from south to north (although this is a generalization), and a west-east gradient of assistance exists in Ireland (Yuill and Allen 1988, Yuill *et al.* 1990).

In the 1970s to 1980s, a move to reduce the spatial coverage of problem regions became obvious. This was linked to a fall in the financial resources of the state and to the socio-economic spatial fragmentation. Relatively prosperous areas emerged in Scotland, Wales and southern France, for example. At the same time, as already noted, crisis areas were emerging in the capital agglomerations of west European countries.

However, essential differences in the approaches to the designation of problem regions are now obvious. In Great Britain, in the 1980s and 1990s, the spatial coverage of problem regions changed significantly (see Figures 1.4–1.6) whereas in France, over the same period, they remained relatively stable and encompassed a larger proportion of the national territory. It should be noted, that where the solution of economic problems is the main priority, smaller areas are generally designated. In contrast, where social objectives are central, designated areas tend to be more extensive.

What are the advantages in the designation of extensive problem regions? It is easier to attract private investment due to the natural variety of socio-economic conditions in the region (and guaranteed state assistance throughout the whole territory). In addition, even if new jobs are not created directly in the crisis areas, they are likely to have favourable knock-on effects for these areas. Unemployment levels, for example, can be reduced through commuting and the image of the entire region can be improved. Where assistance is granted to a large territory (including to local authorities), it is easier to support the creation of infrastructure, an important factor in the region's attractiveness for private investors. In the addressing of ecological problems, such as the preservation of nature in national parks or traditional agricultural landscapes, the presence of buffer zone is a vital condition.

However, the higher the spatial coverage of problem regions, the higher the required expenditure by the state. Under the conditions of economic crisis in the 1970s and 1980s, a reduction in the level of finance provided for regional problem area assistance became a way of making public spending cuts. In addition, people were becoming disillusioned with the idea of the *powerful state* (see Chapter One), and various concepts relating to a reduction in state activity and privatization were becoming more popular.

In many cases, companies located in the wealthiest parts of the problem regions can receive significant state assistance. Research shows that, in these cases, their location decisions are based on the availability of good sites, a suitable labour force etc., and not on the availability of state aid (Gudgin 1978). Where this occurs, the transfer of public funds to private companies is simply a side-effect of the decision.

All the above mentioned factors have resulted in a sharp reduction in the spatial coverage of problem regions (see Table 3.1), and newly designated areas have become more 'compact'.

Table 3.1 Share of population living in problem regions (%)

Countries	End of the 1970s	Beginning of 1989	Beginning of 1992
Belgium	39.5	33.1	33.1
Denmark	27.0	19.7	19.9
France	38.2	39.0	39.0
Germany	45.0	38.0	42.5*
Greece	65.0	58.0	58.0
Ireland	28.0	34.0	28.0
Italy**	35.6	35.6	35.6
Netherlands	27.4	19.9	19.9
Spain	36.0	51.6	58.6
Sweden	28.6	13.5	8.0
UK	45.7	36.8	36.8

*   united Germany
**   South
Source: Yuill and Allen 1983, Yuill *et al.* 1990, 1993

This general trend does not apply to areas of environmental protection and regions/areas with poor ecological conditions.

Up to the mid-1970s, the territory of many developed countries could be divided into two macro-regions: in Italy – the prosperous North and crisis South; in Belgium, similarly, Flanders and Wallonia; in France – the Paris region and other territories; in Great Britain – the South and the North; and in the USA – the *sun* and *snow* belts. The changing tastes of the population, as well as a shift in the factors of location, including a move towards non-metropolitan space, have resulted in significant territorial fragmentation. Now crisis regions can be found even in London and Paris, Amsterdam and Rotterdam, whereas relatively prosperous centres and areas exist within problem regions (in the Mediterranean coastal region of France, in Scotland and Wales and in New England in the USA). Given this situation, a shift in the state's approach to the more selective designation of smaller problem regions is logical. This also allows a greater concentration of resources on areas suffering the worst crises.

When assistance is provided only to small areas, the problems of adjacent regions are exacerbated. The chance to benefit from state assistance forces companies to concentrate investment efforts in the officially designated assisted areas where the locational conditions are only marginally worse than in adjacent territories. As a result, the situation of the latter deteriorates markedly. This dilemma forced the British government in the 1960s to define a new category of problem region (*intermediate areas* or *grey areas*) along the borders of *development areas*, and to establish certain measures to encourage their socio-economic development. Without this, these adjacent areas would have undergone rapid stagnation, which would have resulted in the territorial expansion of many depressed regions. Before the final decision was made, the issue was discussed in the press and scientific literature, and a special commission was created, and the conclusions of this research formed the basis of the government's practical steps (The intermediate 1969).

The borders of compact problem regions often do not correspond to natural ones eg. landscape features, river basins etc. This hinders the realization of measures aimed at ecological or environmental improvement. Such problems are highlighted in measures such as the preservation of traditional agricultural landscapes, where features located within official designated areas are saved, while similar features located in adjacent areas are allowed to deteriorate.

Many ecologically sensitive areas – national parks, valuable natural-historical landscapes etc. – receive a permanent designated status. Problem regions, however, generally only retain designated status until the objectives of the original designation are achieved eg. the elimination of derelict land or the increase in the quality of life or level of economic development. The withdrawal of state assistance following the achievement of objectives, can result in a rapid deterioration of the regional economy, and a sharpening of regional social and ecological problems. In countries of western Europe, in the 1950s and 1960s, there were many examples of this *sine wave* of development. The state, therefore, has tried to grant assistance for longer-term periods, maintaining continuity even when there is a change of ruling political party. The Thatcher government, for example, came to power in 1979, but the reform of regional policy was not completed in 1989. Similarly in France, during the 1980s, the main objectives (and measures) of regional policy were maintained despite the changes of government.

In the designation of problem regions, the countries of western Europe use units at various levels as *basic* territorial units eg. regions, provinces, and communes. Currently, a 'transition' towards the utilization of smaller-sized territorial units as the base units for area designation can be observed. The majority of these basic territorial units have an institutional infrastructure which supports the implementation of regional policy (local authorities, for example, receive help from the EU). In Great Britain, travel-to-work areas are used as the base unit, reflecting the focus on the struggle with unemployment and the general increase in quality of life, given that places of residence and places of employment are often spatially separate. In general, one can see different approaches to the selection of base units, as this process allows the particular situation of individual countries and regions to be taken into account, as well as including a more geographical focus in regional policy.

Originally, the main criterion for the inclusion of a region into the problem category was its high level of unemployment, and currently this is still one of the main parameters. This parameter is, to a certain extent, synthetic – a high level of unemployment is not only an indicator (or consequence) of the crisis, but also an underlying reason for it. Unemployment levels are influenced by the structure of the economy, the professional–educational structure of the population, and the investment climate in the region. It is necessary to establish to what degree the regional unemployment has a structural or stagnant character. An important indicator is also the level of youth unemployment. The existence of significant expanses of derelict land, as well as air or water pollution, can also form the basis of new problem region designation.

The designation process is usually defined by a whole range of socio-economic and ecological parameters, which can broadly be sub-divided into those describing the quality of life, and those indicating the level of economic development. In terms of *quality of life*, researchers and official institutions identify different sets of parameters. However, the level of income and unemployment, housing conditions, the state of the education and public health services, and the availability of social infrastructure are included in virtually all of them. In many countries, demographic indicators, the development prospects, and the geographical position are also taken into account (Allen *et al.* 1994). Another important parameter is the environmental situation which, in turn, is assessed using indicators such as the level of water and air pollution, the condition of the land, the richness of fauna and flora etc. Quality of life has been particularly appreciated in recent years in developed countries, and significant groups of the population are now often prepared to forego higher incomes to live in areas with a better quality of life. This quality is determined by the conditions of the natural and social environment in the place of residence.

The *level of economic development* is determined using indicators such as GDP per head, the structure of the economy and its individual sectors, the level of export production (at regional level), and the state of the infrastructure (including the existence of up-to-date communications).

It is clear that many parameters are used in the designation process (both official and *de facto*), some of which are purely qualitative. Various techniques for the quantitative evaluation of regional socio-economic (and ecological) conditions do exist, but they tend to be used principally in scientific research. However, in the EU and, for example, in Turkey, official institutions (in co-operation with scientists) do calculate complex indexes of socio-economic development, using a range of techniques (Keles 1985, *The Regions* 1991). In practice, the designation of problem regions involves not only a quantitative exercise, but also the opinions and more qualitative knowledge of experts, based on a *weighting* of various parameters. Political and ethnic factors play an extremely important role and include, for example, the presence in a region of an ethnic minority grouping, the electoral system of the country, and the degree of regional autonomy.

As already mentioned, there has always been the possibility of taking qualitative or subjective factors into account in the decision-making process. For example, in the EU, a specified criterion exists for the designation of underdeveloped regions ie. that the regional GDP per head should be less than 75 per cent of the EU average. However, where 'special reasons' can be cited, territories where this criterion is not met can also be included. In addition, territories where the level of GDP per head increases above the 75 per cent cut-off point are not automatically excluded.

Regions can also be included in the designation of problem regions following pressure from local authorities or interest groups in the population. Interest groups are particularly active in the designation of new ecological areas. Local authorities and the population can have a voice through their parliamentary representatives, various 'green' organizations etc.

As stated above, the preparation of the necessary legislative decisions is carried out by national institutions or, in the case of the EU, by the Commission. The decisions are usually then presented to parliaments by the councils of ministers for the final decision. Details on the institutional structure for regional policy have already been outlined.

The following conclusions can be drawn about the designation process:

1. The designation of problem regions cannot be undertaken solely on the basis of objective socio-economic parameters. A range of political-ethnic, historical, and even purely subjective factors must be taken into account.

2. The optimum method of problem area designation involves not only a quantitative exercise, but also the inclusion of more qualitative expertise from specialists.

3. An increase in the spatial fragmentation of development does, at a given stage
    of development, support the designation of smaller problem regions/areas,
    with the continuation of several grades of assistance (decreasing in intensity
    with distance from the core of the crisis)

4. It is necessary (even taking the above point into account) to maintain a level
    of stability in the borders of problem regions, as this promotes the inflow
    of capital into the designated areas.

Direct financial assistance

The development and diversification of new industries, the availability of local
business and advanced infrastructure, and the existence of a qualified labour force
are the only real routes to improving the socio-economic position of a region,
creating a 'sustainable' economy within it and improving its image. These conditions can currently be seen in certain areas of southern France or coastal Wales
and Scotland. These factors are considered by potential investors as an improvement of the investment climate and will stimulate the growth of investment.

The principal key question, therefore, is which methods can ensure the
necessary change in the industrial structure and, wider, in the level of socio-economic development of problem regions which will lead to the creation of the above
conditions. It is clear that, where private companies are the dominant force in the
economy, it is only through stimulating their development that the future of
problem regions can be ensured. However, private companies will not invest
sufficiently in problem regions if the state does not compensate them for the
additional costs associated with location in *disadvantaged* territories. These higher
costs result from the peripheral position of problem regions, the insufficient
qualification levels of the local labour force, the small size of the local market,
poor environmental conditions etc. Lastly, state assistance should counteract the
geographical inertia inherent in private business development whereby companies
gravitate naturally towards already *developed* regions/areas. The example of Greece
shows that even significant levels of financial and other support within the
framework of regional policy cannot ensure that economic development can be
diverted away from Athens and Salonica towards the problem regions (Tsoukalas
1988).

In advanced countries, especially in western Europe, emphasis has traditionally
been placed on direct financial assistance: grants, favourable loans and tax
concessions (in the USA, greater focus is given to the realization of the regional
programmes). It is considered that, within the framework of a functioning
economy, this type of assistance is *the most easily understood* by private business. It
has already been stated that regional policy will only become an important factor
of location when the level of assistance provided is comparable with the costs of
project realization.

Grants

Grants are usually given to companies (both private and state) either as a contribution to the costs of project realization, or as a fixed sum for the creation (or maintenance) of an employment place. The rates of grant award, and the form in which they are paid, are generally set for relatively long time periods (although the period of their validity is not usually stated at the outset and they generally run until a new law is adopted).

However, essential distinctions exist in the approaches of the state to private and state companies. State companies, regardless of whether or not they have received assistance within the framework of regional policy, can also apply for additional state aid. State (and mixed) companies, operating in old crisis sectors, have received multi-million targeted grants to cover losses and modernization – a trend principally evident during the 1950s, 1960s and early 1970s. This was done for two reasons: first, to prevent the socio-political problems (including of individual regions) linked to mass unemployment; and second, to maintain the low costs of production of these sectors which underscored, in many respects, the high rate of economic development in the countries of the West (in the 1950s and 1960s – see above).

Any company applying for a grant must complete the required forms, providing all the necessary information (and the state guarantees its 'confidentiality'). It is sometimes necessary to show that the project could not have been realized in the absence of state assistance. As a rule, the application for a grant can only be done prior to the start of the project. It is particularly important that the appropriate state *bodies* provide, free of charge, all the necessary information pertaining to the grants (and other state assistance measures) to all interested companies. Large and medium-sized companies (less often the case for small firms) can address any questions relating to the possible receipt of a grant to a consulting company, which will explain to them any common rules regulating grant allocation, will analyze the possibilities within the given project, and assist them in the completion of forms etc.

The decision on the award of grants is generally made by central institutions in the case of large projects, and regional ones for smaller projects. In some countries, such decisions are made by *sectoral* ministries and their regional departments, while in others, the specially created central institutions (see above) are involved.

The nature of the decision-making process is an established one. Grants are subdivided into automatic and 'selective'. In the first case, the management bodies only ensure that the project meets the required eligibility conditions. In the second case, however, they must decide (at a qualitative level) on the necessity of the project for the region, its contribution to employment, and also the extent of the likely multiplier effect etc. In cases where the award decision is positive, the rate of award is then set. While it is often officially stated that the rate of award should be at the minimum required level, the actual award rate is generally worked out in the course of negotiations.

Automatic awards have the advantage of allowing companies to take the grant into account in the project planning stage, but have the disadvantage of often providing assistance to companies which would have undertaken the project in the region even without the grant aid. This results in wasted expenditure of public funds. Selective grants, on the other hand, which are more 'economical' for the state, can be perceived as so uncertain that firms will choose locations outside the problems regions.

In modern times, with state spending cuts in vogue, ever more countries are moving towards the provision of selective grants in an attempt to minimize the costs to the state of creating new employment places. However, there are drawbacks to this trend. First, additional costs are incurred through the increased bureaucracy required for project evaluation. Second, there is an inevitable increase in the subjectivity of award decisions, and therefore of the possibility of error. Third, the creation of a new job at minimum cost to the state is not necessarily a positive development for the problem areas. The wider regional effect of this job (i.e. the multiplier effect), and its integration into local markets (goods, services, labour) etc. must also all be taken into account (Swales 1988).

The deadline for award decisions is fixed and does not usually exceed two or three months. The payment procedure is also stipulated. The grant provider will monitor the project throughout its realization and, in the case of infringement by the company of the conditions on which the grant was awarded, the payment of the grant can be suspended or the possibility of the clawback of the award can be raised. The time period in which the project must be completed is also generally stipulated.

Originally, grants were paid to industrial (manufacturing) companies and comprised a fixed share of the cost of the project. This approach is obvious, given the capital-intensive nature of this sector. However, by the 1950s and 1960s, some contradictions in this method because apparent. The main issue in crisis (problem) regions was unemployment but, at the same time, the underlying principle of grant assistance encouraged the creation of capital-intensive, rather than labour-intensive, *investment*. Two ways of addressing this contradiction were identified: setting predetermined limits for each new working place (as a fixed share of the project cost) or identifying separate fixed amounts for each new job created, unrelated to the overall costs of the project. However, a focus on the financing of capital-intensive projects does have a certain logic. In the long-term, capital-intensive projects are generally more stable and durable, and constructed capacities are more difficult to transfer to other regions. The inertia inherent in these projects can be advantageous to problem regions (Prestwick and Taylor 1990).

The transition of developed countries to a post-industrial society has required the reorientation of the system of state aid to the sphere of services. However, while virtually any industrial company can apply for a grant, significant restrictions exist in service sector eligibility – only those companies offering business services (R&D, legal help, advertising and marketing etc.) can apply for grants. In some cases, assistance is also provided for companies operating in construction, transport and communication, and agriculture, although usually only for projects which radically modernize the sector or introduce a new scientific or technological innovation. Within agriculture, often only projects promoting the industrialization of the agrarian sector can be subsidized.

Emphasis, however, is still placed on the development of the manufacturing industry in problem areas (naturally focused on the newest sectors). Given the role of manufacturing in regional economies, particularly in crisis areas, this *focus* appears reasonable.

The state always provides grants for new construction in a problem region, the 'transfer' (migration) into the region of capacities from outside, and the significant expansion or radical reorganization of existing companies. Small changes in production, the modernization of individual sectors etc. are not usually financed by the state within the framework of regional policy (although they may be eligible for aid from other state programmes). Sometimes grants are provided to companies purchasing a firm located in a problem region/area. The fact that grants are awarded principally only for new construction/expansion projects means that, in many respects, a certain sectoral *bias* exists. The creation of new industrial capacities tends, in the majority of cases, to be in the most modern sectors. Thus, while all industries technically have equal opportunities in the application for grants, in reality there is a focus on the newest industries.

In recent years, grants have focused more on the provision of aid to small- and medium-sized enterprises (SMEs), and a number of grants are only available to this type of firm. In other cases, fixed maximum grant awards are set for a single project. The highly dynamic nature of SME development and, at the same time, the difficulties for these firms of operating in problems regions in the absence of state support, are taken into account in this trend. An attempt is also made by the state to avoid the situation where a certain geographical area is dependent principally on one or two large employers. Experience in the 1970s and 1980s has shown that the closure of several large industrial enterprises can almost paralyze the economy even of large centres (Townsend 1983). In other cases, grants are not provided to small-sized projects (which can be financed through other channels), and a certain minimum level of investment or number of jobs to be created are stipulated.

In all the countries where grants are available, three or four grades of award level exist, corresponding to designated zones within the problem areas – the rate of award is linked to the location of the project in a particular zone. Usually, the rate of award increases as one moves away from the centre towards the periphery of the country. However, numerous exceptions can be seen – including, once again, the inner city areas of the largest agglomerations. Table 3.2 shows the various levels of award rate in west European countries.

Table 3.2 Rates of grants in problem regions, 1991 (% of investments)

Countries	Maximum grant	Real share of maximum grant in investments	Maximum share of all financial help*	Maximum share permitted permitted by EU
Belgium	25	12.6	12.6	20
Denmark	25	15.3	15.3	25
France	25	15.2	15.2**	25
Germany	23	11.1	14.8	23
Greece	55	30.4	38.7	75
Ireland	60	37.8	37.8	75
Italy	56	36.3	48.0**	75
Luxembourg	25	14.4	14.4**	25
Netherlands	20	10.8	10.8	20
Portugal	75	49.9	49.9	75
Spain	75	39.9	39.9	75
Sweden	35	18.0	18.0**	–
UK	23.1	25.3	25.3	30
North Ireland	50	30.5	30.5**	75

– no data
*   equivalent of grant share (after tax) in cost of project
**   additional help can be provided
Source: Yuill *et al.* 1993

The value of state assistance is really determined by the issue of whether or not the grants are taxed. Different rates of assistance can be given for investment involving land, equipment, infrastructure, buildings, motor vehicles etc. (and certain costs cannot be subsidized at all). The taxation of grants, the provision of aid for only part of the investment cost, and the system of delayed payments (where part of the award is given only following the completion of the project) all result in considerable differences between the declared maximum award rates and the real value of assistance (see Table 3.2).

The detailed analysis of the grant system permits several general comments to be made. First, this tool of government regional policy is accessible in all problem areas. Second, it is clear that the state can use grants to adjust the industrial structure of new investments, and influence their location within the boundaries of problem regions, the sizes of the new projects etc. Third, it is clear that regional policy cannot exist without its own institutional structure, involved in the drafting and adoption of laws, the distribution of assistance and the monitoring of projects.

The grant procedure is not only the work of officials, but has also been the subject of scientific research, especially in the 1980s (Begg and McDowall 1987). It is important to understand as fully as possible how the maximum regional effect can be achieved under conditions of diminishing state financial resources.

The example of grant assistance also highlights how complex regional policy tools have become in recent years. This is linked partly to the recurring theme in this book of spatial fragmentation and, in this case, within problem territories. Smaller problem areas have more specific requirements as regards the type of assistance offered within them. On this basis, a more complex system of grants can be considered as one of the areas where the 'geographization' of regional policy is occurring (and is not yet completed)

Favourable loans

This type of measure is less widespread than grant assistance in many developed countries. The price of capital has always played an important role in determining the level of investment activity. Favourable loans provided in problem regions not only stimulate the initiation of a project, but also partially secure the position of the company thereafter (i.e. during the period of returns), and thereby reduce running costs. A survey of more than 9,000 companies has shown that this type of loan is particularly important for the attraction of investors to underdeveloped regions (An empirical 1990).

The loans are provided at 'prices' or conditions below the market rates. The rates of the loan can either be fixed or determined on a case-by-case basis in negotiations with the company (ie. attempting to identify the minimum 'discount' necessary for the project to proceed). It is necessary to show that companies could not receive the same finance on the free capital markets.

In the provision of a range of different types of assistance, the state is not attempting to transform regional policy simply into one more channel of private sector development. Increasingly the companies have to prove that the realization of the project in the selected problem region would only be possible with the provision of state assistance.

As a rule, favourable loans are provided by commercial banks, and the state compensates the banks for the difference between the preferential and market rates, and guarantees the loan. Sometimes the money is given directly from state institutions. The volume of the loan comprises either a certain amount and/or a fixed share in the total cost of the project. The receipt of a loan generally does not preclude the company for applying for other types of state aid (such as grants), but the maximum rate of cumulated award value is limited by national or EU legislation.

Frequently the company has a certain repayment-free period, ie. repayment of the loan begins two to three years after it was given. The term of loan repayment is, usually, between 10 and 25 years, although this corresponds broadly with normal terms of any loan in west European countries (although shorter repayment terms are possible).

The procedures for the provision of favourable loans, and the sectoral and project type restrictions are similar to those which apply to grants (see above).

These factors permit the state to select the most viable projects, which are most favourable for problem regions. In addition, the state can partially influence their location decisions within problem regions. In this, the state attempts to be not simply a supervisory, but also a decision-making and influencing body.

Tax concessions

Tax concessions are currently relatively seldom used as a regional policy measure, and, in the countries of the EU, are only operated in France, Italy and Luxembourg. Their abolition in a number of West European countries was linked to the harmonization of tax laws within the framework of the common market.

Tax concessions are mainly provided for the payment of local taxes, and take the form either of a decrease in the normal rates of these taxes, or their complete waiving for a period of five to ten years (from the start of company activity in the problem region). These tax privileges encourage reinvestment of profits in the problem region. In France, the issue of tax privileges is decided by regional and local authorities, and in Italy, tax concessions are awarded automatically when projects comply with the legal norms.

The procedures for application and selection, the criteria used and the system of monitoring etc. are all fixed (as with grants and loans). Given that the rates of specified taxes, in some cases, are well in excess of ten per cent of profit, such concessions are of particular interest to firms operating in problems regions.

The increased depreciation allowance is a particular type of tax privilege (typically found in Germany and Greece). In each country – depending on the kind of industrial 'property' and the sector– fixed norms of amortization exist. Clearly, as building and equipment costs reduce with time, so taxes payable by the company also decline. By permitting accelerated rates of amortization – one to five years instead of ten to twenty – the state allows companies to make significant savings. This encourages location in the worst crisis areas (within the limits of problem regions) and the more intensive use by firms of equipment (clearly, the higher the equipment use, the greater the savings). In Germany, such privileges are granted by the *Lander* authorities, and in Greece, by local authorities.

It should be noted, that the receipt by a company of any form of financial assistance from the state gives the state the right to carry out additional checks. The state can require a company to provide additional information where necessary.

As can be seen from Table 3.3, the intensity of state assistance is determined, first of all, by the severity of regional problems. As expected, the leader is Italy, followed by Great Britain/Northern Ireland, the Irish Republic and Belgium. The wealth of the country is also of significance, and explains the high indicators of Luxembourg and Germany. Although the requirement for assistance is higher in the Irish Republic, more resources are given to the north of the island as London is 'richer' than Dublin.

**Table 3.3 Direct financial help within
the framework of regional policy (1990 prices)**

Countries	Total expenses mln pounds			Per head of population in problem areas, pounds		
	1985	1988	1990	1985	1988	1990
Belgium	116	208	105	34.1	63.3	31.9
Denmark	9	8	4	7.5	8.3	4.1
France	180	146	122	8.2	6.7	5.6
Germany	433	757	516	23.2	41.7	28.4
Greece	149	217	–	25.6	37.2	–
Ireland	145	124	146	41.5	35.4	41.6
Italy	3463	3916	5921	169.0	191.1	288.9
Luxembourg	6	34	19	16.4	88.9	50.9
Netherlands	109	87	70	29.2	29.3	23.6
Portugal	–	–	193	–	–	38.1
Spain	95	371	520	5.9	16.2	22.6
UK	762	642	485	39.1	32.9	24.9
North Ireland	163	105	71	101.6	65.4	44.2
– no data						

Source: Yuill *et al.* 1993

A wide range of direct financial assistance is generally available for project set-up costs. However, the *disadvantages* inherent in problem regions are constant and on-going. This means that the greatest difficulties are encountered in the day-to-day operation of enterprises and offices, but, by this point, only a minimal amount of state assistance is available. This explains the high turnover of new enterprises and offices in problems regions, particularly during periods of crisis (Townsend 1983). Given this, state measures to improve the investment climate in problem regions are of particular value and, in the long term, this type of state activity can be more effective. Accordingly, regional policy is giving ever more attention to this problem in virtually all developed countries.

The improvement of the investment climate

An increase, over the last 15–20 years, of the importance of *indirect* factors of location, i.e. those not directly changing production costs, have resulted in a shift of emphasis in the tools of regional policy. The state is giving increasing attention to the creation of a favourable investment/business climate, rather than focusing, as was earlier the case, on the provision of direct financial assistance to companies.

A good investment climate is defined as the existence of a set of conditions which are favourable for business development. In developed countries, for a number of reasons, this definition now also includes a high quality of life. First, labour, and especially qualified staff, has become the main factor of economic location and plants/offices migrate to areas selected by such staff (i.e. to the areas with the best living conditions). Second, plants and offices use the same facilities and resources as the population. Thus, a motorway serves not only vehicles delivering goods to a factory, but is also utilised by people going to the cinema, theatre or university. Similarly, a fax can transmit and receive business, as well as personal, messages. Good environmental conditions in an area are not only favourable for the health of the local population, but also increase the number of potential customers for local businesses. The availability of land provides the opportunity to build houses with gardens but also facilitates the construction of a single level manufacturing unit with space for staff car parking.

It has already been stated that it is very difficult (in many areas of state activity) to isolate what is *pure* regional policy. The measures/programmes discussed below, therefore, are those which are widely used for the solution of regional policy problems.

The development of infrastructure

As discussed above, virtually all direct financial assistance measures are offered once, either at the start of the project or during the first years of activity. In the long term, therefore, the availability of advanced production (and social) infra- structure in the problem region is of particular significance.

Strictly speaking, state spending on infrastructure often does not come under the heading of regional policy. At the same time, however, the state transfers significant resources to problem regions through industrial management bodies and regional and local authorities. The same is also true through the provision of social security payments.

The problem regions generally occupy peripheral positions in a national context, many are sparsely populated, and the level of income per head is low. All these factors necessitate significant (per inhabitant) costs for all various kinds of infrastructure provision. For this purpose, significant resources are transferred to them through the system of regional and local budgets, and through various government programmes. These resources are higher than those allocated purely for regional policy measures (through direct financial assistance). The state not only creates new infrastructure in problem regions, but its use also leads to savings both for private companies and the local population. The unique system found in Sweden should be mentioned in particular: long-distance cargo transportation (ie. more than 250 km) from problem regions is subsidized, thereby encouraging the development of regional export industries in these areas. The state also plays an important role through the provision of cheap housing for the local and 'incoming' populations – considered a key part of social infrastructure. Through all these measures, the state aims *to reduce* the level of peripherality of problem regions.

In some cases, the creation and maintenance of infrastructure is officially included within regional policy. In EU regional policy, for example, there is an obvious stress on the stimulation of infrastructure construction (see above). Traditional regional policy in Switzerland also includes the financing of infrastructure creation in mountain regions (Rossi 1994).

While the development of infrastructure, particularly transport and communication systems, is very important for the attraction of new investment, it also provides an 'exit route' for the out-migration of the population (and many problem regions suffer from depopulation and the ageing of the population). Naturally, the extent to which this might occur is closely related to the economic situation in Europe as a whole and in individual countries i.e. on the availability of employment opportunities outside the problem regions. In addition, the level of out-migration depends on the type of problem region, its geographical position, its development prospects, the traditions of the population etc. The creation of new infrastructure, however, should take into account the possible consequences of its continued operation. If the countries of western Europe were to return to a strategy *the people to the work*, virtually abolished in the 1950s, then the out-migration of the population might not be such a negative phenomenon. However, this does not currently seem a very realistic prospect.

The creation of industrial and science parks

Industrial and science parks are now widely distributed through the countries of western Europe, where the first industrial parks were established in the 1940s. They are generally created directly by the state, with the aim of attracting private companies. For the companies, the lease or purchase of buildings already equipped with all the necessary infrastructure in industrial parks represents a considerable saving of resources and time, and supports the firm during the initial stage of development.

The industrial park (or 'advanced factory', if a single unit is being referred to) is constructed directly under state orders on behalf of the central, regional or local authorities. Constructed buildings are equipped with all the necessary infrastructure – from electrical power to telephone lines. As a rule, future users are not involved in the construction phase, although any alterations required when new users come to the facilities are usually small-scale.

The typical users of industrial parks are small- and medium-sized firms from the local area. However, branch plants of multi-nationals also utilize business park facilities. The buildings are more often leased than purchased (although the possibility of leasing for 99 years exists in some cases). One of the main conditions of the location of an industrial/science park is proximity to a motorway. The motorway link is not only necessary for the deliveries of 'raw materials' and products, but also for staff access as many industrial parks are on the periphery of cities or in rural areas.

The state (frequently on behalf of local authorities) sometimes creates a kind of mini-park for small business in central areas of the largest agglomerations. This comprises a building (again equipped with necessary infrastructure) within which firms can occupy a number of rooms. The term of use is often limited to several years, during which time either the success of the firm will require it to move to larger premises, or the firm will fail.

Industrial parks are currently being created everywhere – and not only by the state – although in problem regions their creation is not designed to be profit-making (where this is clear from the start, only the state is likely to be able to realize their creation). They are viewed as local poles of growth, able to attract and involve capital from outside and create favourable conditions for local business.

Enterprises located in industrial parks in problem regions are generally oriented towards *external* markets. This promotes the growth of exports from problem regions. However, at the same time, it often means that the companies are poorly integrated into the local economy – both in terms of deliveries and sales. The multiplier effect of the enterprises in industrial parks is, therefore, quite low. Successful programmes of industrial park creation in problem regions contribute more to an improvement of the regional image than the solution of problems such as unemployment, low income levels etc.

Science parks became popular – originally in the USA and Great Britain – in the 1970s, based in universities with private business and/or local authority participation. They act as a kind of 'incubator' for small innovative firms, whose managers are often linked to the university (Gibb 1985). In science parks, R&D activities and the manufacture of higher order, specialized goods is the focus. Where mass production is to be undertaken, firms must leave the science park. Research shows that a significant part of the activity of many firms in science parks is only weakly linked to the universities (more often at a level of irregular consultations), but that these parks represent convenient locations and are considered prestigious addresses (Monk, Porter and Quintas 1988).

Many science parks have been created in problem regions (often using local universities). However, their activity is considerably less effective than in parks located in the wealthiest regions at the best known universities (a classic example being the successful development of a science park in Cambridge, Great Britain). Science parks can, therefore, also be a tool of regional policy although, within this policy area, the level of state assistance tends to be higher, and the results are more modest. In problem regions, programmes for the creation of science parks are smaller and oriented more towards the resolution of 'simple' problems. A similar situation can be seen in Japan (Fujita, 1988).

In general, the creation of a range of different kinds of innovation centre is often currently considered a panacea for problem regions (Cooke 1993). It should be remembered that, in the 1950s and 1960s, the establishment in problems regions of branch plants also promoted similar levels of optimism. The idea that centres of innovation can stimulate the development of local resources is, in itself, certainly a good one. However, the main question is whether or not this can actually be achieved in reality. Will innovation centres, like earlier branch plants, be isolated from the local economy? Is this approach suitable for every type of problem region? The indigenous regional resources which will contribute to the success of innovation centres differ substantially between problem regions – the only commonality between South Wales and South Italy is their sharing of the word 'South'!

A number of conclusions can be drawn at the end of this chapter. *Perestroika* (ie. a period of rapid change, including in state socio-economic policy) was not born in the USSR, but in the developed countries in the mid-1970s and its scope included regional policy and its instruments. The analysis of the latest changes to regional policy tools and the efforts of the state to alter the industrial structure of problem regions deserves special attention.

Many countries have considerably reduced the spatial coverage of regions receiving state help (see Table 3.3). While earlier they encompassed entire economical-geographical regions, they now often comprise only parts of cities. 'Points' where the maximum level of assistance can be given have been designated within larger *regions of development*. A reduction of the spatial coverage of designated regions certainly saves the state considerable resources. In addition, a rapid fragmentation of the socio-economic space of developed countries has taken place: in peripheral problem regions, quite prosperous areas exist while, conversely, crisis territories can be found in the most prosperous central areas.

Grants and loans remain the basis of the regional policy 'toolbox' (Table 3.2 testifies to their scale), in addition to measures for the creation and maintenance of infrastructure. Financial assistance is increasingly being provided on a selective basis i.e. following the analysis of a project applying for assistance, and its effect on the local economy, employment and environmental situation etc. The state is less often involved directly in economic activity, and greater emphasis is placed on the attraction of private capital into problem regions.

The process of privatization in the 1980s and 1990s in advanced countries has included the denationalization of certain sectors and enterprises. A significant part of the denationalized sector (especially in the manufacturing industry) is concentrated in problem regions and, therefore, privatization and subsequent rationalization exacerbates the difficulties of these territories (certainly in the short term). The weakest regions will always emerge as the losers in the process of privatization, and this should be taken into account when planning steps in this field.

A dominant, although not general, trend is the decentralization of regional policy. New regional management bodies have been created, while those which already exist have received more extensive powers. Frequently, powers transferred downwards are not accompanied by sufficient financial resources. Certainly, regional and local authorities have a better understanding of the problems in their own areas. However, regional policy begins the moment that the state places regions/areas in an unequal 'situation' ie. favours certain areas over others.

Ultimately, the efforts of the state are focused on the creation in problem regions of a diversified economic structure. Dependence on old sectors, such as coal mining or traditional agriculture, is not bad in itself (and by the 1960s, their share in the economic structure of crisis regions was not that significant). However, in old-industrial or agro-industrial regions, such old crisis sectors were closely linked to many other regional firms and industries, and thus their demise prompted a negative chain reaction in the region.

The structural backwardness of many problem regions is seen not purely in the share of old crisis industries. Enterprises engaged in mass production and offices providing routine services tend to be concentrated in these regions. Only a few company headquarters, R&D centres, advertising and sales divisions, and plants manufacturing specialised products exist in problem regions. The dynamic of small business development, especially in high-tech industries, is weak. All these factors force the state to pay particular attention to the development of business services and small business. In the 1970s, in almost all the countries of western Europe, government offices were transferred to problem regions (although in no countries were these programmes carried through to completion, as seen in the Dutch, French and British experience). New high-level educational establishments have been created in problem regions, or existing ones have been extended.

The experience of western countries has shown that the dependence of a region on two or three industries in a single economic sector represents a serious threat, even when the sector currently appears to be flourishing. In the long term, the stability of the regional socio-economic situation is directly proportional to the degree of diversification in the economy. Thus, the dependence of the West Midlands on the motor industry, which flourished during the 1960s, 'pushed' it into the category of problem region by the 1970s. A high level of diversification reduces structural unemployment and provides a wider choice of occupations for the young population. The diversification of a regional economy should, therefore, be encouraged in every possible way within the framework of regional policy.

Attracting different economic sectors and industries appears to have been easier than stimulating different types of activity. The creation in problem regions of R&D units, business services and plants with an innovative production range is a key difficulty. In the 1980s, it was no longer possible, as had previously been the case, to correlate the industrial structure (the share of the newest sectors) and the socio-economic situation in a region (Artobolevskiy 1992). For crisis regions, the danger of 'growth without development' is becoming ever more real.

In general, the restructuring of the economy does not simply mean the replacement of one sector with another. An institutional and technological reorganization of the economy, and a 'change' in the educational, professional and even moral level of the labour force etc. are all necessary (Albrechts et al. 1989). One should not oppose, within the framework of regional policy, the provision of assistance to attract branch plants and offices from 'outside' for the development of problem regions. In the majority of cases, only a symbiosis of branch plants/offices and small local firms can really help problem regions. The fact that anticipated economic growth will sharply increase the *potential* for the creation of new branch plants in problem regions should also be taken into account (Fothergill and Guy 1990).

Once again, it should be emphasized that the variety of regional policy tools opens the way for the 'geographization' of regional policy ie. the opportunity to pay greater attention to the spatial peculiarities of problem regions. This, in turn, will increase the efficiency of this policy area. However, full exploitation of these opportunities will only be possible when officials understand the importance of such an approach – and the task of explaining this may fall to the scientists.

The analysis of state activity in the regulation of the industrial structure of west European problem regions is, without doubt, of considerable practical interest to eastern European countries. However, it should not be expected that it will be able to give precise practical recommendations for the Russian situation. It is possible to 'transfer' the logic behind decisions, to determine the nature of key measures, and to establish their sequence. These themes will be developed further in the next chapter.

CHAPTER FOUR

Regional Policy in the USSR/CIS/Russia and the Opportunities for the Practical Implementation of Foreign Experience

Any Russian researcher engaged in the study of western countries, inevitably asks himself the question of how applicable their experience is to the Russian reality. Although political changes since 1985 have opened the way to free scientific analysis, they have not helped unequivocally to answer the above question. It might initially seem that the transition to a market economy would provide significant scope for the exploitation of western experience, but in practice this has been far from the case. The conditions under which western experience would be applied are simply too different. What can be heard in politicians' speeches, in reference to western experience, is frequently incorrect – incorrect information is a result, at best, of ignorance of the subject.

In all formerly Socialist countries, two extremes of approach can be identified relating to the utilization of western experience, including in the sphere of regional policy (Kaderabkova 1991). The first approach assumes the experience can simply be transferred into 'our' socio-economic conditions: what works in the West will also work in the East. Such statements, however, are rarely attributed to scientists, but rather belong in the realm of politicians, journalists and businessmen. The second approach is that our 'path' of development, psychology, culture, economy etc. is unique, and therefore it is impossible to use western experience.

Returning purely to the area of regional policy, one can propose that the utilization of western experience has some practical significance for the following reasons:

1. It is necessary to understand the global character of regional development processes (and their historical *variability*). On this basis, it may be possible to identify the current stage of development in Russia (and its individual regions) and therefore the range of opportunities open to the state.

2. Where resources are scarce, it is particularly important to identify the most effective ways of utilizing them. Western regional policy has always aimed

at maximum efficiency, and, in this area, important positive and negative experience has been accumulated.

3. The institutional structure for the realization of regional policy has already been developed in western countries, and there is no need to reinvent the wheel.

4. The strengthening of the trend towards disintegration within the Russia territory will inevitably force the government to create a *normal* regional policy (and, before this, a strategy of regional development for the country). The person or people making these decisions should be informed on how this area of state activity has been realized in the countries of the West.

The extent to which western experience in the field of regional policy can and will be used, depends on the *path* of the country's socio-economic development. The individual components of regional policy – regional grants, the creation of industrial and scientific parks, the drafting of regional development plans etc. – will almost certainly be introduced in practice. However, it is less certain that regional policy will become a distinct and important area of state activity. The previous system of state-monopolistic socialism did not allow for the creation of an institutionally independent regional policy. However, under capitalist development, two approaches have been taken. Between 1991–1994 the reforms were carried out basically from a monetarist position (in the hope that the market would act as a universal regulator). Within this, once again, there was no real place for regional policy. Regional policy is part of another, dirigible, approach to the solution of socio-economic problems and it seems that this approach is more suitable for our reality. The current Russian crisis is frequently compared with the great depression of 1929–1932, and the 'escape' from this was achieved only within the framework of a dirigible approach.

The evolution of regional policy in the USSR

Although this chapter focuses on the modern period of development and transformation of state regional policy in the USSR and Russia/CIS, it would be beneficial to start with the historical context, without which it will be difficult to understand the current trends and approaches.

The territorial expansion of the state, characteristic for virtually all the periods of Russian Empire development (including in the political and economic arena), comprised the first domestic regional policy. The development and occupation of new territories prompted and promoted actions to maintain order in the old ones.

The existence of colonies can create serious difficulties – as can be seen in the development of all known *parent states* in the twentieth century. For the Russian Empire (and later for the USSR), the main complexity lies in the territorial 'indissolubility' of its territories. Even if the current process of disintegration were to be undertaken objectively, it is not absolutely clear where the new borders would lie (and even the mass media fails to suggest potential solutions to this issues). The historical processes involved are relatively long-term – a significant part of the territory of the now independent Baltic states, for example, became part of the Empire at virtually the same time as the union of Scotland with England and Wales.

Following the disintegration of the USSR, similar problems have arisen within Russia itself, including the Tatarstan declaration of independence and events in the Northern Caucasus (starting in the Chechen republic). However, the move towards disintegration among separate 'nationalities' represents only part of the problem. Aspirations of 'sovereignty' are also shared by the authorities of the individual administrative regions in the *Russian* part of the country. One of the reasons for this increasing move towards separatism is the disregard by central (both the former and the new so-called 'democratic') authorities of regional problems. These developments underlie the first argument supporting the creation of a genuine regional policy. The state should clearly declare its responsibility for the maintenance of a broadly equal quality of life throughout the country, otherwise a permanent struggle will emerge between the internal *colonies* and the centre, which is perceived as 'robbing' them. Given the low standard of living, and the instability within society, this latter argument can easily be 'proved' within problem regions.

The approach of solving economic problems through the expansion into new territories became more popular in the post-revolution period. Within the spatial plan, the process of industrialization and, partially, of collectivization, were oriented towards the development of new territories and their resources – although real economic processes resisted the *Eastern drift* supported by the central authorities. The aims of the first five-years plans ie. the shift of the economy to the East and the restriction of the growth of the largest cities (starting with Moscow), were not realized (Kistanov 1985). It is interesting that during the period of the New Economic Policy (1921–1926), a rapid development of the country's economy was achieved because of the higher rates of growth in 'old' (central) agricultural and industrial regions. There were also experts who opposed the official ideas of the state vis-a-vis economic development, and proposed that the location of productive forces is determined by its own *laws* (Planning of location, 1985). However, the course of economic development that was adopted did not leave space for these particular ideas.

The roots of many of the current territorial conflicts were laid in the 1920s. The borders between nations were established based on the whims of leaders and as a result of political intrigues etc. Even in mono-ethnic territories, however, the established administrative units tend, above all, to serve the purposes of party management.

Government regional policy, concentrated on the development of new regions, continued in the post-war period (up to the mid-1980s) with the development of virgin lands, coal, petroleum and gas deposits of Siberia, and the creation of hydro-electric power stations and power-intensive industries in the same region. However, many of the officially declared aims relating to a shift of economic activity to the East were not realized. In general, the central and western regions of the country developed more successfully. The exceptions were those regions supplying the most needed and, at each given stage, unique resources. Thus, priority was given first to coal-mining regions, and later to those with oil and gas reserves.

During the 1920s and 1930s, as already stated, the state policy for the development of new territories was focused on necessary political (the creation of a manual workers class in national peripheral regions) and strategic (the economic vulnerability of western regions in the case of war) aims. Declarations were also made about the requirement to achieve greater uniformity in national territorial development, in the interests both of the economy, and of the majority of the population. It is difficult not to support, in principle, the latter social-based rationale – and 30 years later it was formulated by west European countries, united within the EU. However, even in the pre-war period, the main aims of any development, as understood by the state, were economic and, in the post-war period, economic goals dominated completely.

Social policy goals were only principally declared where they would support the resolution of economic problems: housing for the labour force, social infra-structure which supports employment opportunities, holidays granted to the workforce to ensure later higher levels of productivity etc. In official documents, the population are classified as 'labour force' and 'staff', and are considered merely as a means of development, and not the end purpose of development itself. At the same time, the supremacy of the social goals is stated in the West. In order to explain this phenomenon, some elements of the USSR system of management should be highlighted.

In principle, a country's development should be guided through officially agreed plans, for different territorial levels, which combine industrial, political and welfare goals. The State planning committee should develop and monitor the realization of the spatial aspects of these adopted plans i.e. this should comprise the main tool of government regional policy. At the start of the 1930s, branch ministries (then called 'narcomats') were created and, from this point, these super-monopolies took over the implementation of regional policy in the country. The main purpose of the ministries was to achieve a maximum volume of production, and they were able virtually to ignore any negative economic, ecological, and social consequence of their activities. They completely controlled entire industries and economic sectors: electric power industry and oil mining, black metallurgy and ship-building, railway transport and communications, and external economic links. Even during recent years since the start of the reform, a complete demonopolization has not occurred, but rather a shift of management form under conditions of continuing significant concentration of economic power (see below).

The ministries very quickly 'acquired' competences for the construction of economic units, infrastructure and housing, population services (eg. shops, hotels, country homes), transport capacities etc. They were able to provide fully – albeit at a minimum level – for the areas within their remit. The main aim of the ministries – to increase their own production levels (even when it was unnecessary or potentially damaging for the national economy) – determined their desire to create new capacities (in both new and old regions – the latter depending on the sector in question). The result was the hugely important role of ideology within economic development: the larger the economic activity to be created or territory to be developed, the better it was financed and provided for (the latter being particularly important under conditions of *global* deficit), the more apartments were constructed, the greater the choice of goods in local shops etc. The already existing economic activities and capacities, as well as those cities and areas (with some exceptions) where new large scale units were not created, received a considerably lower level of investment of all types (although this was in part also the natural end to a period of rapid development). In cities where new huge industrial capacities were under construction, at the height of development, state flats could be obtained within two or three years, but this time period increased several fold after the enterprise started operation. Examples of this can be seen in the cases of Stariy Oskol, Naberejnie Chelni, Toliatty.

The level of state investment may, as Treivish believes, also be regarded as a major indicator of depression or crisis in the *Soviet* region. It should be taken into account that, in the USSR, many regional indicators commonly used in the West (level of unemployment, migration balance, income per head of population etc.) cannot practically be applied, or at least only to individual types of region. In general, the availability of regional statistics – a necessary base for any regional policy – was and is rather low, although in recent years the situation has improved dramatically. Particularly worth noting is the fact that the complete lack of housing has resulted in very low levels of population mobility, and people are forced to live not where they chose, but where they are able to obtain a flat.

Regional policy in the West, as mentioned above, is oriented principally towards the realization of social purposes. In some countries, such as the Scandinavian countries, USA, Canada, and Australia, the policy area also includes the goal of developing resources in regions with extreme natural conditions, i.e. with both an economic and strategic rationale. The regional policy of the Soviet ministries (as well as their other activities) often solved neither social nor macro-economic problems. The achievement of a higher standard of living in the areas of their activity, in general, went against the aims of the ministries: it increased the costs of production and reduced the opportunities to exploit labour force migrations. The nature and type of use made by ministries of *their* areas frequently damaged the national economy. A very well known example within Russia was the Ministry of Water Economy (ie. of economic problems related to the supply, delivery and use of water), whose aims were the development of the maximum amount of territory at the maximum cost to the state. This led to its specialization in large-scale irrigation projects (virtually ignoring any other methods of land improvement) and many areas of its activity then quickly deteriorated – a fact which did not concern the Ministry as it was not linked to the ultimate purpose of increasing the level of agricultural production and the stability of the crops yield.

Similarly, the Ministry for electrical power production was concerned with the maximum output of electrical power, but not with its rational consumption. As a result, the country had large-scale plans for the construction of new power stations, including hydroelectric ones, which took no account of the damage which their creation could bring to agricultural, ecological and recreational resources. To prove the requirement for new projects, the ministries created their own 'pocket' science, and any assessment of the regional consequences of new projects was carried out at an extremely low scientific level. Many of the current regional problems – both national and social, economic and ecological – were induced by the activities of these ministries.

It is widely known that the problem of the mutual relations between the native and 'new' (Russian-speaking) populations in Latvia and Estonia is very marked. The problem has not declined under the current conditions following the independence of these states. Enforced 'Russification' is no better or worse than the modern policy of discrimination against the Russian-speaking minority. In both states the problem of the Russian-speaking minority also has a regional component and, theoretically, comprises the main element of a future regional policy in these states. However, *educated* in the Soviet spirit, the authorities (and, unfortunately, a large part of the population) appear in no hurry to resolve this regional-ethnic problem and the management of the large-scale migration of the Russian-speaking population from the country is the solution proposed for the problem. It is interesting that the suburbanization of Tallinn is not included as part of the proposed Estonian regional policy as this, among other consequences, could increase the area of potential ethnic conflict. This omission is more obvious given the otherwise very western style approach to other regional problems in the document (Keskpaik 1990).

The mass migration in the 1950s and 1960s of Russian speaking peoples into these republics was connected with the construction, by the ministries, of large industrial and infrastructure capacities in these areas. These projects incorporated, from the start, a principally external labour force – the local labour force was insufficient and its traditions were not taken into account. The ministries did not undertake any steps to minimize or deal with the problems linked to the influx of a huge number of migrants speaking another language and belonging to a different culture. No compensation was provided for any inconvenience to native inhabitants, and the migrants were not encouraged or provided with any assistance to learn the 'local' language.

The creation of new enterprises in Latvia and Estonia – often compulsorily implemented by the Russian ministries – was also encouraged under the policies of the local Soviet and party authorities. The latter actively pushed their particular areas forward to the ministries and, through this 'solution' to the then current political problems, created the basis of the modern ethno-political difficulties. The construction of new large scale projects provided an inflow of investment into all spheres, including the social sphere. Ministries also tried to locate new capacities in the Baltic republics because of their advanced infrastructure provision, high quality labour force, good standard of living etc.

The regional policy undertaken by the ministries was carried out within the context of competition between individual republics, regions and cities for the new projects. The decisions reached in Moscow were frequently connected to subjective factors (personal connections, effective lobbying, the political status of a territory etc.). In Azerbaijan in the 1970s, for example, a number of industrial enterprises were created because of the strong position of the leader of the republic's Communist party, Aliev, in Moscow.

Examples such as Azerbaijan or Armenia highlight the fact that the created capacities did not provide the optimum economic output. The local labour force, infrastructure and other factors of location contributed both to 'underproduction' and to a poorer quality of goods. In theory, this is not a disastrous situation – in many western countries, economic activities located in crisis regions for the combating of social problems operate at a *lower* level of efficiency. In the case of the USSR, however, the creation of these economic units has also frequently aggravated local political and social problems.

The domination of mercenary monopolies, the absence of any regulating activities by the centre, and the weakness of regional and local authorities resulted in the sharpening of regional disparities in the USSR. Currently within Russia (CIS), the full range of crisis region types exist: depressed old-industrial; depressed agrarian; underdeveloped (both agricultural and with extreme natural conditions); ecological disaster areas; and overcrowded agglomerations. Even in scientific literature, however, it is not possible to find a comprehensive designation of problem regions within the country and it is thus impossible to calculate accurately the share of crisis areas in the total national territory, population and economy. Real scientific research on the designation of problem regions has only been carried out in the last three to four years.

The crisis situation in the country, as well as the contiguous borders, in many places, of areas with ethnic and economic problems, provide important seedbeds for all separatist and nationality movements.

Under the conditions of an 'economy of deficit', mining and heavy industrial enterprises, located in old-industrial regions, had few difficulties with their production sales. However, ecological and social problems, and the dependence of these enterprises on very large multi-million rouble grants, forced the state to 'think through' their structural reorganization and the retraining of their staff. It should be remembered that, as in *western* regions, coal-miners in the CIS countries did not, and still do not, want to move out of well paid underground work.

Depressed old-agricultural regions are typical only in the CIS/Russia, and are a consequence of a 70 year policy to develop the peasantry. While in western countries, the farmers can be included in the 'Red book' of endangered species and comprise some of the primary targets of state care (and, accordingly, agrarian areas), in Russia/CIS many of the agricultural regions which were flourishing in the 1920s are now in deep depression.

Prime examples of such negative transformation can be found in the Non-Blacksoil zone of Russia. Programmes to develop this zone adopted in the 1970s and 1980s have failed, partly because they paid too little attention to geographical factors in the distribution of investment. The whole zone was treated as a uniform homogeneous space – in fact, what was required was the concentration of help on individual, and not numerous, areas/belts with particular potential for development. The attempt to redevelop the entire zone in the absence of sufficient resources was clearly an impossible goal. Equally, the development of the territory on the basis of agricultural development, as formerly, was also impossible and indeed not necessary. The change of location factors in this sector meant that an intensification of agricultural activity in the zone was required, and this was possible only in areas adjacent to large centres (Ioffe 1990).

The 'best' examples of underdeveloped agricultural regions can be found in the republics of Middle Asia (a term of the USSR period) or in the Caucasus region. They are characterized (although to a different degree) by agrarian overpopulation and mass, frequently hidden, unemployment, a low standard of living, poor environmental conditions, and the existence, to some degree, of feudal relations. In many cases, this situation is linked to their conversion (again under the initiative of ministries and local elite) into mono-cultural regions. The enforced specialization of Middle Asia republics on cotton production resulted in a poisoning of both the environment and the population (infant mortality was extremely high). During the collection of the cotton, the normal life of society was destroyed. In the Aral sea region, a vast zone of ecological disaster comparable with Chernobyl was created.

The *mono-cultural* nature of development is also characteristic for northern regions of Russia, with the overriding goal of exploiting of their natural resource base. This also results in environmental degradation and the destruction of the traditional lifestyle of the native inhabitants. The process of exploitation of the petroleum and gas deposits of Tumen region displays all these characteristics.

The rapid growth of population in the large cities in the USSR has, despite a range of official restrictions, resulted in the heightening of their ecological, social, demographic and transport problems. The power of the Soviet monopolies was demonstrated in their ability to push – *'by way of exception'* – decisions on the construction of new plants and the 'import' of additional labour (*limiters*, i.e. guest-workers). The higher quality of life in large cities made the restrictions on their population growth useless, even within the existing system of police control of a person's place of residence (*propiska*). At the same time, large cities were considered separately from their hinterlands, although the official policy of *restriction of growth* does not differentiate between them.

Aid to problem regions provided by the ministries was oriented towards the achievement of economic goals. 'Independent' regional programmes were not common and were frequently not supported either by financial resources or people to implement them. Indeed, even in these cases, their primary rationale was once again economic, and not the socio-economic problems of the local inhabitants. A recent example serves to illustrate this. The 1990 decree on measures to provide incentives for local authorities and their populations to locate atomic energy plants in their territories was drafted and formulated to meet the development needs of the sector. It did not consider the situation of inhabitants compelled to live near unsafe atomic electric power stations, even at a time when the consequences of the Chernobyl disaster were well known.

The disregarding of spatial disparities and the subordination of regional policy to the interests of individual monopolies was also typical for other countries of eastern Europe. In Poland, for example, depressed old-industrial regions, under-developed areas, and a range of problems connected with the rapid growth of the capital all existed, but no regional policy was created. However, in contrast to the USSR, the problems connected to the introduction of a regional policy were analyzed in detail by scientific establishments. This allowed the country to move quickly to the practical implementation of this policy area, although it was really only introduced, at a relatively small scale, in 1991 (Gorzelak and Jalowiecki 1993).

The exceptions in the Socialist camp were Hungary and the former Yugoslavia. In the 1970s and first half of the 1980s, the policy of decentralizing Budapest (and the development of alternative centres) was carried out, and this helped underdeveloped agrarian and depressed old-industrial areas (small ones). There are two obvious reasons for the differing approach in this country: the existence of deeper regional disparities than in other east European countries, and the intro-duction of market reforms in the economy at an earlier stage. However, even in Hungary, the former regional policy did not enjoy huge success and is recognized, at present, to be inefficient and insufficient. The *old* regional policy was created using western experience, but was not suitable for the prevailing socio-economic system (Horvath 1994). A radical reform of regional policy is now being under-taken in Hungary, although it is too early to discuss its results.

Within the framework of Yugoslavian regional policy, significant sums were transferred from the richer to poorer republics. However, this regional policy was also not very successful – considered by the donor republics to be excessive and by the recipient republics to be insufficient. The republics, particularly the rich ones, accused the federal government of disregarding their internal regional problems. Under the conditions of political and cultural backwardness and the apparent artificial nature of the Federal People's Republic of Yugoslavia, regional policy – in that particular form – actually promoted the disintegration of the country. However, within the now independent Slovenia, a regional policy of the western type is already being proposed (Kukar 1992).

Large-scale regional policy (despite the existence of sharp territorial problems) was not established in countries such as the former Czechoslovakia and Bulgaria. In common with the USSR, the main reason for this was the concentration of economic power in the hands of the state monopolies. However, sharp regional disparities (see, for example, Blajek and Kara 1992) were among the main reasons for the acuteness of regional-ethnic conflicts, particularly in the former Czechoslovakia, where political disintegration followed. As a whole, the political-economic system of these countries, mistakenly named *Socialist*, has been unable to solve regional problems, as it was based purely on the strict centralization of the entire system of management. Where its abilities to deal with spatial problems were limited, this immediately sharply aggravated ethnic problems and regional antagonism, even in such relatively rich countries as the former Czechoslovakia and Yugoslavia.

Regional policy after 1985

Perestroika, as well as the current post-perestroika, has had some obvious consequences, including the introduction of market relations into the economy and the democratization of society – although, at the same time, this was a period of deep economic and, later, political crisis. While the political problems were not directly linked to the process of economic and political changes, unprofessional and inconsistent reforms considerably worsened the situation.

Even the first steps towards the market (the liberalisation of prices, partial privatization etc.) have exacerbated the scale of territorial disparities and, accordingly, increased the need for regional policy and particularly its social goals. It is clear that many of the problem regions mentioned above are in a particularly bad position. It is possible to foresee a strengthening of spatial fragmentation in Russia (Treivish 1993) – depending on the process of transition to the market, the prospects of individual regions/areas/centres, even neighbouring ones, will increasingly diverge. Factors such as geographical position, the structure of individual economic sectors and industries, the functions carried out by the region, and the level of specialization in the delivered goods and services etc. will all become more important. The polarization of space will force the state to intervene, whether or not this is desired by the state. State institutions at various levels have already started to be interested in questions of problem region designation, regional policy etc. (although this should have taken place from the very start of the reform process).

The problem lies not only in the existence in Russia of numerous crisis/underdeveloped territories, but also in the fact that these areas are so much worse off (according to all indicators) than more prosperous regions/areas. At a qualitative level (quantitative comparison is still insufficient), regional disparities in Russia are considerably deeper than in western Europe (although one can see the same situation in many developing countries). The regions/areas are also frequently at different 'stages' of development: while Moscow and St. Petersburg are in a post-industrial stage, for example, others are agrarian, while peripheral regions often show a very particular type of economic development (Unity of reform 1992).

The creation of a market economy is not carried out uniformly in space. The majority of new market developments and institutions have emerged in the largest centres of the European part of CIS/Russia, although frequently exploiting the resources of other regions. The centres of market economy management have grown up in the same regions/areas as the former state ones, and an obvious increase in regional disparities can be observed.

A particularly great danger is one of political and economical disintegration, evident in Russia and virtually all CIS countries. As already mentioned, not only republics, but also individual cities (and even their administrative regions), have declared their sovereignty in the economic sphere. This trend is characteristic for the whole period after 1985 (Granberg 1991), although naturally this process had its peaks and troughs.

In the second half of the 1980s, the idea of regional self-accounting achieved wide popularity ie. that territorial units should live using their 'own' resources, gained from the economic activities located within their territory. Many local leaders were particular proponents of this concept and they tried to exploit the discontentment of the population with the worsened living conditions (unfortunately, sometimes, these ideas are supported not only by the 'former' leaders, but also by the new 'democratic' ones). In scientific publications, as well as in the mass media, many accounts and statements could be found stating that certain republics, regions and cities were 'robbing' each other and living one another's expense. Many of these authors, however, failed to pay attention to the fact that all prices were fixed by the state and were not connected with economic factors and thus to use them for calculations of who lives at whose expense was impossible. An analysis of inter-republican and inter-regional exchange data showed a different conclusion: all the territorial units are interlinked to such a degree that any isolationist policy would exacerbate the crisis not only in the breakaway region itself, but also in the country as a whole.

The support of problem regions is in the interests of all the 'components' of the new Russia, and not only for social-political rationale. Virtually all these regions are monopolists in the manufacture of certain kinds of production, and the likelihood of changing this situation in the near future is very small (there are no resources available for imports and the creation of new centres for the production of these goods would be an expensive and time-consuming process). The obvious notion prevalent in the West that the rich regions have an obligation to help poorer ones can be practically excluded from discussion in a Russian context. In the last two or three years, the term *regional self-accounting* has disappeared from publications and the vocabulary of political leaders, although the ideas incorporated within it have lived on under new titles such as *sovereignty* and the *wider rights of the regional/local authorities* etc. Under crisis conditions, such ideas often receive public support.

Since 1985, virtually none of 'our' reforms have included sufficiently strong measures for the social protection of the population (as used to be the case in Poland and Hungary). This has become particularly obvious since 1991. The role of regional and local authorities in the provision of social and local services to the population has been increased, but they have not received the resources required for this to be carried out. It did, however, strengthen their aspirations to control more property, to increase their own economic activity and, even, to have a greater degree of sovereignty.

This fragmentation of the market complicates the realization of regional policy (even the current, small-scale, policy provision). One result of this is the disruption of financial flows between central and regional authorities: fewer resources are flowing into the common budget of Russia, and the opportunities for centralized investment are more limited. Regional policy can only be based on these two areas.

A further necessary requirement for the operation of 'normal' regional policy is that all the institutions and individuals of the country comply with the nationally approved laws. However, although virtually all the required laws are in place, in everyday life, these laws are often ignored and illegal operation is common at all levels of authority, in companies and among the population. One western regionalist has indicated in the Polish case, where the situation is much better, that the movement towards the market should be complemented by a movement towards complying with the law (Regional development 1992, p.47).

Naturally, the functions of the centre should be considerably reduced (as well as the role of the state in general), within specified limits, central management bodies should still 'rule'. It is logical to assign the competence for macro-economic and social policy to the centre. It is possible to identify and evaluate the various driving forces behind the disintegration of Russia (Unity of reform 1992), but it is imperative to realize that the results of such a movement would be terrible. The disintegration of the country could result in total impoverishment etc. – as illustrated in the case of Ukraine, where the rouble is currently a hard currency. In reaction to the process of disintegration, the growth of Russian nationalism and the creation of a fascist-type state is an even greater possibility. Treivish proposes that the preservation of federation unity could become the main official aim of a new regional policy.

In Russia, the first components of a *normal* regional policy can now be identified. This is based largely on the initiative, and under the pressure of, the population and authorities of individual areas (cities). However, the central government, albeit slowly, has legitimized the required changes through, for example, the provision of aid to coal mining and environmentally damaged regions, social assistance to poor regions through the budget (beginning in 1994), and the creation of free economic zones.

Free economic zones are considered both as an instrument to accelerate development in relatively 'wealthy' areas (eg. Zelenograd, St Petersburg) and as a way of aiding underdeveloped regions (eg. Altai republic, Far East). Questions as to whether these zones are viable and have been well-selected are not ones to be analyzed here. The focus of discussion, rather, is the new direction of regional policy, including the special laws, the provision of aid by the state etc.

Adopted measures within the framework of the *new* regional policy frequently remain unrealized. The crisis conditions, and the state budget deficit, mean that insufficient resources are allocated for the realization of regional policy measures (or they are significantly depleted through inflation). The constant pressure on the central government from regional authorities (especially in territories where the production of valuable resources is concentrated) does not permit a real *weighting* of spatial problems and the creation of a hierarchy of problem regions. Those territorial units which place greatest pressure on the centre, as well as those whose internal resources are most in deficit (eg. oil and gas regions and, formerly, coal regions) receive the most resources.

The state now has two possible approaches open to it. Theoretically it is possible to put aside at present the solution of regional problems (particularly social ones) in favour of the build-up of a certain level of national wealth. It should be remembered that regional policy in western Europe only emerged in the 150 years after the Industrial Revolution. Although the existence of crisis regions will always hinder the realization of any reform, and will become an important factor behind political instability, if Russia has to pass through a long period of 'wild' Capitalism, it can exist without a regional policy.

It is necessary, however, to understand exactly what the results of these, as well as other, processes would be in the absence of an adjusting regional policy. In Moscow, for example, one can see a regeneration of central areas (new offices, flats for new elite). If uncontrolled, this process would probably also bolster other rather small territories (only the most 'valuable') and would thereby strengthen the degree of spatial segregation in the capital. At the same time, even a minimum level of intervention could expand the spatial coverage of the regenerated centre, and lower the acuteness of socio-political problems in Moscow. Old industrial areas located in the central part of Moscow could also be regenerated, but only with state intervention given that this process would be more expensive than the revitalization of residential or office areas. As the experience of the West shows, it is dangerous to create areas of concentration of marginal groups, while domestic experience tells us about the danger of the existence of special areas for rich people/elite. The notion that social problems are of secondary importance and that dealing with them should only happen after the resolution of economic ones, belongs to the most conservative political circles of the West.

Within the framework of the second approach open to the state – the introduction of a controlled market – regional policy is necessary. It will promote the stabilization of the socio-political situation and reduce the negative consequences of the market introduction (even the economic ones). In this case, however, it would be necessary to overcome opposition from central, and regional-local authorities, as well as, most importantly, the population. The natural redistribution of resources within the framework of regional policy will be considered by the populations of the donor regions as an attempt to live at their expense. This process of redistribution, however, is completely normal within civilized societies. However, even the current government appears to have recognized that reforms which ignore social problems could not be stable – leading to the hope that a regional policy may be created.

The last sentence was written in March 1992 – rewriting this text four years later, the author wanted to exclude it and thus avoid inaccuracy. Unfortunately, however, the government still has not understood that any reform has social limitations imposed by the population, and this understanding forms part a different, softer approach to the reform of the economy and society (what the newspapers now class *less shock, more therapeutic*). In July 1993, two Americans – a university professor and a company vice-president – asked the West not to push Russia the way of shock therapeutics (ie. rapid reform with little protection for the population), insisting that the failure of reform in Russia would be a disaster. In their opinion, the West should not finance this approach in Russia and should insist that Russians accept softer reforms (Hanke and Walters 1993). It appears that the authors of this article predicted the Zirinovski phenomenon and it would be good if his success could be a lesson to those adopting decisions within Russian society. The geographical analysis of the election results has shown a high level of territorial concentration of his electoral support in medium-sized cities dominated by heavy and/or military industry. These areas are, from every viewpoint, currently areas of crisis and would be the potential recipients of state assistance were a regional policy in operation. Perhaps this argument will validate the need for regional policy.

It is interesting that many of the former Socialist states placed great emphasis on the economic goals of a new regional policy. In the programme of reform proposed by the then Prime Minister Gaidar in 1992-93, the main purpose of regional policy was to provide assistance to the most advanced regions for the overall development of the national economy. Similarly in Bulgaria, given the understanding that regional disparities will increase in the process of transition to the market, some experts proposed that aid should be concentrated on the 'strongest' regions (Panusheff and Smatrakalev 1992). Comparable ideas have been put forward in Croatia – regional policy as a part of the macro-economic strategy of development (Frohlich and Malekovic 1994). The concept of the decentralization of power has also, for some unknown reason, also been considered popular as part of regional policy and has, for example, been proposed in Poland

(Regional development 1992). However, the earlier large-scale and more socially oriented regional policy of the 1960s and early 1970s in the West may be of more relevance to the post-socialist realities than the current approaches of western countries.

An example of a more balanced regional policy oriented, largely, towards the solution of social problems, is found in Hungary. Its main declared aim is to provide assistance for crisis regions, ranging from traditional ones to those 'damaged' during the transition to the market. Western experience has been exploited to the maximum in the formulation of the new regional policy in this country. It should be noted that, of all the former Socialist countries, Hungary has the most favourable conditions for such a transfer of experience (Horvath 1994).

Possibilities for the practical implementation of foreign experience

It is clear why western experience in the field of regional policy would currently be useful in Russia (as well as in other CIS countries). First, in the course of the operation of regional policy over 60 years, virtually every possible problem and type of territory has been encountered. The regional problems in Russia are not fundamentally new and unique, and western counterparts can easily be found for the majority of them (although clearly not all). Second, a range of 'success stories' can be included on the 'credit side' of western regional policy: the decentralization of the largest agglomerations; the development of new towns and other growth poles; the economic growth in a number of depressed areas. Even the failures of regional policy – such as the development of certain depressed and underdeveloped territories – are of great practical interest. The underlying reasons for the failure can be established, or an understanding can be gained of the impossibility of economic growth in certain types of territory even despite the provision of state assistance. Third, western regional policy succeeds in combining the interests of various territories, and, within the EU, both national and Community interests. Finally, the use of foreign experience (in any sphere) in Russia is currently perceived by the population as more positive than the search for an individual and unique Russian approach. This is also typical for other former Socialist countries (Kader-abkova 1991, Panusheff and Smatrakalev 1992). Conversely, it is also true that, linked to the growth in nationalism in times of crisis in Russia, opposition to the use of western experience is on the increase. The incorrect or inappropriate use of western experience exacerbates this opposition.

Having established the desirability of the practical implementation of western experience, it is necessary to address the question of the 'legitimacy' of its transfer to the Russian situation – even if only the process of adaptation is being talked about. Objections about the impossibility of financing such large-scale regional policy, under the current economic conditions in Russia, are often heard. Many economists consider that, under conditions of such deep economic crisis, the country only has the resources to cope with macro-economic problems. Given that this question has not been resolved even at a theoretical level, it would be pointless to begin a discussion here. It is possible, once again, to remember that regional policy was 'born' during the world economic crisis of 1929–1932, which, by all indicators (eg. fall of production) was quite comparable with our current one.

Regional policy was part of the state's answer to the crisis, a component in its strategy to overcome it. In the USA, regional policy was most significant during the New Deal (Miernyk 1982). Even although the stated aims were not totally achieved, the assistance of the state stabilized the situation in many crisis areas. The analogy with a period of world crisis allows one further conclusion. If regional policy were to emerge at present in the CIS/Russia, it would be comparable in scale not with the modern western regional policy (of the 1980s and 1990s), but rather with the policy area as it existed in the 1930s – although the experience of subsequent decades should also be taken into account.

It is possible to concur with the theory of a lack of sufficient state resources for the realization of large-scale regional policy in Russia. However, it is also true that the central authorities transfer significant grants to regions with little or no consideration of their relative socio-economic position. As a result, regions experiencing approximately the same degree of crisis receive state assistance which differs by a factor of ten or more (per head of the population – see Figure 4.1). It is well known that the share of the taxes given into the federal budget by republics/regions is very different and, again, there are no exact criteria determining the level of tax and its allocation to individual regions/republics. The following is almost a rhetorical question: could regional policy not be started initially on the basis of the laws and official decisions which determine the geography of existing grants, favourable loans and tax privileges? In turn, this geography should be determined by the socio-economic 'position' of each territory.

The state and its central management institutions are also basically obliged to produce a strategy for national regional development (at the very least for the period of transition), and to use their financial (and administrative) 'powers' for the realization of this strategy. The regions actually *more often choose the direction of development by themselves* (Treivish 1993) – although within the framework of the country with tens of regions, this is a direct route to chaos and meaningless competition. This leads to a further problem for regional policy: the co-ordination of the development strategies of the separate territorial units of the federation. Any delay in resolving this problem will only hamper the realization of regional policy. Malezieux, describing the revision of the Ile-de-France development plan, indicates that it was too late for the creation of a complex regional plan capable of combining the various interests of the state, region, departments and communes, as all the involved persons had already gone the route of individualist strategies which met their own mercenary interests (Malezieux 1991).

The expectation that the transition to the market will immediately bring all the aspects of the welfare state into Russia is absolutely utopian. The creation of the welfare state is a product of the long term evolution of a market society. Currently,

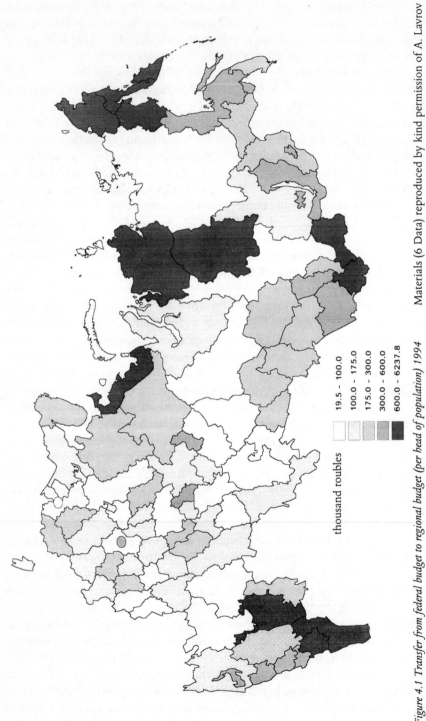

thousand roubles

19.5 - 100.0
100.0 - 175.0
175.0 - 300.0
300.0 - 600.0
600.0 - 6237.8

Figure 4.1 Transfer from federal budget to regional budget (per head of population) 1994

Materials (6 Data) reproduced by kind permission of A. Lavrov

the market is causing a heightening of regional disparities and this requires a response from the state.

Is our (*soviet*) socio-economic system unique and, depending on the response, does this open the door for exploitation of western experience? Within the framework of both systems, the same problem arises ie. the debate between *efficiency and equity*. The increase in the number of crisis regions often leads to a fall in the efficiency of economic location, but the maximizing of national economic efficiency strengthens the existing spatial social disparities. Equally within the framework of both systems, there are numerous social, ethnic and political 'limitations', and it is impossible to take purely economic factors into account.

An example of this can be given in the comparative analysis of Russia and Belgium. It is as impossible to imagine a mass migration of the native population from the Northern Caucasus region to other regions of Russia as from Wallonia to Flanders, even if the level of unemployment in the place of residence was very high and employment options in the new region were very favourable. In both cases, the creation of new working places in the crisis regions themselves is required. This example leads to a further observation: the development both of the Northern Caucasus region and of Wallonia on the basis purely of external resources – i.e. through branch plants and offices of large companies (including multi-nationals) and ministries – has not provided a sufficient number of new working places, has failed to ensure the stability of the economic situation, and has encouraged the emergence of new problems, including the rise of nationalism (although its form clearly differs between the two regions). Thus a conclusion can be drawn which is of relevance to both regions: the new strategy of development should be based more on local resources and the development of small business. The underestimation of socio-ethnic interests consequently threatens the unity of Russia and Belgium. The approaches and logic behind the solution of regional problems in western Europe can, therefore, be suitable for Russia (and other CIS countries), although clearly, the selected methods of tackling unemployment (as well as its cause) will vary and the small (local) businesses in the two regions will be from different industries and take different forms etc.

In the competition between territorial units, the 'weakest' will lose. A hierarchy of regions/areas, and the provision of assistance to those most requiring it, is only possible within the centralized policy of the state. In developed countries, the state has forced companies to take regional policy into account – and under Russian conditions there is no other *way out*. This does not imply a transfer of former powers to the centre, and indeed most of the rights in the economic sphere should, in general, move away from the state and its institutions – this is the main task of the process of privatization. Even when state-controlled companies still exist, it should still be possible to separate the economy from the state by allowing such companies to operate independently (valuable lessons can be learned from the functioning of similar state companies in the West). The state should only determine the rules and framework for the functioning of the economy, and these should be more or less uniform in all territorial units. Thus, within the framework of regional policy, the state stimulates or limits the development of certain territories. Where this occurs in developed countries, the experience is of relevance to the Russian situation.

Scientific and technological progress, and its spatial diffusion, are developed within a common model (although with an appreciable time lag in the USSR/Russia). As a result, similar regional problems emerge, starting with a split between the core and the periphery. Routine production and services are concentrated in the periphery leading to the under-utilization of resources and the discontent of the population. As a result, the pressure on central government to stimulate the development of peripheral regions increases.

Recently in the CIS/Russia (as earlier in the USSR) and in developed countries, national/ethnic problems, which also comprise regional problems, have become more acute. As already stated, their current rise in the West is frequently connected with the events in the USSR and Russia, where national borders which disappeared hundreds of years ago have been restored (see Chapter One). While these problems have not been fully resolved in developed countries, regional policy does include the protection of the interests of native populations, assistance for the assimilation of migrants, and the development of peripheral areas populated by ethnic minorities or inner city areas of large cities where there is a concentration of non-white immigrants. To western experts the disintegration of Russia/CIS does not represent the optimum way out of the current situation. The majority of problems could be (or, unfortunately, it may already be necessary to say *could have been*) resolved through other methods, such as federalism (Dostal 1989).

All ex-Socialist countries have now been faced with the worsening of ethnic (regional, linguistic) problems, 'concentrated' in certain territories (Szul 1993). Although the same situation can be observed in the countries of Western Europe, they partially address these problems through regional policy (among other areas). On the other hand, one can see the break-up of the USSR, Yugoslavia and Czechoslovakia, and the disintegration of Russia and Ukraine etc. Thus, while similar uniform trends can be observed throughout Europe, the reaction of countries varies, and the end results are correspondingly also different.

It is possible to identify many regional analogies which have a similar economic history and industrial structure etc. Both the West and East have old-industrial, depressed and underdeveloped regions (as well as agro-industrial regions, and regions with extreme natural conditions), and there is a requirement in both areas to regulate the development of the largest agglomerations. The simultaneous development of the Urals and the Donbas has begun – in the same direction as many British and French old-industrial regions. It is now necessary in both these regions to undertake structural reorganization, such as that which was carried out in their western counterparts in the 1950s and 1970s. In both CIS/Russia and in the West, such regions are characterized by a poor environmental condition, obsolete infrastructure, a lack of investment and qualified labour force etc.

It is also possible to identify many similarities between the problems of west European Mediterranean regions and those of the republics of Middle Asia and Caucasus. These include an 'excessive' dependence on agriculture (largely 'single-crop'), the low educational and professional level of the population, agrarian overpopulation and environmental problems... In the CIS, as well as in western Europe, one can see the most powerful mafia (and a higher level of corruption) and ethnic and nationalities movements take the most extreme form.

The northern regions of Russia and Scandinavia (and equally of the USA and Canada) are, primarily, the sources of the natural resource base. Their development represents a considerable danger to the environment. The basic problem is one of combining development interests with those of the native inhabitants. In the West, the latter are, naturally, in more favourable conditions achieved through the spatial 'separation' of development centres and traditional areas of the native population. Once again, western experience can be useful.

The common regional policy of the EU has become a large-scale phenomenon, and within its framework, a compromise between national and EU interests has been attempted. In an ideal situation, such an approach could help solve the problems of the CIS – if the efforts of the individual republics could be coordinated and the highest possible rates of state assistance and uniform regional funds could be created, the development of border territories could be stimulated etc. In the current situation, these abstract concepts seem unreal. However, either further disintegration will result in the complete break-up of the CIS, or common interests will lead to a period of re-integration.

There is one difficult problem relating to the implementation of western experience. On the one hand, our disadvantaged position in terms of economic and political conditions must be taken into account – if one were to calculate this in Kondratievs cycles, Russia/CIS would be at least one cycle behind. On the other hand, however, this is not correct: Kondratiev (1989) considered his cycles to be global i.e. one set of countries cannot be in the third cycle while others are in the fourth. Using western experience of regional policy in the CIS/Russia, therefore, would require a combination of measures from the 1930s and the 1990s.

In the conclusion to this chapter, the author wants to focus on other factors which hamper the creation of a regional policy, as well as the implementation of western experience in this area. The options open to the state (in the CIS or in any of the republics) – both financial and socio-economic – are small, and the regional disparities and problems (including ethno-religious ones) are considerably sharper. The socio-economic system in the CIS/Russia (if indeed it is possible to speak of it as a single one) is unstable. Real movement towards the market is only really beginning and it is not clear which *approach* will be chosen (see above). Regional policy can exist only within the boundaries of common socio-economic space, i.e. where there are no significant barriers to the movement of people, goods and capital. It is, therefore, only possible within the limits of a state or integrated group of territories.

It has already been stated that regional policy – in the western understanding – is a tool for the transfer of resources from rich to poor regions. All the difficulties of achieving this idea in practice are clear. However, it is necessary to instill into the consciousness of the population all the advantages of true integration: access to an extensive market and the chance to exploit economies of scale; lower prices (although achieved through the absence of customs duties); greater convenience etc. If this is understood, then neither the cost of integration will appear excessive, nor will regional policy seem unnecessary. Territorial justice should, in Russia/CIS, become the basis of regional policy (Smirniagin 1992) and the general 'backwardness' of society will be the main barrier to domestic regional policy and to the use of foreign experience in this field.

Practical recommendations

It is clear that, in the near future, the creation of a large scale regional policy is impossible. However, it is possible to take the first steps towards this: the scientific and institutional base for regional policy can be created; and, individual measures and plans can be introduced step-by-step. The analysis of western countries experience provides the following recommendations:

1. The creation of a scientific base for regional policy is necessary (although this is impossible
    without adequate regional statistics). The first step should be the
    designation of problem regions in Russia/CIS, based on existing
    administrative-territorial divisions. Any attempt to change this existing
    base, under current conditions, can only lead to the emergence of new
    centres of instability. Independent scientific assessment of decisions taken
    in the field of regional policy and spatial monitoring in Russia/CIS is also
    necessary. The results of scientific research should always be available to
    the people making key decisions, as well as to the population (including
    the populations of problem regions).

2. It is necessary to rank all problem regions by the degree of crisis and the
    probable level of state assistance. It should be remembered that
    ethno-religious and political factors can be considerably more important –
    in the determination of priorities – than socio-economic ones.

3. Regional policy can operate at various levels – the CIS, individual countries,
    regions. However, the maximum level of aid should be limited (for each
    type of problem territory), otherwise competition will occur between
    individual territorial units and maximum award values will be become
    available in wealthier areas.

4. A common management institution ('Ministry') with territorial departments is
    necessary for regional policy. Other Ministries, however, are also likely to
    participate in the implementation of regional policy.

5. The adopted decisions should remain in place for at least three to five years, even in the event of changes in government or leaders. At the same time, a rapid response to changing or worsening regional problems is also necessary.

6. Regional policy measures in the form of incentives ie. grants, favourable loans etc. are more effective. Restrictive measures, even where they are less open to corruption, do not appear to be effective.

7. Particular emphasis should be placed on the provision of assistance to small and medium-sized enterprises. First, SMEs are currently more dynamic, and exploit local resources more widely. Second, the development of this sector will encourage the demonopolization of the economy.

8. The stable development of crisis regions is impossible without the promotion, through state assistance, of infrastructure in these territories. Without a good infrastructure base, the attraction of foreign investment is virtually impossible.

9. The easiest problem is the transfer of concrete measures of western regional policy.

10. Regional policy should focus on the solution of socio-political problems. Ideally, it would highlight the care of the state for the whole population, and could thus be considered a factor of political/social stabilization. Only once such stability has been achieved, will it be possible to discuss the potential for a more economically-oriented regional policy.

11. Within the framework of regional policy, the spatial consequences of all state decisions should be monitored and officially assessed. This will help to compensate for (or forewarn) their negative spatial consequences.

12. The development of domestic regional policy has *to involve* domestic and western experts – and both scientists and officials should be engaged in its implementation.

Conclusion

In concluding this work, the very basic question of the efficiency of regional policy must be the focus. At present, both in scientific literature and in the policy arena, there is a *polarization* in the evaluation of the role of the state (and regional policy). Former Socialist countries more often support the notion of the unlimited opportunities of the free market. Conversely, in the West, the rise of the dirigist approach, planning and the state regulation of socio-economic life is once again evident (Artobolevskiy, 1990). It appears that *controlled Darwinism* (a term of Professor Kuklinski) ie. the controlled competition between regions, is most appropriate for the Russian case. The importance of social factors needs to result in greater attention being paid to regional problems (as well as national-political issues).

At this point, a further aspect of regional policy criticism should be mentioned. Hindsight is a very useful tool and all the miscalculations of the past are very clear. However, the question remains as to whether the regional policy measures of the 1950s and 1960s could *lead to differing outcomes*. It is understood that the development of problem regions through the branch plants of large companies does not lead to economic stability, or an increased qualification of the labour force. Were there opportunities, however, for the conversion of all of these problem regions into 'Silicon valleys', and the state, through obstinacy and/or stupidity, prevented this from happening? Regional policy is rooted in reality (*policy is the art of the possible*) and these *branch plants* have, in many respects, helped problem regions. Equally, the support of old sectors was also not so stupid – it slowed the recession within them and has created time for industrial reorganization (Hassink 1992). Closing an enterprise is always quicker than constructing a new one.

The above argument is not an appeal for the preservation of traditional regional policy. The *old* regional policy was good for the Fordist stage of development (Danielzyk 1992), but the current post-Fordist stage requires a different type of regional policy – and this is what underlies the transformation of this policy area (see Chapter One). It is necessary, however, to assess the efficiency of any regional policy in the context of the situation in which it was implemented.

The efficiency of regional policy

It should be remembered that regional policy is, ultimately, still an area of public policy and, thus, its efficiency determines its necessity. During the entire history of its existence, regional policy has been subjected to criticism from the Left (for its insufficient scale) and from the Right (as a waste of taxpayers' money). And in scientific research, the question of the efficiency of regional policy has always been the main priority (Diamond and Spence 1983, Turok 1990).

The efficiency of regional policy is usually assessed on the basis of the dynamics of change of socio-economic indicators in areas which have received state support – above all, through the level of unemployment, GDP per head, and the balance of migration. The options for applying such an approach are, however, rather limited (particularly during crises – see below). The shifts in all these specified indicators, even within problem regions, depend ultimately on macro-economic factors (and not just on regional policy). Thus, in the crisis years of the 1970s and 1980s, the universal growth of unemployment in the West resulted, in a number of countries, in the levelling of regional disparities. The high level of unemployment everywhere led to less outmigration of population from problem regions – but this did not testify to the success of regional policy. The level of GDP per head in a region is determined, largely, by the industrial structure of its economy. Under these conditions, quite a 'dynamic' growth of the service sector can result in a relative decrease of per capita GDP, for example through the lower labour costs in service sectors (compared with industry).

Another approach to the evaluation of regional policy efficiency is the comparative assessment of certain indicators between periods when there was significant regional policy activity and periods when there was not. Under this approach, the data which are generally compared include the migration of industry and services (including the movement of official institutions). Certainly, rates of migration of economic activities were higher during periods of active regional policy implementation – it is not, however, clear to what extent this was prompted purely by regional policy. In western countries, the intensity of the migration of the economy was, in many respects, determined by the ongoing process of suburbanization, initiated in the 1950s. However, even considering only migrations to problem regions, their high levels in the 1950s and 1960s is a consequence of the significant rates of economic growth during this period. Already by the end of the 1970s, under conditions of zero growth, the previous regional policy approach of encouraging economic migrations appeared considerably less effective. In addition, routine enterprises and offices were largely superseded in problem regions by modern industries and professional services.

In using either of the above mentioned approaches to regional policy evaluation, the general conclusion would be reached that the efficiency of regional policy fell from the mid-1970s, and that this policy area was more effective in the 1950s and 1960s. Whether these conclusions are reasonable will be analysed below.

The efficiency of regional policy is frequently judged by the extent to which it is taken into account by companies in their location decisions (either for the creation of new capacities or the transfer of existing ones). The limited efficiency

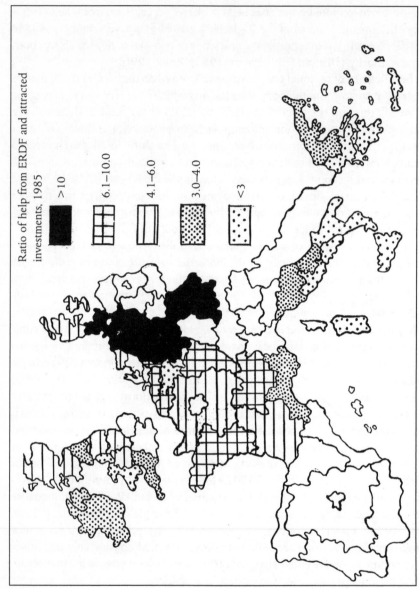

Figure 5.1 Efficiency of regional policy (Source: Regions 1987)

of restrictive measures can be noted, which have decreased as the internationalization of the world economy has risen. The decisions of companies to create new capacities outside the largest agglomeration/regions, or to transfer them from existing locations, are determined, as a rule, not by state restrictions, but rather by the conditions in the new areas, other labour requirements, the desire to make savings on land rent and transport costs etc.

The choice of the new location depends on the likelihood of receiving state assistance. This is shown in survey results of companies (see, for example, Ashchoft and Ingham 1979). However, the surveys also showed that it was those companies which had already decided to site economic activities in problem regions which placed a high value on the availability of state aid. They clearly will take the offer of state assistance into account, and evaluate it highly, although it less clear to what extent purely the assistance provided within the framework of regional policy influences the locational decisions of all companies.

The efficiency of regional policy is evaluated using the quantitative ratio of costs and effects. Thus, the total sum of costs are compared with the number of new/secured jobs. In recent years, the efficiency of regional policy has increasingly been assessed on the basis of the ratio of state investment and the private investment attracted by it. It is proposed that, the higher the rate of private investment attracted by each pound/ecu/dollar etc. of state investment, the higher the efficiency of the policy area – although this approach is not always correct. It allows the comparison of policy efficiency only between the same type of region. In general, the share of state assistance should be greatest in the regions with the worst crisis conditions, and a low grant component in the total volume of investment in relatively wealthy areas is not evidence of the high efficiency of regional policy (see Figure 5.1). Even the conclusions of comparisons within the same type of region, using this approach, should be treated with caution.

It is clear from the above, that strict objective methods for the evaluation of regional policy efficiency do not exist (Armstrong and Taylor 1985, Turok 1990). Frequently, the impossibility of any form of quantitative evaluation of regional policy efficiency is linked to the lack of necessary statistics (Nijkamp and Blass 1992, Armstrong and Taylor 1985). Various models do exist which propose a possible quantitative evaluation of efficiency (Folmer 1986, Nijkamp and Blass 1992). These models use 'existing' statistics, as well as 'ideal-case' statistics ie. those which do not exist in collected or published form. However, in many of these models, a complex and important question remains unresolved: how the effects of regional policy can be separated from other factors. Without this, any evaluation of the real efficiency of regional policy is impossible. Expert or analogous models could be used more productively (ie. the comparison of areas with similar socio-economic features, one of which has received state regional assistance, and one of which has not, or to a lesser degree – Nijkamp and Blaas 1992).

At present, it is rather fashionable to criticize regional policy (even in scientific literature) and to consider its efficiency as low. This argument is based on the fact that currently, more than 50 years after the emergence of this area of state activity, regional disparities in almost all advanced countries have not fallen, and, in some cases, have even increased. This is true both in terms of the level of economic development and the quality of life. Certainly, successes of regional policy are generally recognized – the new towns programme in Great Britain, the creation of new scientific centres in France, the development of Limburg in the Netherlands – but these are only isolated examples. In Italy, for example, the country with the highest levels of regional policy provision, the gap between the North and the South has not been reduced.

All these negative assessments of regional policy are quite fair, but what is not taken into account is that, in the absence of regional policy, the spatial disparities would have been even sharper. In discussing crisis in certain areas, data concerning the job losses (for the specified period) are often cited. This indicator, in reality, is a combination of a certain number of new jobs and a considerably greater number of 'lost' ones – and new jobs created in problem areas are frequently connected purely with regional policy. It is possible, therefore, to assert that in the absence of regional policy (or if its scale was much reduced), the situation in many problem areas would be much worse than is currently the case.

In itself, the existence of spatial socio-economic disparities is not evidence of the low efficiency of regional policy. These disparities are a consequence of many factors and the extent of the influence of regional policy alone (not the most important factor) is impossible to estimate and any econometric approach will be largely incorrect (see above).

The obvious defects of all the above mentioned evaluation methods of regional policy efficiency are linked to an incorrect initial approach to the problem. It has already been stated that socio-political goals are of primary importance in regional policy. On this basis, it is necessary to evaluate the political and social efficiency of regional policy, which, in general, cannot be assessed in quantitative terms. The only possible method of evaluation is to use a qualitative approach, and this can only be undertaken by experts. How can the contribution of regional policy to the unity of a country, the achievement of social stability, the adaptation of migrants, the reduction of criminality etc. be evaluated? It should be remembered that, in the majority of western countries, it would simply be impossible to curtail current regional policy without risking the creation of political problems. Perhaps this situation in itself is the best proof of the efficiency of regional policy. Even all the recent reforms of this policy area – except under Thatcher – have been focused on a shift in the targets and methods of regional policy, but have never placed the necessity for it in doubt.

In Chapter 1, it was stated that the *natural* shifts in the territorial structure of the population and economy can be only accelerated or slowed by the state, including through its regional policy. It should be possible, therefore, to assess the efficiency of regional policy by the extent to which it has affected these natural trends, although this would be difficult to achieve with the existing range of data (it is indirectly possible using surveys of the companies). It is also reasonable to talk about the propagandist efficiency of regional policy. This policy area can be realized for purely political aims – an attempt of the state to show its care for the population and for minorities in particular.

It is necessary to separate the question of the efficiency of regional policy *per se* from the efficiency of its individual measures – grants, loans etc. In the latter case, an evaluation of the ratio of costs and particular effects (eg. new jobs) is reasonable, but, again, has to be adjusted with the macro purposes of regional policy. However, a key conclusion is that a calculation of the ratio of costs and effects should not become the main criterion for decision-making on the future of regional policy.

The strategic economic goals of regional policy have already been discussed. In regions with extreme natural conditions, for example, regional policy fosters the development of resources. The exploitation of indigenous resources may be more expensive than comparative imports, but will reduce the import dependency of the region concerned. This, as already stated, is particularly important for developing countries. In certain cases, the strategic efficiency of regional policy should be discussed, understanding its potential current lack of profitability for the treasury.

In recent years, as already stated, the 'economization' of regional policy has occurred. When regional policy is used to tackle issues such as the increasing of economic competitiveness (as at present in the Netherlands), it should be evaluated on the basis of its economic efficiency, i.e. the ratio of costs and achieved results (increase of GDP, growth of exports, improvement of the foreign trade balance etc.).

In summary, the complex question of the efficiency of regional policy (ie. including its economic, social, political, ecological aspects) is not one that can even be posed. In the majority of cases, its social/political efficiency can be discussed and assessed at a qualitative level. Certainly attempts made in scientific works are interesting, but often do not give the real picture. The important role of regional policy both as a factor of location, and in the stabilization of social and political life, means that it can, without doubt, be evaluated highly. It is an integral part of a civilized state. Changes of approach and methods in the formulation and implementation of regional policy are not evidence of its decline, but rather represent a normal adaptation to new conditions of operation.

Regional policy in western and eastern Europe: two approaches

The main intention of this part of the book is to identify common features and differences in the regional policy approach of western and eastern European countries. The differences between the two 'blocks' in the framework of regional policy are obvious. However, can we use common terms in our research? Are there any options for further convergence? Only after answering such questions can one consider the possibility of using western experience of regional policy in eastern Europe.

In the field of regional development and policy, the countries of both groups have some common features, and significant spatial disparities in economic development, the quality of life, and the density of infrastructure provision are evident in all of them. In the West, this can be regarded only as a potential threat to the countries' unity – although it is one of the main obstacles to EU integration (The Regions 1991). Spatial disparities in eastern European countries, however, played an important role in the break-up of the Federal People's Republic of Yugoslavia, the Republic of Czechoslovakia and the USSR, as well as, to a lesser extent, in the disintegration process in Russia or Ukraine.

Both systems have the same type of problem areas: old industrial, underdeveloped, agglomerations. In some cases, the evidence of their crisis is similar eg. derelict land in old industrial areas, lack of adequate infrastructure in underdeveloped regions etc, while in others it differs. At the present time, for example, the rate of unemployment is a good indicator for western development areas but not for eastern ones. However, the regional problems of both the West and the East could not be solved without state assistance as both systems require regional policy.

These common features can be explained by several factors. First of all, a common economic history from the Industrial Revolution until 1917 (and until 1945 for the majority of East European countries) was shared. Even after these dates, there were some common processes of economic development. The restructuring of industry and employment, and the changing of factors of location were very similar (although they did not take place at the same time – see later). Scientific progress followed similar lines, and affected the location of the economy and population.

Another very important common feature is the high level of monopolization. Monopoly companies in the West and Ministries in the East were, and are, synonymous, although, at 100 per cent, the level of monopoly was higher in eastern countries. The decision-making of monopolies in both systems created similar spatial problems – while monopolies tackled efficiency problems, they created others difficulties in terms of equity.

Even on the assumption that the East and the West would have followed the same development trajectory, it is clear that they have now come to different stages. The leadership of the West is well-defined and has been greatly improved since the late 1950s. This can be illustrated by some examples taken from the regional development sphere. The crisis in old industrial areas emerged in the West in the late 1930s – 1950s, while in the East it occurred between the 1970s – 1980s (and indeed the move towards a post-industrial society is only now beginning). The process of suburbanization took place in the West immediately after World War II and the problems of the inner city areas emerged in the 1970s – in the East, the growth of large cities has just finished, and in the next two or three years, the importance of the inner city areas question will become apparent. If capitalism is to be our bright future, we should be able to predict some of our likely future regional problems and thus be ready to tackle them. All eastern European countries require a regional policy approach which is appropriate for new market societies. Until now, regional policy, as it is understood by the West, has been practically non-existent in all the eastern European countries (Artobolevskiy and Treivish 1992).

In theory, planning was indirect in the West and direct in the East. Speculatively, the direct approach had more opportunities to influence the economy and society, although in reality western planning was more effective in achieving set goals. The regional policy approach of the East shows that the state was trying to fulfill economic and social functions simultaneously: the state was the principal, and virtually only, provider and organizer of society life, and thus faced the dilemma of *equity or efficiency* – and chose the latter. Regional problems were regarded as secondary, and only when they hindered the process of economic development did the state pay any attention to them. The Western state should be the guarantor for social and political stability, but this cannot be achieved where severe regional disparities exist. The state is responsible for the entire territory and all of the population and, even in the face of difficult areas such as North Ireland or South Italy, the State tries to fulfill its obligations.

It was mentioned above that monopolies can create regional problems. The Western states were more capable of correcting these through the system of tax-redistribution and the provision of aid to areas which have suffered from the monopolies' activities. In the East, the state was a conglomeration of monopolies, i.e. ministries, whose primary motivation was to operate in their own areas and raise associated production levels. No margin was left for general regional problems and every ministry carried out its own regional policy, providing limited support to areas of their own activity. Within the framework of this policy approach, individual areas or urban communities were considered of secondary importance to factories, enterprises or mines.

It is interesting that regional policy emerged during the 1920s in both systems. Having much in common, it was regarded by both as institutionally independent and with the aim of providing assistance to problem areas. The late 1920s and early 1930s marked a turning point in both systems (proving once again that a single universal process of development, or the interdependency of development processes, can be seen). The welfare state was the outcome of economic crisis in the West, including regional policy. Russia stopped all market-experiments and established a system of state-monopolistic Socialism, as well as political dictatorship. From this point onwards, every ministry, rather than the state, carried out its own regional policy (Artobolevskiy and Treivish 1992). During the 1930s, the policy of industrialization and collectivization impoverished the central agricultural areas of the country, which had formerly been the most prosperous ones. A new and unique type of problem area was artificially created – the depressed old agricultural region.

Before World War II, regional policy, as an independent activity of the state, emerged only in the most developed countries of Europe. The countries of central Europe (later the *Socialist countries of Europe*) did not reach the necessary level of development, including in the area of regional policy, before the war and, after 1945, they still had to follow the Socialist path. Even with the introduction in some of these countries of a centralized regional policy, it proved neither adequate for the scale of the regional problems, nor suitable within the centrally planned economy.

Different methods of development did lead to different results. By the end of the 1970s and the start of the 1980s, regional policy in west European countries was a predominantly social activity, although utilizing economic methods. In the countries of eastern Europe, conversely, the principal aims of regional policy were economic.

Regional policy methods also differ greatly between the two blocks. In the West, measures principally involve the provision of positive incentives. Practice showed the limited efficiency of restrictive measures such as the Industrial Development Certificates or Office Permits which existed in the 1960s and 1970s in Great Britain. These kinds of regional policy tool had virtually disappeared in all western countries by the beginning of the 1980s.

In the East, all regional goals were integrated into the official plans concerning the location of the economy, population and development. In reality, the regional component of all state plans were the sum of the spatial proposals of the various ministries, and regional socio-economic development and the reduction of spatial disparities were not considered as independent goals. If the plans had to be adjusted due to insufficient resources, the regional components were the first to be excluded.

In spite of all these real differences, a scientific base for regional policy has been largely developed both in the East and the West, although, in general, western studies are more practically oriented. Poland and Hungary, for example, were ready to establish a regional policy some years ago (Gorzelak and Jalowiecki 1992, Hajdu and Horvath 1994). The level of spatial research and monitoring was very high in the USSR, being consistently encouraged by various scientific centres. Many of the plans developed for individual territories, specific regions, cities and towns in the USSR are scientific documents of a very high quality and comprise a valuable source of information.

In discussing a division of the regional policy approach in Europe between East and West, this does not imply that, within each division, all the countries are equal in terms of the territorial and financial scale, methods, institutional structures or other elements of regional policy. In general, the intensity of regional policy provision in western Europe increases from the centre to the periphery. The most active regional policy can be found in Italy, Spain, Portugal, Greece, and Ireland.

The largest underdeveloped area in western Europe is the Scandinavian North. The same pattern of regional policy provision can be seen in individual countries, although there are some exceptions to the centre-periphery model. The factors determining the intensity of regional policy are numerous – among the most important are regional socio-economic disparities, the actuality of national and/or religious difficulties, the organization of the state (unitarian or federal), the financial potential of the state, and the ideology of the ruling party (Hansen *et al.* 1990).

The leading countries in the field of regional policy in the East were Hungary and Yugoslavia, where, in both cases, it was operated as an institutionally independent state activity. The approach of Hungary to the *decentralization* of Budapest or to the fostering of development in certain problem areas had much in common with western methods. The limited efficiency of regional policy in Hungary can, among other factors, be explained by its lack of correlation to the general socio-economic system in the country.

A relatively intensive regional policy was carried out in Yugoslavia, based on the correct notion that it was a method of maintaining the unity of the country. However, ultimately, a combination of national, historical and political factors proved stronger. While a regional policy based on a redistribution of wealth from richer to poorer regions is absolutely natural – in the same way that adults help children within families –, Slovenia complained that it contributed too much while Serbia thought it received too little. All the republics showed more interest in their own regional problems than in those of the country as a whole. The scale of the regional policy was insufficient to combat spatial problems – although even the existing spatial redistribution was determined principally by political factors (Plestina 1992).

In both systems, reforms took place during the 1980s which included major changes in regional policy. In the West, this policy area was considered a 'disappearing phenomenon', while in the East, the term *regional policy* became increasingly popular and, although not actually put into practice, was used by many politicians. From the author's point of view, the developments in the West during the 1980s can be regarded as natural improvements to regional policy, making it more suitable for the new post-industrial system characterised by fragmented space.

In the East, the old regional policy of the ministries disappeared together with them. In Russia, a disintegration process is currently evolving – similar to the previous events in the USSR. The political struggle in Moscow, and pressure from the regions, is leading to the 'emancipation' of parts of the country – often with an insufficient economic base. For unknown reasons, politicians, and unfortunately also some scientists, are labelling this *regional policy*. In reality, such developments represent considerable obstacles to the achievement of a genuine regional policy, based exclusively on the principle of *unequal rights* for regions. However, the current situation does not permit such an approach to emerge, and Russia is not the only country facing such a conflict. Other examples of devolution can be found in Poland and Croatia. Devolution is suitable principally within societies where consensus has been, or can be, reached, and otherwise it can lead to disintegration, as illustrated by the Yugoslavian experience (Plestina 1992). The paradox is that, as Russia moves towards a market economy, it requires a regional policy to prevent the increase of regional disparities. The correlation between the market and regional problems is clear for many western scientists, although the transition period, characterised by severe crisis and political instability, has little room left for regional policy.

Regional policy can be considered a by-product of civilization and the development of society and the state. It emerged when the state understood its total responsibility for the whole country and the entire population, including the crisis regions. Regional policy laws on the distribution of state assistance are precise, and preclude, to some extent, corruption and political considerations. And, given that regional assistance implies the redistribution of wealth from richer to poorer regions, it also requires the support of the population, which has to understand the necessity for such a redistribution. The people of the contributor regions have to understand that they are forwarding the unity of the country, the market, and political stability. This situation was evident in the West when regional policy emerged between the 1930s – 1950s in individual countries, and could also be seen within the EC in the 1970s when a common regional policy was created. The level of civilization of the population was sufficient to provide support for cross-border redistribution.

What is the future of regional policy? It will definitely not disappear in western countries. The example of the Thatcher administration in Great Britain shows that, in spite of all attempts to reduce regional policy, the government was ultimately forced merely to reorganize it. The problem area map was adjusted, old industrial regions were replaced by inner city areas, and some direct automatic measures were substituted by indirect and selective ones. As the notion of the welfare state is starting to restore the popularity of regional policy, a future renaissance or revival of this policy area can be anticipated – naturally in a form appropriate to the new economic, social and geographical reality (Albrechts *et al.* 1989, Fothergill and Guy 1990). The experience of the 1980s showed that a long-term strategy has many advantages over frequently changing approaches. In theory, the exploitation of indigenous resources is a good thing, although clearly the region must first possess an adequate resource base (Garofoli 1992).

Regional policy has better prospects in the most developed of the eastern European countries. In this context, Hungary appears to be the leader, where regional policy comprises a part of the new market oriented system. In Slovenia, the first practical steps can also be seen and, in Poland, regional policy will be implemented in the near future. It has been stated that regional policy can develop only in countries where positive results have been achieved in the transition to a market economy. In Russia and Ukraine, the perspectives are still undefined; both countries face similar obstacles which have already been outlined. Regional policy is certainly imperative to avoid both the further disintegration of the country and new problems at regional/national level, and now is the time to begin the creation of such a policy. Even under severe financial constraints, initial steps towards the legislation of laws and regulations for existing aid distribution and the designation of problem regions could be taken.

A more dirigist approach to market reforms seems generally more reasonable ie. the consideration of a larger role of state regulation. At the same time, the state has to clarify its role and responsibilities. The recognition by the state of its responsibility for the country's unity and society would be the first step towards practical regional policy, and once this was achieved, western experience would be valuable.

In spite of the differences in state approaches to regional problems, the overall natural process of development leads to universally similar spatial consequences. Regional problems in western countries are more 'advanced', and this means that their present regional problems will be our own future ones, as its old ones are our current ones. This must be borne in mind in the utilization of western experience. Recent years have been transitional ones for regional policy in both the West and the East. This illustrates, once more, the requirement for each period of development to have a unique regional policy approach. It would be more beneficial for regional policy to be altered appropriately in advance, but political and economic considerations usually prevent this.

Main conclusions

The majority of the previous chapters and sections have ended with a number of principal conclusions. This final section aims to present, in the author's opinion, the main 'results' of the book. The purpose and tasks of the book were set out in the Introduction and it is hoped that these conclusions correlate broadly with them.

1. It is impossible to maintain genuine national unity, and to undertake a process of integration, if deep regional socio-economic disparities exist. The reduction of such disparities is impossible without large-scale regional policy.

2. Regional policy should encompass all territories of the country, and it emerges as soon as individual regions/areas receive *unequal rights*. The devolution of power (including economic power) does not help to achieve the goals of regional policy, and can often hinder their realization. As a result, the winners are the most prosperous regions/areas.

3. Regional policy can operate at various territorial levels – *international*, national etc. Its co-ordination, as well as the imposition of maximum award rates and levels of assistance, are necessary – otherwise competition occurs

between territories for investment and, as a consequence, an unavoidable over-expenditure of public funds occurs.

4. Regional policy, in the majority of cases, forms part of a state's social activity – thus it promotes equity at the expense of efficiency. However, in the achievement of social purposes, regional policy principally encourages economic development.

5. Regional policy also represents the provision of care by the state for its minorities. This indicates both a high level of societal development, and a degree of common sense among politicians.

6. Regional policy evolves on the basis of the transformation of the economy and society. Each stage of development requires a regional policy approach which is suitable for it. The transformation of regional policy corresponds closely to the shift of Kondratiev cycles and waves (within the framework of each cycle).

7. Each new stage of development leads to shifts in factors of location (for economy/population). This, in turn, results in the emergence of new problem territories. The 'overlapping' of problem areas, which emerged at various stages of development, increases the fragmentation of space. All these trends increase the need for regional policy.

8. The increasing real fragmentation of space requires the transition within regional policy to increasingly limited territorial units (by area). While in the 1950s and 1960s, regional policy operated, as a rule, within entire regions, it is currently confined sometimes even to individual parts of a city. Thus the reform of regional policy is a reflection of real spatial shifts.

9. The fragmentation of socio-economic space leads to the greater territorial selectivity of regional policy. Greater selectivity is also the result of more limited state resources.

10. The regionalization/geographization of regional policy is necessary. 'Typical' measures for the development of all types of problem regions should be supplemented *by an individual approach* to each area. Taking into account the particular geographical features of each area can considerably increase the efficiency of state activity.

11. The 'geographization' of regional policy can be achieved through the grading of problem territories, the decentralization of certain regional policy activities (eg. provision of small grants and the realization of smaller projects), and a greater consideration of ethnic and religious problems. This is possible even within the framework of existing institutional structures for regional policy, and its current range of measures.

12. In the post-war years, growth without development was characteristic for many problem regions. Routine functions were concentrated in them and they were transformed increasingly into internal colonies. This was promoted by the attraction of external resources to these territories. However, the economic structure created in these regions is relatively effective from an economic point of view.

13. In developed countries, despite all the efforts of the state, sharp regional disparities still exist. Accordingly, the niche for regional policy is maintained.

14. In western Europe, the level of provision of regional policy assistance increases from the centre to the periphery (i.e. from the centre to the south, north, west and east). A similar core-periphery model of increasing regional policy support can also be seen in individual west European countries.

15. Within the framework of regional policy, the development both of territories and of the local population, can be stimulated. Economic goals are achieved in the former case, and social goals in the latter.

16. Regional policy appears to be most effective when it corresponds to the natural trends in the changing location of economic activities and population. Regional policy can slow or accelerate these trends, but cannot halt them.

17. Regional policy, and particularly the successful realization of individual programmes, creates a new image for problem regions, and this is very important in the West.

18. Regional policy will always be a public policy area and, in its realization, takes into account not only social and economic, but also ethnic and electoral factors.

19. Regional policy measures which provide incentives are considerably more effective than those which impose restrictions. The latter, at present, cannot by implemented under conditions of economic recession and the internationalization of economy.

20. The range of possible regional policy measures is rather limited, and a key to success is their correct combination and an optimum grading system. This is the art of regional policy.

21. The basis for the efficiency of regional policy is its conformity – at each stage of development – to the shifts in the territorial structure of the economy and population, the changing factors of location, and macro-economic and social developments.

22. The changes in regional policy in developed countries in the 1980s and 1990s do not indicate its decline, but rather a shift in its measures and industrial and territorial targets in accordance with changing socio-economic conditions. Statements about the 'economization' of regional policy do not correspond with reality, as this policy area basically remains part of the social activity of a state.

23. In more than 50 years of operation, regional policy has become an integral part of socio-economic life. The crises in regional policy were linked to a delayed reaction to macro-economic, political and spatial shifts.

24. Fluctuations in the coverage and location of problem regions will be determined by economic processes, political rationale etc. However, it is possible to predict with certainty that their location will become increasingly dispersed, due to the process of growing spatial fragmentation. There will be areas of crises in currently prosperous regions and vice-versa. Thus, small areas with different socio-economic conditions, will often be neighbours.

25. In Russia/CIS, large-scale regional policy is certainly necessary to promote stabilization. However, the lack of resources in the state budget, and the opposition of part of the population and regional authorities (principally in donor regions) to any redistribution of wealth or assistance, comprise the most serious obstacles to the achievement of regional policy in these countries.

References

Agranat, G.A. (1988) *Development of the North: Global Experience.* Moscow: VINITI. (In Russian.)

Agranat, G.A. (1988) 'A territory: increase of role in life of society.' *Izvestia AN SSSR, Geographical Series 2,* 5–16. (In Russian.)

Agranat, G.A. (1984) *Use of Resources and Development of the Foreign North Territory.* Moscow: Nauka. (In Russian.)

Alaev, A.B. (1973) *Regional Planning in Developing Countries.* Moscow: Nauka. (In Russian.)

Alaev, A.B. (1982) *Socio-economic Geography: Concept-terminological Dictionary.* Moscow: Misl. (In Russian.)

Albrechts, L., Moulaert, H., Roberts,P. and Swyngedouw, E. (eds) (1989) *Regional Policy at the Crossroads.* London: Jessica Kingsley Publishers.

Albrechts, L. and Vinikas, B. (eds) (1986) *Managing the Metropolis.* Leuven; Amersfoort: ACCO.

Aldcroft, D.H. (1984) *Full Employment: The Elusive Goal.* Brighton: Wheatsheaf books.

Allen, K., Bachtler J. and Yill D. (1994) 'Regional Policy-making in Western Europe.' In Z. Hajdu and G. Horvath (eds) *European Challenges and Hungarian Responses in Regional Policy.* Pecs: Centre for Regional Studies.

Alymov, A.N. (1981) *Productive Forces: Problems of Development and Location.* Moscow: Economica. (In Russian.)

Amersfoort, H. van and Knippenberg (eds) (1991) *States and Nations: The rebirth of the 'nationalities question' in Europe.* Amsterdam: RNGS.

Annual Abstract of Greater London Statistics, 1985–86. (1987). London: GLC.

Annuario Statistico Italiano 1990. (1990) Roma: Institute National di Statistica (ISTAT).

Archibugi, F. (1993) 'European regional policy: critical appraisal and foresight.' In G. Gorzelak and B. Jalowiecki (eds) *Regional Question in Europe.* Warsaw: EIRLD.

Armstrong, H. and Taylor, J. (1985) *Regional Economics and Policy.* Oxford: Philip Allan.

Artobolevskiy, S.S. (1985) 'Geography of production and non-production spheres in the manufacturing industry of Great Britain.' *Izvestia AN SSSR, Geographical Series 3,* 75–84. (In Russian.)

Artobolevskiy, S.S.(1987a) 'Regional Policy in the countries of Western Europe at the present stage of scientific-technological revolution.' In G.V. Ioffe (ed) *Territorial Organization of Economy as a Factor of Economic Development.* Moscow: IGAN. (In Russian.)

Artobolevskiy, S.S.(1987b) 'Regional Policy in developed capitalist countries and territorial problems in the USSR.'In A.B. Alaev, S.S.Artobolevskiy and U.G. Lipets (eds) *Regional Problems of Developed Capatalist Countries*. Moscow: IGAN. (In Russian.)

Artobolevskiy, S.S. (1989a) 'Post-war shifts in settling in Great Britain and France.' In P.M. Polian (ed) *Evolution of Settling in USSR. Part I*. Moscow: IGAN. (In Russian.)

Artobolevskiy, S.S. (1989b) 'Purposes, objects and methods of regional policy in developed capitalist countries.' *Izvestia AN SSSR, Geographical Series 4*, 77–84. (In Russian.)

Artobolevskiy, S.S.(1990) 'The capability of the state to solve regional problems.' *Geoforum 21*, 4, 449-454.

Artobolevskiy, S.S. (ed) (1990) *Development of Urban and Rural Areas of Great Britain and the USSR*. Moscow: IGAN. (In Russian.)

Artobolevskiy, S.S. (1992) *Regional Development in Britain*. Moscow: IGAN. (In Russian.)

Artobolevskiy, S.S. and Privalovskaya, G.A. (eds) (1989) *Geography and Problems of Regional Development*. Moscow: IGAN. (In Russian.)

Artobolevskiy, S.S. and Savchenko, A.B. (1989) 'Regional policy in COMECON and EC states.' In S.S. Artobolevskiy and G.A. Privalovskaya (eds) *Geography and Problems of Regional Development*. Moscow: IGAN. (In Russian.)

Artobolevskiy, S.S. and Treivish, A.I. (1992) 'Regional development and state policy in Eastern and Western Europe.' Glasgow: EPRC Research Papers 12.

Ashcroft, B. and Ingham, K.P.D.(1979)'Company adaptation and response to regional policy.' *Regional Studies 13*, 1, 25-37.

Bachtler, J. (1988) *EC Regional Policy and the Member States: The Regional Implications of the Single European Market*. Glasgow: University of Strathclyde.

Bachtler, J. (1988) 'Regional Policy: European perspectives and the comparative experience.' Belfast (unpublished report).

Bachtler, J. (1989) 'North versus South in European Regional Policy.' Glasgow, (unpublished report) p.8.

Bachtler, J. and Clement, K. (1990) 'Regional peripherality in the single European market, with particular reference to Ireland and Scotland.' EPRC Research Paper 10. Glasgow.

Bachtler, J., Clement, K. and Raines, Ph. (1991) *The Impact of the Single European Market on Direct Investment in Norway*. Glasgow: University of Strathclyde.

Baklanov, P.I. (1986) *Spatial Production Systems: Macro Structural Level of the Analysis and Management*. Moscow: Nauka. (In Russian).

Balchin, P.N. (1990) *Regional Policy in Britain. The North-South Divide*. London: Paul Chapman.

Ballantyne, E. and Bachtler, J. (1990) 'Regional policy under scrutiny: the European Commission and regional aid.' EPRC Research Paper 9. Glasgow.

Bandman, M.K. (1990) *Territorial-industrial Complexes Under New Conditions of USSR Economy Management*. Novosibirsk: Institute of Economy and Organization of Industrial Production. (In Russian.)

Barquero, A.V. and Hebbert, M. (1985) 'Spain: economy and state in transition.' In R. Hudson and J.L. Lewis (eds) *Uneven Development in Southern Europe*. London; New York: Methuen.

Begg, H. and McDowall, S. (1987) 'The effect of regional investment incentives on company decisions.' *Regional Studies 21*, 5, 459–470.

Bellu, R.R. (1988) 'A behavioral explanations of the different economic development of the Center-North and Mezzogiorno of Italy.' *Journal of Regional Policy 8*, 1, 67–82.

Benko, G. (1993) 'Spatial dynamics in France: past and present.' *GeoJournal 31*, 3, 289–299.

Bergman, E., Maier, G. and Todtling, F. (eds) (1991) *Regions Reconsidered*. London, New York: Mansell.

Berquin, A. (1984) *Towards a European Regional Planning Strategy*. Strasbourg: Council of Europe.

The Brixton Disorders 10–12 April 1981. (1982) London: HMSO.

Blazek, J.and Kara,J.(1992) 'Regional Policy in the Czech Republic during the period of transition.'In G.Gorzelak and A.Kuklinski (eds)*Dilemmas of Regional Policy in Eastern and Central Europe*. Warsaw: EIRLD.

Brunt, B. (1993) 'Ireland as a peripheral region of Europe.' Dublin: Geographical Society of Ireland. Special Publications 8.

Burns, P. and Dewhurst, J. (eds) (1986) *Small Business in Europe*. London: Macmillan.

Bylund, E. and Wiberg, U. (eds) (1986) *Regional Dynamics of Socio-economic Change – Experiences and Prospects in Sparsely Populated Areas*. Umea: CERUM.

Camagni, R. and Cappelin, R. (1985) *Sectoral Productivity and Regional Policy*. Luxemburg: European Commission.

Castillo, I. (ed) (1989) 'Regional development policies in areas of decline.' Bilbao: University of Bilbao working paper.

Centre et Peripheries: La Belgique Parmiles Douse. (1988) Brussels; Luxemburg: Internal document of the European Commission.

Cesaretti-Bianca, G.P. and Torquati, B.M. (1990) 'The European community and regions.' *Journal of Regional Policy 10*, 1, 79–104.

Cheshire, P.C. and Hay, D.G. (1989) *Urban Problems in Western Europe*. London: Unwin Hyman.

Cheshire, P., Hay, D. and Carbonaro, G. (1988) *Urban Problems and Regional Policy in the European Community*. Luxemburg: European Commission.

Chisholm, M. and Smith, D.M. (eds) (1990) *Shared Space: Divided Space*. London: Unwin Hyman.

Clarke, I.M. (1985) *The Spatial Organization of Multinational Corporations*. London; Sydney: Croom Helm.

Clout, H. (1986) *Regional Variations in the European Community*. Cambridge: Cambridge University Press.

Competitiveness and Cohesion: Trends in the Regions (1994) Brussels; Luxemburg: European Commission.

Cooke P. (1993) 'Regional innovation centres.' In G. Gorzelak and B. Jalowiecki (eds) *Regional Question in Europe.* Warsaw: EIRLD.

Danielzyk, R. (1992) 'Gibt es im Ruhrgebiet eine "postfordische regionalpolitic".' *Geographische-Zeitschrift 80,* 2, 84–105.

De Witte, B. (1990) *The Integrated Mediterranean Programmes in the Context of Community Regional Policy.* Florence: European University Institute.

The Development of Maritime Islands as Extreme examples of Peripheral Regions (1986) Strasbourg: Council of Europe.

Diamond, D.K. and Spence, N.A. (1983) *Regional Policy Evaluation: A Methodological Review and the Scottish Example.* Aldershot: Gower.

Dieleman, F.M. and Musterd, S. (eds) (1992) *The Randstad: A Research and Policy Laboratory.* Dordrecht: Kluver Academic Publishers.

Diem, A. (1979) *Western Europe: A Geographical Analysis.* New York: Wiley.

Dmitrieva, O.G. (1990) *Regional Policy and Regional Structure in USSR.* Leningrad: LFEI. (In Russian.)

Dostal, P. (1989) 'Regional interests and the national question under Gorbachev.' In A. Bon and R. van Voren (eds) *Nationalism in the USSR. Problems of Nationalities.* Amsterdam: Second World Centre.

Dostal, P.F. (1984) 'Regional policy and corporate organizational forms: some questions of international social justice.' In M. de Smidt and E. Wever (eds) *A Profile of Dutch Economic Geography.* Assen; Maastricht: Van Gorcum Assen.

Drudy, P.I. (1991) 'Demographic and economic change in Dublin in recent decades.' *Trinity Papers in Geography 5,* 17–25.

Dunford, M.F. (1988) *Capital, the State and Regional Development.* London: Methuen.

Dunford, M.F. (1994) 'Winners and losers: the new map of economic inequality in the European Union.' *European Urban and Regional Studies 1,* 95–114.

Dunford, M. and Kafkalas, G. (1992) *Cities and Regions in the New Europe.* London: Belhaven Press.

EC Regional Policies 1 (1994) Brussels: European Commission.

EC Regional Policies 3 (1994) Brussels: European Commission.

'An empirical assessment of factors shaping regional competitiveness in problem regions.' (1990) Luxemburg: European Commission.

'The ERDF [European Regional Development Fund] in 1989.' (1991). Brussels; Luxemburg: European Commission.

Eskelinen, H. (1991) 'The Nordic model at the crossroads: Consolidated periphery in a state of flux?' *Nord REFO 4,* 55–64. Copenhaven: Academic Press.

Europe 2000: Outlook for the Development of the Community Territory. (1991) Brussels; Luxemburg: European Commission.

Europe at the Service of Regional Development (1994). Brussels; Luxemburg: European Commission.

European Regional Development Fund. *UK Regional Development Programme, 1986–90.* (1987) Brussels; Luxemburg: European Commission.

European Research Centres (1986). Harlow: Longman.

Evaluation of Industrial and Commercial Improvement Areas (1986). London: HMSO.

Ewers, H.J., hGoddard,J.B. and Matzerath, H. *et al.* (eds) (1986) *The Future of the Metropolis: Berlin, London, Paris, New York: Economic Aspects.* Berlin; New York: De Gruyter.

Finnish Regional Policy in a Period of Radical Changes (1992) Copenhagen: Nordic Council.

Flockton, C. and Kofman, E. (1989) *France.* London: Chapman.

Fogarthy, P.M. (1949) *Prospects of Industrial Regions of Great Britain.* Moscow: IIL. (In Russian.)

For the Southern Regions of the Community: The Integrated Mediterranean Programmes (1983) Luxemburg: European Commission.

Fothergill, St. and Gudgin G. (1982) *Unequal Growth: Urban and Regional Employment Growth in the UK.* London: Heineman Educational Books.

Fothergill, S. and Guy, N. (1990) *Retreat from the Regions.* London: Jessica Kingsley Publishers.

Freeman, O. (1992) 'Swiss regional policies in a changing international environment.' In G. Gorzelal and A. Kuklinski (eds) *Dilemmas of Regional Policies in Eastern and Central Europe.* Warsaw: EIRLD.

Frohlich, Z. and Malekovic, S. (1994) 'New approaches to regional development policy in Croatia.' In Z. Haiju and G. Horvath (eds) *European Challenges and Hungarian Responses in Regional Policy.* Pecs: Centre for Regional Studies.

Fujita, K.(1988) 'The Technopolis: high technology and regional development in Japan.' *International Journal of Urban and Regional Research 12,* 4, 566-594.

Garofoli, G. (ed) (1992) *Endogenous Development and Southern Europe.* Aldershot: Avebury.

Giaoutzi, M. (ed) (1988) *Small and Medium Size Enterprises and Regional Development.* London: Routledge.

Gibb, J.M. (1985) *Science Parks and Innovation Centres.* Amsterdam: Elsevier.

Glickman, N.J. (1979) *The Growth and Management of Japanese Urban System.* New York: Academic Press.

Goddard, J.B. (1987) *Research and Technological Development in the Less Favored Regions.* Brussels; Luxemburg: European Commission.

Gore, Ch. (1984) *Regions in Question: Space, Development Theory and Regional Policy.* London; New York: Methuen.

Goria, G. (1988) 'Government's action and Mezzogiorno: Guiding principles in the just ended phase.' *Journal of Regional Policy 8,* 1, 5–10.

Gorkin, A.P. (1978) 'Influence of capitalist reproduction cycles on territorial structure of USA manufacturing industry.' *Izvestia AN SSSR, Geographical Series 6,* 80–92. (In Russian.)

Gorkin, A.P., Gohman V.M. and Smirniagin L.V. (1976) 'Territorial-industrial structure of industry (an example of the system in"Industry of capitalist countries").' *Izvestia AN SSSR, Geographical Series 6*, 107–114. (In Russian.)

Gorzelak, G. (ed) (1988) *Regional Dynamics of Socio-Economic Change*. Warsaw: ISE.

Gorzelak, J. and Jalowiecki, B. (eds) (1993) *Regional Questions in Europe*. Warsaw: EIRLD.

Granberg, A.G. (1991) 'USSR – regions in the new political and economic situation.' *Nederlandse Geografische Stadies 130*, 25–34.

Greater London Plan 1944 (1945). London: GLC.

Grieco, M.S. (1983) 'Corby: New town planning imbalanced development.' Warwick economic research papers 240, 1–18.

Gritzai, O.V. (1988) *Western Europe: Regional Contrasts at New Stage of Scientific-technological Revolution*. Moscow: Nauka. (In Russian.)

Gudgin, G. (1978) *Industrial Location Processes and Regional Employment Growth*. Westmead: Saxon House.

Hajdu, Z. and Horvath G. (eds) (1994) *European Challenges and Hungarian Responses in Regional Policy*. Pecs: Centre for Regional Studies.

Hall, P. (1989) *London 2001*. London: Unwin Hynman.

Hall, P.G. (1992) *Urban and Regional Planning*. London: Routledge.

Halvorsen, K. (1993) 'European integration and the effects on regional development in Norway.' In L. Lundquist and L.O. Persson (eds) *Visions and Strategies in European Integration. A North European Perspective*. Berlin: Springer-Verlag.

Hanke, S.H. and Walters, A.(1993) 'High Cost of Jefferey Sachs.' *Forbes 21 June 1993, 151*, 13, p.152.

Hansen, N., Higgins, B. and Savoie D.J. (1990) *Regional Policy in a Changing World*. New York, London: Plenum.

Harvey, D. (1985) *The Urbanization of Capital*. Oxford: Blackwell.

Hassink, R. (1992) *Regional Innovation Policy: Case Studies for the Ruhr Area, Baden Wurtemberg and North East England*. Utrecht: Rejksuniversiteit Utrecht.

Healey, M.J. and Ilbery, B.W. (1990) *Location and Change: Perspectives on Economic Geography*. Oxford: Oxford University Press.

Higgins, B. and Savoie, D.J. (eds) (1988) *Regional Economic Development*. Boston: Unwin Hyman.

Hilpert, U. (ed) (1991) *Regional Innovation and Decentralization*. London; New York: Routledge.

Hoggard, K. and Green D.R. (eds) (1991) *London: A New Metropolitan Geography*. Sevenoaks: Edward Arnold.

Horev, B.S. (1989) *Regional Policy in USSR*. Moscow: Misl. (In Russian.)

Horvath, G. (1994) 'From the micro-regionalization to the research of the cooperation of the European regions.' In Z. Hajdu and G. Horvath (eds) *European Challenges and Hungarian Responses in Regional Policy*. Pecs: Centre for Regional Studies.

Houterman R.P.A. 'East-West: Regional policy in transition (a Dutch approach)' (1992). In G. Gorzelak and A. Kuklinski (eds) *Dilemmas of regional Policies in Eastern and Central Europe.* Warsaw: EIRLD.

Hudson, R., Rhind, D. and Mounsey, H. (1984) *An Atlas of EEC Affairs.* London; New York: Methuen.

The Intermediate Areas (1969). London: HMSO.

Ioffe, G.V. (1990) *The Agriculture of Non-Black Soil Zones: Territorial problems.* Moskow: Nauka. (In Russian.)

Ioffe, G.V. (ed) (1987) *Territorial Organization of Economy as the Factor of Economic Development.* Moscow: IGAN. (In Russian.)

Italian Statistical Abstract 1989 (1989). Rome: ISTAT.

John, B.S. (1984) *Scandinavia: A New Geography.* London: Longman.

Joseph, R.A. (1989) 'Silicon Valley myth and the origins of technology parks in Australia.' *Science and Public Policy 16,* 6, 353–365.

Jull, P. (1986) *Politics, Development and Conservation in the International North.* Ottawa: CARC.

Kaderabkova, A. (1991) 'Restructuring in South Limburg – Inspiration for Czechoslovakia.' Maastrict. (unpublished report).

Karpov, L.N. (1972) *New Regions in Economy of Developed Capitalist Countries.* Moscow: Misl. (In Russian)

Karpov, L.N. and Bogdanov, O.S. (eds) (1974) *Regional Programming in Developed Capitalist Countries.* Moscow: Nauka. (In Russian).

Keating, M. and Jones B. (eds) (1985) *Regions in European Community.* Oxford: Calderon Press.

Keles, R. (1985) 'The effects of external migration on regional development in Turkey.' In R. Hudson and J.L. Lewis (eds) *Uneven Development in Southern Europe.* London; New York: Methuen.

Keskpaik, A. (1990) 'Estonian regional policy: proposals for upbuilding.' Tallinn. (Unpublished report.)

King, R. (1985) *The Industrial Geography of Italy.* London; Sydney: Croom Helm.

King, R. (1987) *Italy.* London: Harper and Row.

Kistanov V.V. (ed) (1985) *Planning of USSR Productive Forces Location. Part 1 and 2.* Moscow: Economica. (In Russian.)

Knaap B. van der and Wever E. (eds) (1987) *New Technology and Regional Development.* London: Croom Helm.

Kolosov, V.A. (1988) *Political Geography.* Leningrad: Nauka. (In Russian.)

Kondratiev, N.D. (1928) *Large Cycles of Conjuncture.* Moscow. (In Russian.)

Kondratiev, N.D. (1989) *Problems of Economic Dynamics.* Moscow: Economica. (In Russian.)

Kukar, S. (1992) 'Regional policy in Slovenia in comparison with EC countries.' In G. Gorzelak and A. Kuklinski (eds) *Dilemmas of Regional Policies in Eastern and Central Europe.* Warsaw: EIRLD.

Kuklinski, A. (1990) 'Efficiency versus equality: old dilemmas and new approaches in regional policy.' EPRC Research Paper 8. Glasgow.

Lambooy, J.G. (1986) 'Urban development and employment.' Report on INTA conference in Hungary, June, 1986.

Lappo, G.M. and Treivish A.I. (eds) (1988) *Moscow Capital Region: Territorial Structure and Natural Environment.* Moscow: IGAN. (In Russian.)

Larsson, M. (1989) 'The history of regional policy in Britain and Sweden.' *University of Liverpool Working Papers 37*, 1–84.

Lavrov, S.B. (1967) *Geography of FRG Industry. Parts 1 and 2.* Leningrad: LGU. (In Russian.)

Limburgse Social Ekonomische Verkenning 1991 (1991). Maastricht: Economisch Technologisch Instituut.

Lythe, Ch., Majmudar, M. (1982) *The Renaissance of the Scottish Economy?* London: Allen and Unwin.

MacLaran, A. (1993) *Dublin.* London; New York: Belhaven Press.

MacLaran, A. (1992) 'Inner area decline, state policy and the property development sector in Dublin.' In G. Gorzelak and A. Kuklinski (eds) *Dilemmas of Regional Policies in Eastern and Central Europe.* Warsaw: EIRLD.

Maergoiz, I.M. (1981) *Technique of Small-scale Economic-Geographical Researches.* Moscow: MFGO. (In Russian.)

Maergoiz, I.M. (1964) *Czechoslovakia Socialist Republic. Economic Geography.* Moscow: Misl. (In Russian.)

Maksimova, M.M. (1971) *Main Problems of Imperialist Integration.* Moscow: Misl. (In Russian.)

Malecki, E.J. and Nijkamp, P. (1988) 'Technology and regional development: some thoughts on policy.' Environment and Planning. C: *Government and Policy 6*, 383–399.

Malezieux, J. (1991) 'New economic development zones in the Paris agglomeration.' In G. Benko and M. Dunford (eds) *Industrial Change and Regional Development.* London; New York: Belhaven Press.

Massey, D. (1984) *Spatial Divisions of Labour: Social Structures and the Geography of Production.* London: Macmillan.

McCrone, G. (1969) *Regional Policy in Britain.* London: Croom Helm.

Miernyk, W.H. (1982) *Regional Analysis and Regional Policy.* Cambridge (Mass.): Oelgeschlager, Gunn and Hain.

Mileikovski, A.G. (ed) (1981) *New Tendencies in State-Monopolistic Regulation of Economy of Main Capitalist Countries.* Moscow: Nauka. (In Russian.)

Minorities and Autonomy in Western Europe (1991). London: A Minority Rights Group.

Mita, de C. (1987) 'A new phase in the Southern problem.' *Journal of regional policy 7*, 1, 5–11.

Monk, C.S.P., Porter, R.B. and Quintas, P. (1988) *Science Parks and the Growth of High Technology Firms.* London: Croom Helm.

Monnesland, J. (1992) 'Sparsely populated regions in an integrated Europe: the regional challenge in Norway.' EPRC Research Paper 11. Glasgow.

The Movement of Manufacturing Industry in the UK 1945–1965 (1968). London: HMSO.

Muegge, H. and Stohr W.B. (eds) (1987) *International Economic Restructuring and the Regional Community*. Aldershot: Avebury.

Nanetti, R.Y. (1988) *Growth and Territorial Policies: The Italian Model of Social Capitalism*. London; New York: Pinter.

National Accounts 1960–1986 (1988). Paris: Orginization for European Cooperation (OECD).

Nekrasov N.N. (ed) (1980) *Features and Problems in the Location of Industrial Forces in the USSR's Underdeveloped Socialism*. Moscow: Nauka. (In Russian.)

'New location factors for mobile investment in Europe.' Final report Brussels; Luxemburg: European Commission.

Nijkamp, P. and Blaas, E. (1992) *Methods of Regional Impacts Assessment*. Amsterdam: Free University.

Nord REFO, N 4 (1991). Copenhaven: Academic Press.

Nordic Regions and Transfrontier Co-operation (1991) Copenhaven: Nordic Council.

Oakey, R. (1984) *High Technology Small Firms: Regional Development in Britain and the US*. London: Pinter.

Panusheff, E. and Smatrakalev, G. (1992) 'Bulgaria towards Europe: meeting the challenge.' EPRC Research Paper 13. Glasgow.

Pavlov, U.M. (1970) *Regional Policy of Capitalist States*. Moscow: Nauka. (In Russian.)

'Peripheral regions in a Community of twelve member states.' Draft Final Report (1986). Cambridge (unpublished report).

Pinder, D. (1983) *Regional Economic Development and Policy. Theory and Practice in the European Community*. London: Allen and Unwin.

Plestina, D. (1992) *Regional Development in Communist Yugoslavia*. Boulder: Westview Press.

Polskaya, N.M. (1974) *Great Britain: Economic Regions and Cities*. Moscow: Misl. (In Russian.)

Prestwick, R. and Taylor, P. (1990) *Introduction to Regional and Urban Policy in the United Kingdom*. London; New York: Longman.

Privalovskaya, G.A. (1989) 'The territorial factor in socio-economic development.' In S.S. Artobolevskiy and G.A. Privalovskaya (eds) *Geography and Problems of Regional Development*. Moscow: IGAN. (In Russian.)

'The privatization of public enterprises. A European debate' (1986). *Annals of Public and Co-operative Economy 57*, 2, 141–311.

Probst, A.E. (1971) *Questions of Socialist Industry Location*. Moscow: Misl. (In Russian.)

'Proposals on reorganization of territorial planning and management' (1988) Novosibirsk (Unpublished report) (In Russian).

Raskov, N.V. (1979) *State-monopolistic Capitalism (Theory Issues)*. Leningrad: LGU. (In Russian.)

Ravet, V. (1993) 'Regional policy in public opinion.' *European Planning Studies 1*, 3, 398–401.

Rees, J. (ed) (1986) *Technology, Regions and Policy.* Totowa (N.J.): Rowman and Littlefield.

Regional Development Problems and Policies in Poland (1992) Paris: Organization for Economic Cooperation.

Regional Economic Strategy for North West England (1992) Wigan: North West Planning Authority.

Regional Imbalances and National Economic Performance. Report (1985). Brussels; Luxemburg: European Commission.

The Regional Impact of Community Policies (1991) Regional Policy and Transport Series 17. Brussels; Luxemburg: European Commission.

Regional Problems and Policies in Greece (1981) Paris: Organization for Economic Cooperation.

Regions 1987 (1987) Luxemburg: EUROSTAT.

Regions 1993 (1993) Luxemburg: EUROSTAT.

Regions: The Community's Financial Participation in Investments 1985 (1987) Luxemburg: EUROSTAT.

The Regions in the 1990s. Fourth Periodic Report (1991) Brussels; Luxemburg: European Commission.

The Regions of the Enlarged Community. Third Periodic Report (1987). Brussels; Luxemburg: European Commission.

Restructuring the Regions (1986) Paris: Organization for Economic Cooperation.

Richardson H.W. (1978) *Regional and Urban Economics.* Hardmondworth:

Richardson, H.W. (1969) *Regional Economics.* New York; Washington: Praeger.

Robert, J. (1982) *Mobilising the Indigenous Potential of Disadvantaged Regions.* Strasbourg: Council of Europe.

Rodwin, L. and Sazanami, H (eds) (1991) *Industrial Change and Regional Economic Transformation, the Experience of Western Europe.* London: Harper Collins.

Rossi, A. (1994) 'Structural change and regional policy: The stand of the debate in Switzerland.' In Z. Hajdu and G. Horvath (eds) *European Challenges and Hungarian Responses in Regional Policy.* Pecs: Centre for Regional Studies.

Royal Commission (1940) Report of the Royal Commission on the Distribution of the Industrial Population. London: HMSO.

Sarubbi, A. (1990) 'Basilicata: the "weak" region of the European Community.' *Journal of Regional Policy 10*, 2, 301–325.

Seers, D. and Ostrom, K. (1983) *The Crises of the European Regions.* London; Basingstoke: Macmillan.

Sickle, J.V.van (1943) *Planning for the South.* Nashville (Tenn.): Vanderbilt University Press.

Smirniagin, L.V. (1992) Thesis on regional strategy. Moscow. (unpublished report) (In Russian).

Smirniagin, L.V. (1989) *USA Regions.* Moscow: Misl. (In Russian).

Statistiques et indicateur des regions francaises 1989 (1988). Paris: National Institute of Statistical and Economic Studies (INSEE).

Statistisk arsbok for Sverige 1989 (1989). Stockholm: Statistiska Centralbyran (SCB).

Stillwell, F.J.B. (1972) *Regional Economic Policy.* London; Basingstoke: Pergamon Press

Submission to the European Commission on the post–1993 reform of the structural funds from the European parliamentary labour party. (Date not indicated.)

Swales, J.K. (1988) 'Are discretionary regional subsidies cost-effective?' EPRC Research Paper 5. Glasgow.

Szul, R. (1993) 'Some problems of regionalism in contemporary Europe with special reference to Eastern Europe.' In G. Gorzelak and B. Jalowiecki (eds) *Regional Question in Europe.* Warsaw: EIRLD.

'Territorial organization of economy' (1990) Sverdlovsk. Budapest: Institute of Economy (unpublished report) (In Russian).

Territorial Statistical Abstract 1985 (1988) Budapest: Central Statistical Office. (In Russian.)

Thumerel, P.J. (1989) Le Nord-Pa-de-Calais: Affaiblissement economique et resistances demographiques. *Hommes et terres Nord 1–2,* 9–23.

Townroe, P. and Martin, R. (eds) (1992) *Regional Development in the 1990s.* London: Jessica Kingsley Publishers.

Townsend, A.R. (1983) *The Impact of Recession: On Industry, Employment and the Regions, 1976–1981.* London; Canberra: Croom Helm.

Treivish, A.I. (1993) 'Regional policy.' *Vash vibor 1,* 6–7. (In Russian.)

Tsoukalas, D.A. (1988) 'Regional development incentives and industrial location.' EPRC Research Paper 4. Glasgow.

Turok, I. (1990) 'Evaluation and accountability of spatial economic policy.' *Scottish Geographical Magazine 106,* 1, 4–11.

'Unity of reform and reform of unity (1992).' Moscow: Expert Institute of the Russian Union of Industrialists and Businessmen. (In Russian.)

Vandermotten, C. (1989) 'Le comportement spatial des industries en Belgique avant et après 1974.' *Hommes et terres du Nord 4,* 265–271.

Vanhove, N. and Klaassen, L.H. (1980) *Regional Policy: A European Approach.* Westmead: Saxon House, 1980.

Volski, V.V. and Kolosova U.A. (eds) (1975) *State Regulation of Productive Forces Location in Capitalist Countries.* Moscow: Misl. (In Russian)

Watts, H. (1981) *The Branch Plant Economy: A Study of External Control.* London; New York: Longman.

Williams, A.M. (1987) *The Western European Economy: A Geography of Post-War Development.* London: Hutchinson.

Wise M. and Chalkley B. (1990) 'Unemployment: regional policy defeated.' In D. Pinder (ed) *Western Europe: Challenge and Change.* London; New York: Belhaven Press.

Yearbook of Nordic Statistics 1985 (1986). Stockholm; Copenhagen: Nordic Council.

Yearbook of Nordic Statistics 1989 (1990). Stockholm; Copenhagen: Nordic Council.

Yuill, D. and Allen, K. (eds) (1983) *European Regional Incentives 1983*. Glasgow: University of Strathclyde.

Yuill,D. and Allen,K.(eds) (1988) *European Regional Incentives 1988*. Glasgow: University of Strathclyde.

Yuill, D. and Allen, K. (1993) 'Regional incentives policies in the eighties.' In G. Gorzelak and B. Jalowiecki (eds) *Regional Question in Europe*. Warsaw: EIRLD.

Yuill, D., Allen, K., Bachtler J. and Wishlade F. (eds) (1988) *European Regional Incentives 1988*. Glasgow: University of Strathclyde.

Yuill, D., Allen, K., Bachtler, J. and Wishlade F. (eds) (1990) *European Regional Incentives 1990*. London: Bowker-Saur.

Yuill, D., Allen, K., Bachtler, J., Clement, K. and Wishlade, F. (eds) (1993) *European Regional Incentives 1993–94*. London: Bowker-Saur.

Zimin, B.N. (1976) 'Shifts in location of industry of the capitalist world.' In N.V. Alisov (ed) *Geography of Industry*. Moscow: MFGO. (In Russian.)

Author
Index

Agranat 9, 70, 72, 73
Alaev 9
Albrechts, 7, 10, 68, 82, 83,
    128, 162
Aldcroft 10, 22
Allen 11, 25, 26, 58,
    104,111, 112, 114
Alymov 9
Amersfoort 47
Archibugi 95
Armstrong 10, 155
Artobolevskiy 9, 21, 22, 31,
    53, 55, 59, 73, 88, 128,
    152, 159
Ashcroft 155

Bachtler 11, 24–26, 58, 98,
    100
Baklanov 9
Balchin 10, 81, 83, 84, 102
Ballantyne 98
Bandman 9
Barquero 49
Begg 120
Bellu 69
Benko 10, 23
Bergman 22
Berquin 10
Blajek 139
Blass 155
Bogdanov 9
Brunt 29
Burns 61
Bylund 29, 71

Camagini 10
Capellin 10
Carbonato 58
Castillo 28, 38
Cesaretti–Bianca 94
Chalkley 108
Cheshire 58, 73, 76, 80, 82,
    84, 87
Chisholm 47
Clarke 26
Clement 100
Clout 19
Cooke 126

Danielzyk 152
Dewhurst 61
De Witte 93
Diamond 153
Dieleman 28, 110
Diem 17, 70–72
Dmitrieva 9
Dostal 28, 148
Drudy 83
Dunford 19, 28, 62, 68, 99

Eskelinen 29
Ewers 81

Finnish 29
Flockton 10
Fogarthy 32, 60
Folmer 155
Fothergill 61, 81, 128, 162
Freeman 10
Frohlich 143
Fujita 10, 126

Garofoli 66, 162
Gibb 126
Glickman 33
Goddard 31
Gohman 9
Gore 10
Goria 69
Gorkin 9, 14
Gorzelak 20, 138, 160
Granberg 140
Green 107
Grieco 56
Gritzai 9
Gudgin 31, 82, 112
Guy 61, 128, 162

Hajdu 160
Hall 5, 10, 73, 83
Halvorsen 100
Hanke 143
Hansen 10, 38, 46, 106, 161
Harvey 6, 28, 46
Hassink 60, 152
Hay 58, 87
Healey 29
Hebbert 49
Higgins 10, 19, 23, 28
Hilpert 20, 22
Hoggard 107
Horvath 138, 144, 160
Horev 9

Houterman 30
Hudson 11

Ilbery 29
Ingham 155
Ioffe 9, 137

Jalowiecki, 138, 160
John 10
Jones 10
Joseph 10
Jull 70

Kaderabkova 57, 130, 144
Kafkalas 19, 62, 99
Kantzbovskaia 14
Kara 139
Karpov 9, 62, 63, 70, 72
Keating 10
Keles 115
Keskpaik 135
King 10, 17, 67
Kistanov 9, 132
Klaassen 10
Knaap 55
Knippenberg 47
Kofman 10
Kolosov 9
Kolosova 9
Kondratiev 19, 22, 45, 53,
    149
Kukar 139
Kuklinski 3, 152

Lambooy 85
Lappo 9, 76
Larsson 49
Lavrov 9
Lythe 10

MacLaren 83, 101
Maergoiz 9
Maier 22
Majmudar 10
Malekovic 143
Malezieux 145
Maksimova 10
Malecki 22
Martin 10, 20, 28
Mashbitz 14
Massey 36
McCrone 19, 32
McDowall 120
Miernyk 5, 33, 60, 145

Mileikovski 10
Mita 69
Monk 126
Monnesland 70
Moulaert 7
Mounsey 11
Muegge 10
Musterd 28, 110
Nanetti 68
Nekrasov 9

Nijkamp 21, 155

Oakey 36
Ostrom 10, 21

Panuskeff 143, 144
Pavlov 9
Pinder 10
Plestina 161, 162
Polskaya 13
Porter 126
Prestwick 27, 118
Privalovskaya 9, 14
Probst 9

Quintas 126

Raines 100
Raskov 10
Ravet 32
Rees 36
Rhind 11
Richardson 26, 28–30
Robert 10, 21, 61
Rodwin 10
Rossi 63, 125

Sarubbi 10, 69
Savchenko 88
Savoie 10, 19, 23, 28
Sazanami 10
Seers 10, 21
Sickle 10
Smatrakalev 143, 144
Smirniagin 9, 150
Smith 47
Spence 153
Stillwell 30, 51
Stohr 10
Swales 118
Swyngedouw 7
Szul 148

Taylor 10, 27, 118, 155
Thumerel 10, 54
Todtling 22
Torquati 94
Townroe 10, 20, 28
Townsend 20, 119, 123
Treivish 9, 76, 139, 145, 159
Tsoukalas 23, 69, 113
Turok 153, 155

Vandermotten 59
Vanhove 10
Vinikas 83
Volski 9

Walters 143
Watts 60
Wever 55
Wiberg 29, 71
Williams 17, 18, 19, 23, 47,
    70
Wise 108
Wishlade 58

Yuill 2, 11, 25, 26, 37, 58,
    63, 64, 68, 71, 100, 102,
    104, 110, 111, 112, 123

Zimin 9

Geographical Index

Ile-de-France *see* Paris

Lancashire 53
Lapland province 70, 72
Latvia 135
Limburg 28, 54, 101, 156
Lisbon 63, 67
Liverpool 58, 102
London 20, 21, 30, 53, 77, 79, 81–84, 85, 86, 101, 103, 113, 122
Lorraine 25, 33, 54

Maas river valley 56
Madrid 69
Manchester 102
Mediterranean 66, 69, 70, 93, 102, 113, 149
Merseyside 89
Midlands 57
Milan 20, 38
Molise 68
Moscow 76–78, 79, 85, 86, 102, 132, 136, 140, 142, 161

Naberejnie Chelni 134
New England 32, 113
Non-Blacksoil zone 21, 137
Nord Pas-de-Calais 52, 54
Nordland county 70
Norrbotten county 70, 71
North region, Italy 58, 67, 69, 113, 156
North region, UK 32
North Sea 102
North West region UK 58, 107
North East region UK 60
Northern Caucasus 132, 147
Novosibirsk 102
Northern Ireland 27, 28, 40–44, 47, 48, 66, 122, 159

Oporto 63, 69
Orly 18
Oxford 108

Palermo 38
Paris 20, 28, 34, 50–54, 77, 79, 80, 84, 85, 86, 101, 113, 145
Paris region 52, 113

Aberdeen 102
Abruzzi 68
Alsace 33, 47, 53, 54, 56
Altai region 142
Amsterdam 18, 50, 78, 79, 85, 101, 109
Antwerp 18
Appalachian region 33
Armenia 136
Athens 22, 63, 69
Azerbaijan 135, 136

Basilicata 68, 69
Basque country 47, 49
Birmingham 21
Borinaige 34
Brittany 47, 101
Brussels 20, 84, 87, 99, 101, 103, 110
Budapest 77–80, 138

Cambridge 126
Catalonia 47, 49
Chernobyl 137, 138
City 30, 83
Corsica 27, 47
Croatia 143

Dublin 63, 69, 83, 122

Estonia 135

Far East region 142
Finnmark county 70
Flanders 48, 59, 107, 110, 113, 147

Galicia 47
Glasgow 58, 102
Grampian region 57, 102
Greater London *see* London
Groningen 28

Hainaut 54, 89, 107
Heathrow 18

Quebec 27

Randstad 2, 27, 30, 46, 52, 77, 78, 79–84, 107
Rotterdam 18, 79, 113
Ruhr 33, 34, 56, 60, 62

Saambr river valley 56
Saar 33
Salonika 22, 63, 69
Scandinavia 17, 33, 58, 70–73, 101, 149, 161
Schipol 18
Scotland 25, 28, 32, 47, 56–58, 63, 84, 89, 102, 111–113, 127
Serbia 161
Shannon 67
Siberia 21, 132
South region, Italy 34, 37, 58, 67–69, 106, 111, 127, 159
South Limburg 57
South East region UK 52, 107
South West region UK 101
Stariy Oskol 134
St. Petersburg 140, 142

Tennessee river valley 33
Toliatty 134
Troms county 70
Tumen region 137

Wales 8, 28, 32, 47, 56, 57, 63, 101, 102, 111–113, 127, 132
Wallonia 8, 28, 34, 48, 53, 56, 59, 62, 84, 107, 110, 113, 147
West Midlands 54, 57, 128
Westerbotten county 70
Zelenograd 142

Subject Index

Agency of the South 68, 106
Agglomeration 22, 34, 51, 54, 73–84, 103
Airports 18
Allocation of regions 110–116

Branch plant economy 20, 22, 61, 152

'Cassa' of the South 34, 68
Central authorities 105, 106
Centre and periphery 19, 20, 58, 104, 160

DATAR 106
Delores J. 100
Decentralization 2, 3, 21, 38, 50
Denationalization 17, 127
Department of the South 68
Depressed regions 17, 33, 34, 52–62, 136
Devolution see Decentralization
DG-XVI 12, 92, 106
Diffusion of innovations 60
Disintegration 4, 12, 20, 27, 131, 132, 139, 140, 161

Efficiency and equity 31, 37
Efficiency of regional policy 152–157
Environment 56, 57, 72, 114
ERDF 87, 92, 93
ESF 93
European integration 57, 63, 87–100, 101, 149
European Policies Research Centre 11
Expanded towns 77

Factors of location 31
Fragmentation of space 36, 159, 163, 164
French desert 34

Gentrification 5, 18, 103
Grants 83, 116–121

Greater London Council 50, 107
Growth poles 66, 68

Immigrants 79, 85, 101
Industrial Development Certificate 160
Industrial parks 125, 126
Industrial Revolution 51–55, 141, 158
Inflation 29
Infrastructure 18, 24, 31, 61, 64, 65, 67, 71, 84, 85, 103, 123, 124
Inner city areas 23, 72, 79–86
Institute of Geography (Russian Academy of Sciences), 9
Internal resources 36, 39, 61, 62, 71, 72
Investment climate 123

Keynes J.M. 5, 86
Kondratiev cycles 46, 53, 57

Loans 61, 121–122
Local authorities 18, 26, 39, 105–110

Migration of industry 34, 77
Migration of population 18, 22, 71, 76, 135, 147
Ministry of trade and industry UK, 17
Millan B. 100
Ministry of electric power production 134
Ministry of water economy 134
Moscow State University 9
Multi-national corporations 24, 38, 56, 57

National Economic Institute 11
National problems 23, 27, 28, 48–50, 111, 148
Nationalization 1, 16
Natural resources 29, 62, 69–73
Neo-Keynesian 22
New Deal 145
New Towns 77, 155

Office Permit 159
Old-industrial regions 23, 32, 50, 51–62, 69, 89, 90

Periphery 57, 62, 63, 90, 101–104
Perestroika 138
Planned decentralization 34, 73–87
Planning control 18, 78, 108
Planning Research Centre 11
Ports 18
Positive discrimination 3
Post-Fordism 23
Post-industrial society 20, 103
Privatization 1, 16, 127
Problem regionalization 6

Quality of life 60, 114

Reagan R. 37
Regional authorities 106, 107
Regional antagonism 4
Regional programs 2, 21, 32, 38, 136
Regional statistics 11
Regional strategy 1, 2

Scientific and technological 'revolution' 36, 147, 148
Scientific parks 125, 126
Social efficiency 156, 157
St. Petersburg State University, 9
Suburbanization 5, 18, 21, 79

Territorial justice 28
Tax concessions 122, 123
Thatcher, M. 37, 38, 107, 114, 156, 162

Underdeveloped regions 33, 51, 62–73, 90, 137
Unemployment 18, 79, 114, 115

Welfare state 15–17
World economic crisis 15, 27, 32

Zirinovski V. 143